TESI GREGORIANA

Serie Filosofia

17

MUHIGIRWA F. RUSEMBUKA

THE TWO WAYS OF HUMAN DEVELOPMENT ACCORDING TO B. LONERGAN
Anticipation in *Insight*

EDITRICE PONTIFICIA UNIVERSITÀ GREGORIANA
Roma 2001

Vidimus et approbamus ad normam Statutorum Universitatis

Romae, ex Pontificia Universitate Gregoriana

die 31 mensis octobris anni 1997

R.P. Prof. CARLO HUBER, S.J.
R.P. Prof. SALVINO BIOLO, S.J.

ISBN 88-7652-890-3

GREGORIAN UNIVERSITY PRESS
Piazza della Pilotta, 35 - 00187 Rome, Italy

ACKNOWLEDGMENTS

Philosophy, as a field of human knowing, is to be considered as life reflected upon, thought of and founded by reason. The philosopher is the one who, as a friend of wisdom and truth, seeks by critical refection to give sense and meaning to his/her existential and problematic living in the world. All the traditional schools of philosophy, its treatises and history are but contributions to a coherent articulation of sense and meaning of human living.

The present dissertation lies within the scope of this understanding of philosophy. And if, according to G. Bastide, what defines a philosophy is its problems, my problem is human development. In fact, this dissertation examines the theme of human development which constitutes for me and for Africa a truly existential problem which requires philosophical reflection. My philosophical reflection, within the limits of this dissertation, is based on the Lonerganian understanding of the two ways of human development.

Furthermore, my philosophical reflection is part of a dynamic process of research and self-appropriation of a *modus philosophicus*. This *modus philosophicus* is as a critical investigation. All along the way of this research and self-appropriation, several persons have helped, sustained, advised and encouraged me.

This is why I want first of all to give thanks to God the Almighty for all the blessings that he has bestowed upon me throughout my formation. How shall I thank him for all his blessings and wonders? I will try in return to make of my existence, a gift received from him, an eternal offering to the praise of his glory, convinced that he is, for humankind, «the Way, the Truth and the Life» (Jn14, 6). I specially thank him for all the persons that he has placed on the path of my life in order to render me more attentive to the signs of his steadfast and unfailing Love.

I sincerely express my gratitude to all my parents, formators, professors and friends who have instilled in me the love of God, the critical passion of the true, the good, the beautiful, the just and the reasonable. I am exceedingly grateful to Professor Carlo Huber S.J. who, in addition to his position as Dean of the Faculty of Philosophy at the Pontifical Gregorian University in Rome, has directed my doctoral dissertation with great competence and a high sense of responsibility.

I express my acknowledgement to the Society of Jesus, to my dear companions of Jesus residing at Collegio Bellarmino, to all my dear fellow companions of Jesus of the Central African Province, friends in the Lord and servants of Christ's mission. Together, as companions of Jesus, rooted in Christ and ever searching for the Ignatian *Magis*, we are courageously going to face the contemporary challenges of human development, service of faith, promotion of justice, inculturation, and interreligious dialogue.

My acknowledgement is addressed to the professors of Regis College and the scholars of the Lonergan Research Institute in Toronto, namely, Frederick Crowe, for his personal value, his insightful exploration and expansion of Lonergan's thought; Robert Doran who has helped me to grasp an insight into *Insight*; Jean Marc Laporte, Robert Crocken and Michael Schields for their availability and their encouragement.

I also wish to thank the staff members of the Lonergan Institute at Boston College, most particularly, Professors Joseph Flanagan and Fred Lawrence for all that I have received from them through their writings and our exchanges. I am exceedingly grateful to Professor Fred Lawrence who did the proof-reading of this dissertation. I equally thank Professors Salvino Biolo of the Pontifical Gregorian University in Rome, Michael Vertin of the University in Toronto and Giovanni Sala of Berchmanskolleg in Munich for their advise and insights. I would like, in a particular way, to mention Carol and Bill Olson, Joachin Ciervide, Muhigirwa Bernard, Michael Paul Gallagher, Echaniz Ignazio who have helped to translate this doctoral dissertation into English.

It goes without saying that I cannot, in the limits of this preface, mention all the persons who have inspired, helped, advised, encouraged and sustained me throughout the writing of this dissertation. To all the people who, in some ways, have contributed to the completion of this thesis, I offer my sincere thanks. May all find in this doctoral thesis, the fruit of collaboration and creativity, the expression of our profound gratitude. *Nasa. Bakonkwa*: May all be thanked. To all my Relatives and to all the Jesuits who, in the present world, consider integral human development, as a challenge, a value and a mission, I dedicate this book Ad Majorem Dei Gloriam.

GENERAL INTRODUCTION

Bernard Lonergan (1904-84), Canadian philosopher and theologian, is «widely regarded as one of the most significant thinkers of the twentieth century»[1]. His original and coherent philosophical investigations focusing on human knowing as a dynamic event and a philosophical field have led him to an elaboration of cognitional theory, epistemology, ethics, metaphysics, and philosophy of God. The same philosophical investigations and the intellectual force of his literary output also brought him to address fundamental questions that pertain to human development. His exploration of the two ways of human development constitute a major theme in his post-*Method* articles, written during the final stage of his career, namely, between 1974 and 1980.

In his May 15, 1975 article entitled «Healing and Creating in History», Lonergan asserts that authentic human development follows two fundamental and complementary ways, an ascending one, the way up from below upwards, the way of achievement, and a descending one, the way down, from above downwards, the way of heritage:

> For human development is of two different kinds. There is development from below upwards, from experience to understanding, from growing understanding to balanced judgement, from balanced judgement to fruitful courses of action, and from fruitful courses of action to new situations that call for further understanding, profounder judgement, richer courses of action. But there also is development from above downwards. There is the transformation of falling in love: the domestic love of the family; the human love of one's tribe, one's country, mankind; the divine love that orientates man in his cosmos and expresses itself in worship[2].

Lonergan's description of the two ways of human development is based on his cognitional theory composed of four levels of conscious

---

[1] M. MORELLI – E. MORELLI, *The Lonergan Reader*, 3.
[2] B. LONERGAN, «Healing and Creating in History», 106.

and intentional operations. Thus development from below upwards begins with an attentive experience of data, then evolves from an understanding of the data to critical reflection on this understanding, and from this critical reflection to responsible decision. Development from above downwards, on the other hand, begins with the gift of human or divine love which creates the conditions within which one better apprehends the meaning of responsible decision, critical reflection, intelligent understanding and attentive experience.

Lonergan, however, did not elaborate a systematic study of the ways of human development, even if they constitute a major theme in his later writings. Neither did he show any historical progress in his thought concerning the two ways. We have noticed throughout our research that very few commentators on Lonergan, philosophers as well as theologians, considered this theme in depth as the fundamental subject of their investigations. Thus, Frederick Crowe states rightly that the two ways of human development are an important, unexplored theme in Lonergan's philosophy.

> I underline the need to appropriate one's interiority in two directions, which Lonergan calls «the way up» and «the way down»[...] The second way has its source in gift, but the first is the way of achievement [...]This double way is an important unexplored idea in Lonergan. Neglect of it is bound to result in undistorted interpretations[3].

The originality of the present doctoral dissertation resides precisely in a systematic, philosophical study of this important unexplored theme. Throughout this systematic study, we will underline the interdependence and the complementarity of the two ways of human development.

If the two ways of human development constitute a major theme in Lonergan's philosophy, which method are we going to use? Method — *meta hodos* — is not to be conceived as a set of rules that everyone must follow blindly. Method is rather a normative pattern composed of a set of directives aiming at creativity and collaboration. This normative pattern is principally a *modus procedendi* which leads inquiry towards precise results and clear objectives. And our main objective is to grasp, in a critical and synthetic manner, the Lonerganian understanding of the two ways of human developement and to show their anticipation in *Insight*, his philosophical masterpiece.

To reach our objective, we will use as method «an intellectual hermeneutics» which, according to Lonergan, is «a matter of understanding

---

3 F. E. CROWE, *The Lonergan Enterprise*, 72-73.

the thing, the words, the author, and oneself, of passing judgement on
the accuracy of one's understanding, of determining the manner of expressing what one has understood»[4].

As defined, this intellectual hermeneutics includes the two first
functional specialities of which Lonergan speaks in *Method in Theology*, namely, research and interpretation. Our research is not general
but special because it endeavours to gather Lonergan's writings relevant
to the two ways of human development. Our interpretation aims at understanding the meaning of these writings in their proper context.

Intellectual hermeneutics, in a spiral movement, focusing on research and interpretation, will allow us to grasp the meaning and the
historical progress of Lonergan's thought pertaining to the two ways of
human development. We will point out how the two ways of human
development are operative in *Method in Theology* (1972), explicit in
post-*Method* writings published between 1974 et 1980 and anticipated
in *Insight* (1957).

The present dissertation is entitled «The Two Ways of Human Development according to Bernard J.F. Lonergan. Anticipation in *Insight*»
(*De duabus viis progressionis humanae secundum Bernard J.F. Lonergan. Anticipatio in libro Insight*). From the title of our dissertation the
two main parts of our study emerge, structured around the two following questions: 1. What does Lonergan mean by the two ways of human
development? 2. Can we find an anticipation of the two ways in *Insight*? Each part of the dissertation has two chapters. In the first part,
chapter one deals with development from below, chapter two with development from above. The second part examines the anticipation of
the development from below (chapter three) and of development from
above (chapter four) in *Insight*.

What does Lonergan mean by the two ways of human development?
The first chapter spells out Lonergan's understanding of the two ways
of human development in *Method in Theology* and in post-*Method*
writings. For Lonergan, development from below upwards corresponds
to the result of his cognitional theory. This cognitional theory is a formally dynamic process, composed of four levels of consciousness and
intentionality, i.e., empirical, intellectual, rational, and responsible.

The second chapter examines development from above downwards
which comes about with the transformation of love in its threefold
manifestation, i.e. the domestic love of the family, the love of one's

---

[4] *MIT*, 245.

country, and the love of God. We have considered God's love as a gift, as religious conversion and as a dynamic state. Religious conversion, as foundation of cognitive and moral self-transcendence, transforms the knowing subject and establishes him in a dynamic state of being in love with God. The subject realises, therefore, in his existence that *nihil cognitum nisi prius amatum*. In *Method in Theology* and in post-*Method* writings, God's love is conceived as a new and higher integration which promotes development from below.

Chapter three deals with the anticipation of development from below in *Insight*. Development from below corresponds to human knowing which, as dynamic process, explicitly consists in experiencing, understanding, and judging. These three cognitive operations find their anticipation mainly in chapters 9 and 10 of *Insight*. Though not as explicitly analysed, decision finds its anticipation in chapter 18 of *Insight*.

If *Insight* is written «not from above downwards, but from below upwards»[5], how can we justify the anticipation of development from above downwards? The fourth chapter attempts to elucidate this question, by showing its anticipation in chapters 19, 20 and the epilogue of *Insight*. In considering the problem of evil, we argue that God's love is not only its supernatural solution, but equally the topmost integration of development from below.

Our general conclusion, retrospective and critical, sums up the results of the dissertation and highlights the interdependence and the complementarity of the two ways of human development. For it is in their interdependence and complementarity that the two ways of human development contribute to the advent of truly human development of which God remains the *arché* and the *telos*.

---

[5] *IN*, 17.

FIRST PART

TWO WAYS OF HUMAN DEVELOPMENT
1972-1980

Human Development from Below Upwards

1. Introduction

The two ways of human development constitute a major theme in Lonergan's post-*Method* writings. Lonergan argues that truly human development consists of two complementary ways of development: the way up and the way down. The two ways of human development are considered in their unity and complementarity. But, while maintaining their unity and complementarity, we are going to distinguish them without separating them.

However, to avoid any ambiguity, we must from the outset make three points. Firstly, the two ways of human development form one single dynamic process. This means that the upward and downward movements of development constitute two processes of one and the same reality which Lonergan calls «the truly human development». Thus, they can neither be confused nor separated. Still, for the sake of clarity and method, we will distinguish them, while at the same time maintaining their unity and complementarity.

Secondly, the two ways of human development cannot be identified with the *via analytica* and the *via synthetica* which are often found in Lonergan's Latin theological writings[1]. Analysis and synthesis consti-

---

[1] B. LONERGAN, *Divinarum Personarum Conceptionem Analogicam*, 23-28. *De Deo Trino. Pars Systematica*, 31-41. «Qui primus motus dicitur *analysis*, qui ex confuse apprehensis ad causas seu rationes bene definitas procedit [...] Alter motus dicitur *synthesis*, quia rationes fundamentales adhibentur tum ad res definiendas tum ad proprietas earum deducandas» (*De Deo Trino*, 33). The first movement» is named analysis because it proceeds from the confused apprehension of things to justifications or causes clearly defined [...] The second movement is called synthesis because the

tute two ways of organising ideas at the level of thought. The way up and the way down of development, however, essentially evolve from one level of consciousness to another.

Thirdly, in agreement with Frederick Crowe, we maintain the thesis that in *Method in Theology* the two ways of human development are operative but not thematic[2]. It is only during the period from 1974 to 1980 that Lonergan makes the two ways of human development an explicit and major theme of his philosophy.

In the first chapter, we will examine what Lonergan means by development from below upwards, the way up. The present chapter has two parts: the first one is a study of development from below in *Method in Theology*, drawing inspiration principally from its first chapter. The second part deals with the explicitation of development from below in the eleven post-*Method* articles, written between 1974 and 1980.

2. Lonergan's biography

Bernard Joseph Francis Lonergan was born in Buckingham, Quebec, December 17, 1904. He read his first book, *Treasure Island*, at the age of six. He attended St. Michael's school run by the Christian Brothers. At the age of thirteen, Lonergan went off to Loyola College, a Jesuit High School in Montreal. In later years he recalled his first impression of his teachers: «The Jesuits were the best educated people I had met»[3].

In the summer of 1922, at the age of seventeen, he entered the Jesuit Noviciate at Guelph, Ontario for two years of spiritual formation. In 1926, his noviciate and juniorate completed, Lonergan was sent to Heythrop College, Oxfordshire, for three years of scholastic philosophy, to which he added a year for a degree in sciences at the University of London. He appreciated the English ways of living, thinking and doing. It was at Heytrop that Lonergan predicted that the «theory of knowledge is what is going to interest me most of all»[4].

This period was the setting of a decisive commitment to the intellectual life. At the University of London, he read the books of Lewis Carroll, Gilbert Keith Chesterton. Professor Charles O'Hara and John

---

fundamental justifications or explanations are used to define things and deduce their properties.

[2] See F.E. CROWE, «An Expansion», 345.

[3] P. LAMBERT – C. TANSEY – C. GOING, ed., *Caring about Meaning*, 135.

[4] Cited by F.E. CROWE, *Lonergan*, 14.

Henry Newman's *An Essay in Aid of a Grammar Assent* had a profound influence on Lonergan's epistemology. «I was looking for someone who has some common sense, and knew what he was talking about. And what was Newman talking about? About judgment as assent; and real apprehension and notional apprehension, notional assent and real assent. He was answering the liberal view that all judgements are more or less probable but nothing is certain. And he could give examples»[5]. In 1930 he was rewarded a BA in Greek, Latin, French and mathematics. For his regency, he was sent to Loyola College in Montreal where he taught from 1930 to 1933. He devoted his free time to reading Plato's *Doctrine of Ideas*, St. Augustine's early dialogues writings and St. Thomas' *Summa*.

In 1933, Lonergan was sent to Rome to start theology at the Gregorian University in Rome. He lived at the Collegio Bellarmino in the Campo Marzio. In Rome, Lonergan did his undergraduate and doctorate studies in theology. He prepared his doctoral dissertation on the Thomist, i.e. theory on grace. «My philosophical development was from Newman to Augustine, from Augustine to Plato, and then I was introduced to Thomism through a Greek, Stephanos Stephanou, who had his philosophical formation under Maréchal. It was talking to him that I came first to understand St. Thomas, and see that there was something there»[6]. «Already in the pre-war years he was making his personal intellectual pilgrimage: first it was from Newman to Augustine to Plato; then he imbibed Maréchal by "osmosis" from a fellow scholastic at the Gregorian; and through his doctorate work he came to a personal confrontation with Aristotle and St. Thomas that would lead him far from the established 'schools' and be a powerful fertilising influence for further evolution and new creative thinking»[7]. On July 25, 1936, Lonergan was ordained to the priesthood in Rome. In 1937, at Amiens (France), he did his tertianship, a year devoted to the *schola affectus*.

From 1953 on, at his Gregorian alma mater, Lonergan was occupied with a relentless struggle to bring the new ideas into relation with the old. Here are the lines that his thinking has followed. His doctoral dissertation was a study of the concept of *gratia operans* in St. Thomas. The chief benefit of his dissertation was the personal development involved in reaching up to the mind of Aquinas. From 1938 to 1940, he

---

[5] P. LAMBERT - C. TANSEY - C. GOING, ed., *Caring about Meaning*, 14.

[6] *UB*, 350.

[7] *ALI*, 5.

wrote his doctoral dissertation under the direction of Charles Boyer on «A History of St. Thomas' Thought on Operative Grace», a study of the development of St. Thomas' notion of grace and freedom. This held for Lonergan's work on grace and cognitional theory.

Lonergan was sent to Montreal as professor of theology at the Col- lège de l'Immaculée Conception from 1940 to 1946. Pursuing his early interests in economics from 1940-1944, he wrote the initial version of «An Essay in Circulation Analysis». In 1947 he was sent to Regis Col- lege, Toronto, as professor of theology. It was during these years at Regis College *Insight* was written.

The next step in the evolution of his thought was quite personal, moving from study of historical figure to independent affirmation. *In- sight: A Study of Human Understanding*. Insight is Lonergan's original philosophical masterpiece. As Fred Crowe wrote:

> The book is, in fact a profound rethinking of cognitional theory on the basis of seven centuries of mathematics, physics, biology, depth psychology, the social and human sciences, and modern philosophy. The net result was the transformation of the transcendental method as developed by Maréchal in correction and complement of Kant: a critical appropriation of human cogni- tional structure as a basis for a methodical science and philosophy [...] It was a necessary foundation, solid ground for either the methodical promotion of the sciences or that of integration of differentiated cultures and ways of knowing and doing that poses such a problem today. But it dealt mainly with the subject, and the subject was irrevocably oriented to the object in an *in- tentio entis intendens*. The object is always being in its totality[8].

Lonergan returned to Rome and was a professor of theology at the Gregorian University from 1953 to 1965. His lectures in graduate courses at the Gregorian (Trinity, incarnation, and redemption) and in the summers in North America moved with the writing of *Insight* to the question of the meaning that constitutes human historical institutions.

Whatever question he dealt with, Lonergan was concerned with the field of method, of the operations of the subject, of what, since Kant's time, has been known as transcendental philosophy: «The study of the subject results in a style of thinking. Human operations have a built-in normative; to study them is to become aware of the standards intrinsic to their nature, and this awareness is almost certain to be reflected in one's further operations and ways in Lonergan's style of thinking»[9].

---

[8] *ALI*, 7.
[9] *ALI*, 9.

In 1965 Lonergan returned to Canada for a sabbatical but had to undergo an operation for lung cancer. After his recuperation, he remained in Toronto as research professor at Regis College for five years. *Method in Theology* was completed in 1971 and published in 1972. In 1975 he moved from Regis College to Boston College, where he was Visiting Distinguished Professor of Theology until 1983. He continued to expand on his ideas in *Insight* and *Method in Theology*. While in Boston, he taught a course entitled «Macro-economics and the Dialectics of History». In 1983 he became ill and was unable to teach. He retired to the Jesuit infirmary in Pickering, Ontario. Lonergan died on November 26, 1984.

Many people and organisations have recognised the significance of his accomplishments. «Lonergan was made Companion of the Order of Canada in 1970; the Catholic Theological Society of America presented him with the John Courtney Murray Award in 1972; he was made a Corresponding Fellow of the British Academy in 1975; and he was awarded nineteen honorary doctorates»[10]. From their conversations with Lonergan, Mark and Elizabeth Morelli wrote that «in Lonergan's writings and published interviews, there is no evidence of romanticism, moral idealism, or elitism [...] He impressed us as a highly practical intellectual whose deep and broad learning was complemented by good common sense»[11].

3. *Method in Theology*

There are several kinds of development[12] in *Method in Theology*. But we will limit ourselves to human development. In general, human development can be conceived as a «process from initial global operations of law efficiency, through differentiations and specialities, to the

---

[10] R.M. LIDDY, *Transforming Light*, 211-212.

[11] M. MORELLI – E. MORELLI, *The Lonergan Reader*, 11.

[12] Affective development (65), intellectual development (72.230-231.272), personal development (81.118.218.223.236), development of language (87.258.390), development of philosophy (258), moral development (38.110), development of knowledge (38.72.231.258), development of understanding (189-190.216-218.348), development of the community (118.223), religious development (110-112.118.360), cultural development (30.305.353.360.363), doctrinal development (166.305-310.319.353), dialectical development (110.287.319), academic development (139), systematic development (347), theological development (138-144.310.347.353), spiritual development (290.363), scientific development (139.258.353), historical development (41.57), cumulative development (81.302) and human development (99.116.138.170.252.287.310.361).

integration of the perfected specialities»[13]. These conscious and intentional operations are those of «seeing, hearing, touching, smelling, tasting, inquiring, imagining, understanding, conceiving, formulating, reflecting, marshalling and weighing the evidence, judging, deliberating, evaluating, deciding, speaking, writing»[14]. Specifically, development from below upwards is considered as a formally dynamic process composed of four levels of consciousness and intentionality, namely, «empirical, intellectual, rational, and responsible»[15].

These four levels are functionally successive and interrelated, yet qualitatively different. As a dynamic process, development from below proceeds from the attentiveness to data of sense or consciousness to decision, passing through understanding and judgement. «The appropriate image is of the gradual ascent of a mountain on which the arrival at each succeeding plateau provides a broader, farther-reaching vista. Such effort begins with elemental experience regarding a basic situation, and normally rises through the various levels of consciousness»[16].

This conception of development from below is at the heart of Lonergan's writings and is clearly present in the first chapter of *Method in Theology*. Before proceeding to an understanding of the four levels of consciousness and intentionality, it would be appropriate to establish a distinction between consciousness and self-knowledge.

3.1 *Consciousness and Self-Knowledge*

In paraphrasing Lonergan, M. Vertin states that «knowing distinctively consists of conscious intentional operations of attentive experiencing, intelligent understanding, reasonable judging, and responsible evaluating»[17]. This means that according to Lonergan, knowing is not «some single operation or activity but, on the contrary, a whole whose parts are cognitional activities»[18]. These cognitional activities are exercised by a conscious subject.

---

[13] *MIT*, 288.

[14] *MIT*, 6.

[15] *MIT*, 9.

[16] M. SCHEPERS, «Human Development», 141.

[17] M. VERTIN, «Lonergan's Three Basic Questions», 224-228.

[18] B. LONERGAN, «Cognitional Structure», 207. For J.F. Flanagan, «From Lonergan's perspective Kant's basic concern is epistemological not cognitional. Kant's question is what are the conditions necessary in knowing an object. Lonergan's question is what are the conditions necessary for prescinding from the objectivity of the knowing itself». J.F. FLANAGAN, «Lonergan's epistemology», 75-76.

Consciousness is the presence of the subject to himself through his conscious and intentional operations. «Just as operations by their intentionality make objects present to the subject, so also by consciousness they make the operating subject present to himself»[19]. Each time the subject accomplishes one of the operations, he becomes conscious of himself, he is present to himself as the one who performs the operations. In doing this, he develops because it is «only in the process of development that the subject becomes aware of himself and of his distinction from his world»[20].

According to Lonergan, there are two different modes of presence: material and intentional. There is material presence in which no knowing is involved, such as the presence of the house on a mountain. There is intentional presence, in which knowing is involved. There may be the presence of the object to the subject, but there may also be the presence of the subject to himself, which is conscious but not cognitive. Thus in the realm of intentional presence, «the presence of the object is quite different from the presence of the subject. The object is present as what is gazed upon, attended to, intended. But the presence of the subject resides in the gazing, the attending, the intending»[21].

The subject can be conscious, as aware of himself, while giving his attention to the object as attended to. To come to know oneself as conscious subject, one must be attentive to what one is already conscious of, to understand what one has attended to, and to pass a judgement on the correctness of the understanding. «It is a matter of heightening one's consciousness by objectifying it; and that is something each one ultimately has to do in himself and for himself»[22].

Self-knowledge is the result of an objectification by the subject of his conscious and intentional operations. It implies for the subject a reflective movement of his own experience, his own understanding, his own judgement and his own deliberation. As an objectification of knowing, self-knowledge is «experience, understanding, and judging with respect to experience, understanding, and judging. Consciousness, on the other hand, is not knowing knowing but merely the experience of knowing, experiencing, that is of experiencing, of understanding, and of judging»[23]. Therefore some subjects can be conscious empirically intel-

---

[19] *MIT*, 8.
[20] *MIT*, 29.
[21] *MIT*, 8.
[22] *MIT*, 14.
[23] B. LONERGAN, «Cognitional Structure», 208.

lectually, rationally and morally conscious, but they do not know this yet. However, to truly know, one must be fully conscious of himself in the knowing process. Thus consciousness is not identical with self-knowledge, but constitutes a virtual component, an indispensable pre-liminary, a condition *sine qua non*:

> Consciousness is merely the presence of the subject to himself or herself in all the operations and states of which he or she is the subject [...] In all of these operations and states, one is aware of oneself operating and being dis-posed in such and such a fashion. This awareness is not reflexive. It is not self-knowledge. It is simply the experience of the self as self, the subject as subject[24] . Knowledge, by contrast, including knowledge of oneself, is a function of conscious operations [...] Consciousness is a prerequisite for knowledge, a necessary condition. But it is not a sufficient condition[25] .

In other words, according to Lonergan, development from below upwards corresponds to his cognitional theory which is an answer to the first of his three basic questions: «What am I doing when I am know-ing»[26] ? This cognitional theory is a dynamic process which proceeds from the level of experience through the levels of understanding and judgement to the fourth level of value judgement and decision.

3.2 *The Empirical Level*

The empirical level is the first of the four levels of consciousness and intentionality. Intentionality and consciousness differ from one level of consciousness to another. «On all four levels, we are aware of ourselves but, as we mount from level to level, it is a fuller self of which we are aware and the awareness itself is different»[27] .

On the first level one attends to the data of sense or consciousness. The positivists, the behaviourists, the relativists and the determinists

---

24 «The subject-as-subject is the one who establishes by his or her own activities to relate to object, including other subjects. The subject-as-subject is the perceptible human being behaving and acting in the shared, public life [...] Self-appropriation, in the first instance, is a shift of attention from objects, including the subject-as-object, to the subject-as-subject and in the realm of interiority» (M. MORELLI – E. MORELLI, *The Lonergan Reader*, 18).

25 *TDH*, 68-69.

26 *MIT*, 25. The second question is: «Why is doing that knowing»? and the third: «What do I know when I do it»? The answer to the first question is a cognitional theory or gnoseology, the second is epistemology, and the third a metaphysics. See Lonergan's three basic questions in *MIT*, 25.83.261.297.316.

27 *MIT*, 9.

cannot claim to never have had an attentive experience «of seeing or hearing, or touching or smelling, of imagining or perceiving, of feeling or moving»[28]. So, at the empirical level, that of the attentive experience, «we sense, perceive, imagine, come to understand, work, speak and move»[29].

Meanwhile, Lonergan makes a distinction between the external and the internal experience. «External experience is of sights and sounds, of odours and tastes, of the hot and cold, hard and smooth, wet and dry. Internal experience is of oneself and one's apprehensive and appetitive activities»[30]. In other words, the external experience conveys the data of sense whereas the internal experience conveys the data of consciousness.

We make the experience of the data of sense or of consciousness as conscious subjects. But, since we are also intellectual and rational subjects, our consciousness and intentionality on the empirical level are springboards that project us towards further activities. The data of sense or of consciousness concern the four levels of consciousness of the knowing subject. At the empirical level, they «provoke inquiry, inquiry leads to understanding, understanding expresses itself in language. Without the data, there would be nothing for us to inquire, and nothing to be understood»[31]

3.3 *The Intellectual Level*

Through inquiry, an experience attentive to the data on the first level leads to the second level, the intellectual level. This second level is characterised by insight, which, as principal cognitive operation, grasps intelligible relations in the data, images or symbols. Thus, «there is an intellectual level on which we inquire, come to understand, express what we have understood, work out the presuppositions and the implications of our expressions»[32]. Without the data of sense or consciousness of the empirical level, there would be nothing to inquire and nothing to be understood on the second level. For Aristotle as well, at the intelligent level, phantasms are necessary in order to understand, to ex-

---

[28] *MIT*, 17.
[29] *MIT*, 9.
[30] B. LONERGAN, «Cognitional Structure», 208.
[31] *MIT*, 10.
[32] *MIT*, 9.

perience *intelligere*[33]. «*Ta men oun eiden to noetikon en tois phantasmasi noei*»[34].

Intellectual understanding moves us beyond attentive experience in asking the question *quid sit*[35]? what is it? The purpose of this question is to grasp the quiddity[36] of data, to understanding the intelligible relations existing between the data. For the subject, the possibility of inquiry and arriving at an understanding cognitional structure depends on his intelligence, on his desire to know the *quid sit*, the why, the how, and his ability to attain intellectually satisfying answers. It is clearly a question of «understanding the unity and relations of one's experienced experiencing, understanding, judging, deciding»[37].

This desire and effort to understand is indeed the source of a questioning always in progress within which insight occurs as a response to the question of *quid sit*, in relation to the data of sense or of consciousness. Nevertheless, «what is grasped in insight, is neither an actually given datum of sense nor a creation of the imagination but an intelligible organisation that may or may not be relevant to data»[38]. As an intelligible organisation, insight constitutes «the active ground whence proceed conception, definition, hypothesis, theory, system»[39]. Insight is clearly situated at the level of thought, embodied by an intelligently conscious subject. In effect, «as intelligent, the subject seeks the insight

---

[33] According to St. Thomas Aquinas *intelligere* means to understand and we think in order to understand: «Ipsum enim intelligere non perficitur nisi aliquid in mente concipiatur, quod dicitur verbum; non enim intelligere, sed *cogitare ad intelligendum*». See *De Potentia*, q. 9, a. 9. c; my emphasis.

[34] ARISTOTLE, *De Anima*, III, 7, 431b 2. Commenting on the same quotation, F. E. Crowe affirms that : «At the basis of all reasoning (*ratio*) is the simple act of reasoning, the Thomist *intelligere* or the Aristotelian *noein*. Aquinas could say that whenever man tries to understand (*intelligere*) he forms images (*phantasmata*) in which he, as it were, inspects (*inspiciat*) the solution (*S.T.* I, q. 84, a. 7 c), and Aristotle could assert that the noetic faculty (*noetikov*) understands (*noei*) the forms in images (*en tois phantasmasi*)». «Understanding (*Intellectus*)», 391.

[35] For Aristotle, the first act of intelligence is the knowledge of the «to ti estin?» (*De Anima*, III, 8, paragraphs 705-719) and for Aquinas the *quod quid est*? (*S.T.*, q.1, a. 12 c).

[36] «Behind the notion of quiddity, there is a whole speculative activity starting with Socrates, developed by the Academy and finding a climax in Aristotle ; the *quod quid est* is at the centre of logic, philosophy, metaphysics and epistemology» (B. LONERGAN, *The Concept of Verbum*, 79).

[37] *MIT*, 15.

[38] *MIT*, 10.

[39] *MIT*, 213.

and, as insights accumulate, he reveals them in his behaviour, his speech, his grasp of situations, his mastery of theoretic domains»[40].

Accordingly, intelligent understanding is not purely theoretical. It seeks to understand the concrete data of sense and of consciousness. And in this quest for understanding, the human being defines himself as a subject who grasps the intelligible unity of these data. Nevertheless, intellectual understanding is only a stage in the dynamic process of development from below. «With inquiry the intelligent subject emerges, and the process becomes intelligent; it is not merely an intelligible that can be understood, but the active correlative of intelligibility, the intelligence that intelligently seeks understanding, comes to understand, and operates in the light of having understood»[41].

The search, intelligently achieved, shows itself as the term of attentive experience and the beginning of critical reflection which arises from the rational level.

3.4 *The Rational Level*

After the grasp of insight as a response to the question of the *quid sit*, the eros of the human spirit, seeking for an epistemologically valid knowledge, evolves to the third level, that of rationality. This rationality moves one beyond the responses of intelligence and impels him to ask if these responses are true. In face of the question of *an sit*, «we reflect, marshal the evidence, pass judgement on the truth, certainty or probability of a statement»[42].

Judgement is the principal cognitive answer to the question of *an sit*. As such, it consists of affirming the truth or the falsity, the certainty or the probability of a proposition, after having grasped the virtually unconditioned[43]. The grasp of the virtually unconditioned is of «cardinal importance in Lonergan's philosophy, enabling him to avoid Hegel's conclusion that thought ultimately has nothing to think of but of itself,

---

[40] *MIT*, 10.

[41] *MIT*, 16.

[42] *MIT*, 9. According to Frederick Crowe, «Fr. Lonergan has taken Aristotle's two basic questions, *an sit* and *quid sit*, linked them sharply to the *duae operationes intellectus* of St. Thomas Aquinas, understanding and reflection, and made them central to his account of the dynamism of cognitional activity». F.E. CROWE, «The Origin and Scope», 16.

[43] Lonergan makes a distinction between the virtually unconditioned and the formally unconditioned. «The virtually unconditioned is a condition whose conditions are fulfilled. The formally is itself without conditions whatever» (*MIT*, 75).

without embroiling him with Kantian 'things in themselves' such as somehow exist in utter transcendence of our cognitional processes»[44].The grasp of the virtually unconditioned is expressed in judgement. In other words, judgement is a critical instance through which one accepts or rejects hypotheses set forth results of understand the data of sense or consciousness.

Meanwhile, intelligent understanding alone does not constitute knowledge, but rather thinking. It deals with insights as objects of thought. It is up to the rational level to transform objects of thought into objects of knowledge. The transition from thinking to knowing requires «a reflexive grasp of the unconditioned and its rational consequent is judgement. Not taking seriously into account this third level leads to «a resultant failure to break away cleanly and coherently from both empirism and idealism»[45] .

At the rational level, Lonergan distinguishes judgements of fact and judgements of value. He argues that judgements of value differ in content but not in structure from judgements of fact:

> They differ in content, for one can approve of what does not exist, and one can disapprove of what does. They do not differ in structure, inasmuch as in both there is a distinction between criterion and meaning. In both, the criterion is the self-transcendence of the subject, which, however, is only cognitive in judgements of facts but it is heading toward moral self-transcendence in judgements of value. In both, the meaning is or claims to be independent of the subject; judgements of fact state or purport to state what is or is not so; judgements of value state or purport to state what is or is not truly good or really better [46] .

According to Lonergan, the affirmation of the virtually unconditioned by a judgement shows that the knowing subject transcends attentive experience and intelligent understanding, thus manifesting his reflexive and critical consciousness. This is why «as reflectively and critically conscious, he incarnates detachment and disinterestedness, gives himself over to criteria of truth and certitude, makes his sole concern the determination of what is or is not so; and now, as the self, so

---

[44] H. MEYNELL, *An Introduction*, 49.

[45] *MIT*, 213.

[46] *MIT*, 37.

also the awareness of self resides in that incarnation, that self-surrender, that single-minded concern for the truth»[47].

This single-minded concern for truth invites the subject, on the one hand, to pass true judgement when the elements of evidence are sufficient, so it is true that *veritas in formaliter est in solo judicio*. On the other hand, it invites the subject to affirm that a proposition is false, dubitable or probable when the elements of evidence are insufficient. This single-minded concern for truth, characteristic of the third level, is completed by the sense of responsibility of the subject.

3.5 *The Responsible Level*

The responsible level is the fourth level of the ascending human development. It appears when, after having passed a judgement on the facts, the subject deliberates, evaluates, decides, and acts. At this level, «we are concerned with ourselves, our own operations, our goals, and so deliberate about possible courses of actions, evaluate them, decide, and carry out decisions»[48]. The fourth level is thus the level of deliberation, evaluation, decision, and action. The decision occurs as the principal conscious and intentional operation.

However, decision is no longer to be conceived as an act of will. «To speak of an act of will is to suppose the metaphysical context of a faculty of psychology. But to speak of the fourth level on which consciousness becomes conscience, is to suppose the context[49] of intentional analysis. Decision is responsible and it is free, but the work not of a metaphysical will but of conscience»[50].

As an act grasp by intentional analysis, decision is situated at a higher level which presupposes and sublates[51] the other three prior

---

47 *MIT*, 10. For Aquinas, the object of intelligence is *ens*. The *verum* is the final object of judgement in which one recognises the *ens reale*. See *De Veritate*, q.1, 1.a. ad 4m.

48 *MIT*, 9.

49 And in this context, cognitive operations such as attending, understanding, reflecting, and deliberating are those that «man has found to go on in himself, the consequent operations are the operations he has uncovered and identified in his own operating; and the structure within which the operations occur is the pattern of dynamic relations which, as he knows from his own experience, lead from one operation to the next» (*MIT*, 286).

50 *MIT*, 268-269.

51 Lonergan uses the term *sublate* «to mean that what sublates goes beyond what is sublated, introduces something new and distinct, puts everything on a new basis, yet so far from interfering with the sublated or destroying it, on the contrary needs it,

levels. «The fourth level of the intentional consciousness — the level of deliberation, evaluation, decision, action — sublates the prior levels of experiencing, understanding, judging. It goes beyond them, it sets up a new principle and type of operations, directs them to a new goal but, far from dwarfing them, preserves them and brings them to a fuller fruition»[52].

More specifically, the decision sublates judgement and understanding which, in turn, sublates the data of sense or of consciousness. In fact, «observing lets intelligence be puzzled, and we inquire. Inquiry leads to the delight of insight but insights are a dime a dozen, so critical reasonableness doubts, checks, makes sure. Alternative courses of actions present themselves and we wonder whether the more attractive is truly good»[53].

Thus in assuming the role of sublation with regard to the three prior levels, the fourth level is considered as the level of the responsible exercise of freedom and moral development. This responsible exercise of freedom is explained by the fact that «there is a still further dimension to being human, and there we emerge as persons, meet one another in a common concern for values, seek to abolish the organisation of human living on the basis of competing egoisms and to replace it by an organisation on the basis of man's perceptiveness and intelligence, his reasonableness, and his responsible exercise of freedom»[54].

This responsible exercise of freedom allows the subject either to realise himself or to fail to the extent that he is attentive or inattentive in experiencing, intelligent or unintelligent in his understanding, reasonable or unreasonable in his judgements. «Therewith vanish two notions, the notion of the pure intellect or pure reason that operates as on its own without guidance or control from responsible decision; and the

---

includes it, preserves all its proper features and properties, and carries them forward to a fuller realisation within a richer context» (*MIT*, 241). Lonergan's understanding of the term *sublate* corresponds to Hegel's *aufheben* as reinterpreted by Karl Rahner.

[52] *MIT*, 316. Lonergan shows that in the philosophy of history, there has been an awareness of the fourth level of intentional consciousness «from Descartes through Kant to the nineteenth century German idealists. But there follows a more emphatic shift from knowledge to faith, will, conscience, decision, action in Kierkegaard, Schopenhauer, Newman, Nietzsche, Blondel, the personalists, and the existentialists» (*MIT*, 316).

[53] *MIT*, 13.

[54] *MIT*, 10.

notion of a will as an arbitrary power indifferently choosing between good and evil»[55].

Regarding the subject in quest of his own development, it is always a question of perceiving attentively, understanding intelligently, judging correctly, choosing judiciously, and being responsible. And «being responsible includes basing one's decisions and choices on unbiased evaluation of short-term and long-term costs and benefits to oneself, to one's group to other groups»[56].

In effecting a just evaluation of the costs and in choosing judiciously the good, we pass from decision to actions, which permit us «to know and to do not just what pleases us, but what is truly good, worthwhile. Then we can be principles of benevolence and beneficence, capable of genuine collaboration and of true love»[57]. As principles of benevolence and beneficence, we deliberate and evaluate in order to act according to the judgements of value that we have established. Thus, «the process of deliberation and evaluation is not in itself decisive, and we experience our liberty as the active thrust of the subject terminating the process of deliberation by settling on one of the possible courses of action and proceeding to execute it»[58]. Deliberation, decision and execution are to be exercised in a free and responsible manner.

In so doing, individuals attain the existential moment where they discover for themselves that their choices affect them, and they have to decide for themselves what to do with their lives. This existential moment is pre-eminently the place of moral development, of self-transcendence or self-destruction because moral development heads to the existential discovery, the discovery of oneself as moral being, the realisation that one not only chooses between different courses of action but also thereby makes oneself an authentic human being or an inauthentic one. With that discovery emerges in consciousness the significance of personal value and the meaning of personal responsibility[59].

With this discovery, we realise that judgements of value open the way to personal responsibility, self-transcendence or self-destruction.

---

[55] *MIT*, 121.

[56] *MIT*, 53. «Evaluation may be biased by an egoistic disregard of others, by a loyalty to one's own group matched by hostility to other groups, by concentrating on short-term benefits and overlooking long-term costs. Moreover, such aberrations are easy to maintain and difficult to correct» (*Ibid.*).

[57] *MIT*, 35.

[58] *MIT*, 50.

[59] *MIT*, 38.

Furthermore, moral development offers a space for the responsible exercise of freedom. At this level, subjects engage themselves in intersubjective and existential relations in order to better their world. They then become «individually responsible for what they make of themselves, but collectively responsible for the world they live in»[60]. It is a question individually and collectively of an ongoing self-transcendence, a question of free and responsible choice of values, a question of putting these values into practice.

3.5.1 The Notion of Value

The second chapter of *Method in Theology* speaks of the human good, of values as human creations, determined by the person who acts intelligently and reasonably and who makes responsible choices. The attentive, intelligent, reasonable and responsible creation of values permits individuals and groups to transcend and to fulfil themselves. This creation of values arises from development from below, while the reception and transmission of these values belong to development from above. But, the crux of the matter is the complementarity of the two phases of human development, the upward and downward movements.

This complementarity is underlined in the fifth chapter of *Method in Theology* when dealing with functional specialities of theology[61]. In this chapter, Lonergan states that « the two phases possess a dynamic interdependence and unity»[62]. In effect, «as the first phase *rises* from the almost endless multiplicity of data first to an interpretative, then to a normative, and then to a dialectical unity, the second phase *descends* from the unity of a grounding horizon towards the almost endlessly varied sensibilities, mentalities, interests, and tastes of mankind»[63].

Lonergan qualifies this interdependence between the two phases of reciprocal dependence:

---

[60] *MIT*, 402.

[61] *MIT*, 125-145. Lonergan distinguishes two phases and eight functions of theology. The first mediating phase — *in oratione obliqua* — comprises the four first functions: research, interpretation, history, and dialectic. The second mediated phase — *in oratione recta* — concerns the other four functions: foundations, doctrines, systematics, and communications. These eight functions specialities are «intrinsically related to one another. They are successive parts of one and the same process. The earlier parts are incomplete without the latter. The latter presuppose the earlier and complement them» (*MIT*, 126).

[62] *MIT*, 145.

[63] *MIT*, 142.

There is, then, a reciprocal dependence within each of the two phases, and this was only to be expected since the four levels of conscious and intentional operations (which determine the specialities in each phase) are themselves interdependent. Further there is a dependence of the second phase on the first, for the second confronts the present and the future in the light of what has been assimilated from the past[64].

The two phases, in their autonomy and interdependence, are based on the four levels of consciousness and «seek the end proper exclusively to experiencing, understanding, judging, and deciding»[65].

More explicitly, in the mediated phase, *in oratione obliqua*, one recognises the upward movement which deals with the four levels of human consciousness in correlation with the four first functional specialities: «The first of these proceeds from the level of experience (data provided by research) through the levels of understanding (interpretation of the data), judgement (the history of what really happened, of what was going forward) to the fourth level challenge of values impelling us to decision (dialectic)»[66].

The notion of value concerns specifically the fourth level. At this level, judgements of value go much further than judgements of fact to the extent that they permit knowing and doing not only what is apparently good but what is truly good and worthwhile. That is why «judgement of value, then, is a reality in the moral order. By it the subject moves beyond pure and simple knowing. By it the subject is constituting himself as proximately capable of moral self-transcendence, of benevolence and beneficence, of true loving»[67].

Nevertheless, when the subject asks himself whether a thing is apparently good or truly good and worthwhile, he does yet not know the value in question, he intends it. Thus «value is transcendental notion. It is what is intended in questions for deliberation, just as the intelligible is intended in questions for intelligence, and just as the truth and being is intended in questions for reflection. Such intending is not knowing»[68]. Hence, there exists at the core of the human person, a tension of intelligence towards the intelligible, the true, the real and the good. In this context, the person in quest of human development, is the one

---

64 *MIT*, 142143.
65 *MIT*, 134.
66 F.E. CROWE, «An Expansion», 347.
67 *MIT*, 37.
68 *MIT*, 34.

who decides to commit himself to the pursuit of the intelligible, the true, the good, and remains faithful to his commitment.

Let us point out further that Lonergan establishes a hierarchy among vital, social, cultural, personal and religious values[69], in ascending order[70]. What immediately interests us in the here and now is Lonergan's conception of personal value. «Personal value is the person in his self-transcendence, as loving and being loved, as originator of values in himself and his milieu, as an inspiration and an invitation to others to do likewise»[71] Accordingly, the human person is not only a value in himself but is also and above all a source of values and of love, the originating value of transcendence for self and for others.

3.5.2 Self-Transcendence

«Self-transcendence is the achievement of conscious intentionality»[72]. According to Lonergan, the human being is inhabited by a quest of intelligibility, an inquiring and critical mind. In this quest, the human being transcends himself in asking questions for intelligence, questions for reflection and questions for deliberation. These three kinds of questions give rise to two distinct but interdependent forms of self-transcendence: the cognitive and moral.

The first form of self-transcendence concerns questions for intelligence and for reflection. So, on the cognitional plane, the subject transcends himself in transcending the level of sensibility by asking, for example, What is it? Why? How? «On questions for intelligence follows questions for reflection. We move beyond imagination and guess-work,

---

[69] It is a matter of development and independence between vital, social, cultural, personal, and religious values. «Vital values , such as health and strength, grace and vigour are preferred to avoiding the work, privations [...] Social values, such as the good of order conditions the vital values of the whole community, have to be preferred to the vital values of individual members of the community. Cultural values do not exist without the underpinning of vital and social values, but none the less they rank higher. Not on bread alone doth man live. Over and above mere living and operating, men have to find a meaning and value in their living and operating. It is the function of the culture to discover, express; validate, criticise, correct, develop, improve such meaning and value» (*MIT*, 31-32).

[70] «Thus *from below*, more basic levels are required for the emergence of higher levels, but they also set problems that only proportionate developments can solve; and *from above*, these proportionate developments are conditions of possibility of the appropriate schemes of recurrent events at the more basic levels» (*TDH*, 95).

[71] *MIT*, 32.

[72] *MIT*, 104.

idea and hypothesis, theory and system, to ask whether or not this is really so or that really could be. Now self-transcendence takes on a new meaning»[73].

Therefore, on the cognitive plan, questions for intelligence and for reflection and the relevant answers to these questions orient the subject towards a cognitive self-transcendence that shatters the assumption that «all knowing must be something like looking»[74]. This first form of self-transcendence is situated at the level of knowing and not of doing. The subject, engaged in a such process, effectively transcends himself at the cognitive plane, when he comes to truly know the intelligible, the true and the real. In this context, «genuine objectivity is the fruit of authentic subjectivity»[75], exercised by an authentic subject.

The second form of self-transcendence is envisioned when we «respond with the stirring of our being, when we glimpse the possibility or the actuality of moral self-transcendence»[76]. Moral self-transcendence concerns questions for deliberation. One then asks the following questions: Is it worthwhile? Is what I intend apparently or truly good and worthwhile? Should I act in accordance to the values apprehended?

> Because we can ask such questions and answer them, and live by the answers, we can effect in our living a moral self-transcendence. That moral self-transcendence is the possibility of benevolence and beneficence, of honest collaboration and of true love, of swinging completely out of habitat of an animal and and becoming a person in a human society[77].

Accordingly, the human being effects moral transcendence when he seeks what is worthwhile and truly good and manages to do it. He is operating at the moral level and corresponds thus to the virtuous man of whom Aristotle[78]. speaks And so far as the subject opts and decides not for the apparent good but for the real good, he succeeds at the level of moral transcendence to exist authentically and to constitute himself as a personal value. The personal value concerns human being as long as one transcends oneself on the cognitive as well as on the moral plane. One transcends oneself to the extent that one puts into practice the tran-

---

[73] *MIT*, 104.
[74] *MIT*, 239.
[75] *MIT*, 265.
[76] *MIT*, 38.
[77] *MIT*, 104.
[78] ARISTOTLE, *Nichomachean Ethics*, II, 4, 1105b 5-8.

scendental precepts: «Be attentive, be intelligent, be rational, be responsible»[79].

Putting transcendental precepts into practice is at the basis of self-transcendence. Thus «man is his true self inasmuch as he is self-transcending. Inversely, man is alienated from his true self inasmuch as he refuses self-transcendence»[80]. In effect, being attentive, intelligent, rational, and responsible promotes self-transcendence while being inattentive, unintelligent, irrational and irresponsible destroys self-transcendence and fundamentally alienates the individuals. «As self-transcendence promotes progress, so the refusal of self-transcendence turns progress into cumulative decline»[81].

Moreover, moral self-transcendence contributes to the knowledge of self and of others. «Just as it is one's self-transcendence that enables one to know others accurately and to judge them fairly, so inversely it is through knowledge and appreciation of others that we come to know ourselves and fill out and refine our apprehension of values»[82]. One of the main values that the moral self-transcendence allows one to perceive and appropriate is that of authenticity.

3.5.3 Human Authenticity

How does Lonergan conceive it? Negatively, «human authenticity is not some pure quality, some serene freedom from all oversights, all misunderstandings, all mistakes, all sins»[83]. Positively, «man's deepest need and most prized achievement»[84]. Human authenticity is situated at the fourth level, that of responsibility, because at this level we emerge as persons. But how does one achieve authenticity? «Man achieves human authenticity in self-transcendence»[85].

Authenticity thus is seen as the fruit of self-transcendence and is realised when the judgements of values are followed with decisions and actions, when a person knows what is truly good and does it. Nevertheless, it is not sufficient occasionally to decide what is good and to act accordingly in order to be an authentic person. Furthermore, «one has to have found out for oneself that one has to decide for oneself what one is

---

[79] *MIT*, 18, 53, 55, 231, 302.
[80] *MIT*, 356.
[81] *MIT*, 55.
[82] *MIT*, 289.
[83] *MIT*, 252.
[84] *MIT*, 104.
[85] *MIT*, 254.

to make of oneself; one has to have to prove oneself equal to that moment of existential decision; one has to have kept on proving it in all subsequent decisions, if one is to be an authentic human person»[86] . In other words, to develop oneself as an authentic person is an ongoing process, a perpetual advent, a new creation in the constitution of oneself. Thus, «the subject truly knows itself only when it reflectively recognises that it is authentically itself solely in the self-transcending intention of intelligibility, truth, and value»[87] .

But human authenticity is not taken for granted. There are human failures. There exist unauthentic persons. This is why authenticity calls for dialectic. According to Lonergan, «dialectic has to do with the concrete, the dynamic, and the contradictory»[88] . As such, «it discerns processes of development and aberration»[89] to oppose and eliminate inauthenticity. But the elimination of unauthenticity is never total and it is always precarious.

> It is ever precarious, ever to be achieved afresh, ever in great part a matter uncovering still more oversights, acknowledging still further failures to understand, correcting still more mistakes, repenting more and more deeply hidden sins. Human development, in brief, is largely through resolution of conflicts and, within the realm of intentional consciousness, the basic conflicts are defined by the oppositions of positions and counterpositions[90] .

This incompatibility requires that the positions be developed and the counterpositions reversed. In developing the positions and reversing the counterpositions, the dialectic reveals that «our advance in understanding is also the elimination of oversights and misunderstandings. Our advance in truth is also the correction of mistakes and errors. Our moral development is through repentance for our sins»[91] .

When there is a conflict, development from below demands the application of transcendental precepts, which requires us to pay attention to the data, «to advance in understanding, to judge truthfully, to respond to values. Still this possibility and exigence become effective only through development. One has to acquire the skills and learning of a competent human being in some walk of life. One has to grow in sen-

---

[86] *MIT*, 121.
[87] R. DORAN, «The Theologian's Psyche», 123.
[88] *MIT*, 129.
[89] *MIT*, 252.
[90] *MIT*, 252.
[91] *MIT*, 110.

sibility and responsiveness to values if one's humanity is to be authentic»[92].

Taking into consideration the first chapter of *Method in Theology,* we can affirm that development from below upwards exists in according with the four levels of consciousness and intentionality. This development from below upwards is a dynamic process that evolves from the attentive experience of data (empirical level) to the responsible decision (responsible level) passing through the intelligent understanding (intellectual level) and reasonable judgement (rational level).

These four levels, constitutive of development from below, are intrinsically connected and interdependent. But each level of operation has an achievement of its own.

> The proper achievement and end of the first level, experiencing, is the apprehension of data; that of the second level, understanding, is insight into the apprehended data; that of the third level, judgement, is the acceptance or the rejection of the hypotheses and theories put forward by understanding to account for the data; that of the fourth level, decision, the acknowledgement of values and the selection of the methods or the means that lead to their realisation[93].

At the heart of the proper achievement and end pursued by each level, there is the knowing subject as the centre of gravity, the rock of development from below. «The rock, then, is the subject in his conscious, unobjectified attentiveness, intelligence, reasonableness, responsibility»[94].

As a dynamic process, ascending human development invites individuals in a continuous and coherent manner, to attend to the data, to understand intelligently, to judge correctly, to respond to values, to effect cognitive and moral self-transcendence, to commit themselves in an authentic process. For each individual engaged in this process, «it is his coming to be a man, his existing as a man in the full sense of the name»[95].

4. Post-*Method Articles* (1974 -1980)

In this second section of the first chapter, we will examine the articles relative to development from below written between 1974 and

---

[92] *MIT,* 51.
[93] *MIT,* 133.
[94] *MIT,* 20.
[95] *MIT,* 79.

1980. It is during this period that the two ways of human development become a major theme in his thought. As Frederick Crowe so well affirms, it is after *Method in Theology*, published in 1972, «that the two ways, as a general idea of human development, each with its dynamism but each also complementary to the other, came sharply into focus»[96].

We have found eleven articles where Lonergan speaks clearly of human development. Their chronological order of publication is: «Mission and the Spirit» in 1974, «Christology Today: Methodological Reflections» of March 22, 1975, «Creating and Healing in History» of May 13, 1975, «Religious Experience» of March 2, 1976, «The Ongoing Genesis of Methods» in 1976, 1976 Lonergan Workshop held from June 14-18, «The Human Good» of September 1976, «Questionnaire on Philosophy» in 1976, «Natural Right and Historical Mindedness» of April 16, 1977, «Theology and Praxis» of June 16, 1977 and «Questions with regard to Method» of March 31, 1980.

To better understand Lonergan's conception of development from below, we will put these articles in their context and examine them in chronological order of publication. Adopting a historical perspective will permit us to grasp better Lonergan's thought with respect to the two ways of human development in general, and ascending human development in particular.

4.1 Mission and the Spirit

The first explicit mention relative to the two ways of human development is found in «Mission and the Spirit»[97], written in 1974, but published in 1976. In this article, Lonergan asserts that «besides *fides ex auditu*, there is *fides ex infusione*. The former mounts up the successive levels of experience, understanding, judging, deliberating. The latter descends from the gift of God's love through religious conversion to moral, and through religious and moral to intellectual conversion»[98].

Lonergan arrives at this assertion by asking himself how «to apprehend the economy of grace and salvation in an evolutionary perspective and, more precisely, how it enters into the consciousness of man»[99]. To answer this question, he considers vertical finality[100] «inasmuch as

---

[96] F.E. CROWE, «An Expansion», 348.

[97] «Mission and the Spirit», 23-34.

[98] «Mission and the Spirit», 32.

[99] *MIT*, 31.

[100] *MIT*, 24. See B. LONERGAN, «Finality, Love and Marriage», 16-53; *Grace and Freedom*, 76-80.

emergence, development, maturation follow the analogy of evolutionary process»[101].

Distinguishing three kinds of finalities[102], Lonergan speaks of development from below within the framework of intentionality analysis, articulated around three operators. The three operators are the «questions for intelligence, questions for reflection, and questions for deliberation that promote activity from one level to another»[103]. As questions for intelligence the operators, taking the data into account, ask : Why? What? How often? As questions for reflection, the operators, in regard to the discoveries of human genius, ask : Is it so? Is it exactly so? Are you sure? Finally, as questions for deliberation the operators ask if the projected actions are worthy of interest and value.

These operators are in related to each others by sublation: «three types of operators yield four levels of operation. Each lower level is an instance of vertical finality and, that finality is already realised as the higher level functions. The lower level accordingly prepares for the higher and is sublated by it»[104]. Interpreted in the context of the person in quest of development from below, Lonergan considers vertical finality as identical to self-transcendence. Self-transcendence «is experience of man's capacity for self-transcendence, of his unrestricted openness to the intelligible, the true, the good»[105] : ·

---

[101] *MIT*, 158.

[102] «*Absolute finality* is to God. For every end is an instance of the good, and every instance of the good has its ground and goal in absolute goodness. *Horizontal finality* is to proportionate end, the end that results from what a thing is, what follows from it, and what it may exact. *Vertical finality* is an end higher than the proportionate end. It supposes a hierarchy of entities and ends. It *supposes a subordination of the lower to the higher*. Such subordination may be merely instrumental, or participative, or both, inasmuch as the lower serves the higher, or enters into its being and functioning, or under one aspect serves and under another participates» («Mission and the Spirit», 24); my emphasis.

[103] «Mission and the Spirit», 28.

[104] «Mission and the Spirit», 29. «The lower levels of operation are prior as presupposed by the higher, as preparing material for them, as providing them with underfooting and, in that sense, with foundations. But the higher have a priority of their own. They sublate the lower, preserving them indeed in their proper perfection and significance, but also using them, endowing them with a new and fuller and higher significance, and so promoting them to ends beyond their proper scope» («Mission and the Spirit», 30).

[105] «Mission and the Spirit», 32.

By experience we attend to the other; by understanding we gradually construct our world; by judgement we discern its independence of ourselves, by deliberate and responsible freedom we move beyond merely self-regarding norms and make ourselves moral beings. The disinterestedness of morality is fully compatible with the passionateness of being. For that passionateness has a dimension of its own: it underpins and accompanies and reaches beyond the subject as experientially, intelligently, rationally, morally conscious[106].

This passionateness of being, inherent in human nature, invites the subject to transcend himself, to ascend in a conscious and intentional manner the levels of experience, understanding, judgement and responsibility. These different levels are not only in relation to sublation, but also to finality, the one relating to the others, to the extent that the inferior levels are in tension toward higher ends, actualised by the superior levels. Thus,

> we experience to have the materials for understanding; and understanding, far from cramping experience, organises it, enlarges its range, refines its content, and directs it to a higher goal. We understand and formulate to be able to judge, but judgement calls for fuller experience and better understanding; and that demands has us clarifying and expanding and applying our distinctions between astronomy and astrology, chemistry and alchemy, philosophy and myth, fact and fiction. We experience and understand and judge to become moral: to become moral practically, for our decisions affect things; to become moral interpersonally, for our decisions affect other persons, to become moral existentially, for by our decisions we constitute what we are to be[107].

More specifically, the fourth level, that of our moral responsibility, plays the role of vertical finality, in relation to the levels of our concrete experience, our interpersonal understanding and our judgements. In «Mission and the Spirit», therefore, Lonergan views development from below upwards in the context of vertical finality and of human being in quest of his self-transcendence.

4.2 Christology Today: Methodological Reflections

In «Christology Today: Methodological Reflections»[108] of March 22, 1975, Lonergan comes to consider human development in the con-

---

[106] «Mission and the Spirit», 29.
[107] «Mission and the Spirit», 29.
[108] «Christology Today», 74-99.

text of Christology. Evaluating Piet Schoonenberg's contribution to the christological debate, Lonergan finds fault with his christology of presence[109]. The central question around which this christological debate gravitates is as follows : «Can one be truly a man without being a human being»[110]? To answer this question, Lonergan evokes three prolegomena, namely, psychology, philosophy and history.

Concerning the first prolegomenon, — psychology —, Lonergan maintains that «scholastic psychology was a metaphysical psychology. It was a doctrine of the essence of the soul, of its potencies, of their informing habits and acts, and of the objects of the acts. So little did consciousness enter inter into this psychology»[111]. Lonergan wants to include scholastic psychology «within the dynamic of a foundational methodology»[112]. For him, the contemporary challenge flung at traditional christology requires a transcendence of a metaphysical conception of the human being.

In a psychological vein, Lonergan expresses the following postulates: «(1) a person is a psychological subject of interpersonal relations; (2) human development is entry into a symbolic world, a world mediated by meaning; (3) one cannot be a truly human being without being a human person»[113]. He spells out these postulates in clarifying his conception of the development from below upwards:«Human development advances ordinarily from below upwards. It is from experiencing through inquiry to understanding; from intelligent formulations through reflection to judgement; from apprehended reality through deliberation to evaluation, decision, action. Such ordinary process is not the exclusive process»[114].

The second prolegomenon deals with philosophy. Lonergan criticises Piet Shoonenberg's christology of presence, pointing out the difference between the world of immediacy and the world mediated by meaning. «The world of immediacy is the world of data, of what is given to sense and given to consciousness. It is a world as yet without names or concepts, without truth and falsity, without right or wrong»[115]. The presence of Christ to us does not belong to the world of

---

[109] See P. SCHOONENBERG, *Il est le Dieu des hommes*, 1973.
[110] «Christology Today», 75.
[111] «Christology Today», 75.
[112] «Christology Today», 76.
[113] «Christology Today», 76.
[114] «Christology Today», 76.
[115] «Christology Today», 78.

immediacy: as far as «happy are they who without seeing have believed» (Jn 20,9).

In contrast with the world of immediacy, the world mediated by
meaning is a world of questions and answers, a world where one deals
with concepts, symbols, truth and falsity, good and evil. In this world
mediated by meaning, the world is perceived not only as present and
real, but also and first of all «as structured by intelligence, by reasonable judgement, by decision and action»[116]. It is the world of reality, of
knowledge and transcendence:

> The world mediated by meaning is not just reality but reality as known;
> where the knowing is ever in process. The subject that mediates his world by
> meaning is in process of self-realisation for the self-transcendence [...] For
> man's self-realisation is by self-transcendence. Without difference, there is
> no self-transcendence. Without identity it is not one's own but some other
> self that is realised[117].

In the world mediated by meaning self-development is achieved by
self-transcendence, on the cognitive level (that of knowledge and truth)
as well as on the moral level (that of good and values). More specifically, the world mediated by meaning is the world of the existential
sphere where «the cognitional yields to the moral and the moral to the
religious, where we discern between right and wrong and head for holiness or sin»[118].

For Lonergan, development from below consists in entering into the
symbolic world mediated by meaning. «The world mediated by meaning goes beyond experiencing through inquiry to ever fuller understanding, beyond mere understanding through reflection to truth and reality,
beyond mere knowing through deliberation to evaluated and freely chosen courses of action»[119]. Thus, we again recognise the four main operations that structures development from below, i.e., experience, understanding, reflection and deliberation. It is in this world mediated by
meaning that development from below is unfolded and realized.

Taking into consideration the third prolegomenon, the history that is
written and the history that is written about, Lonergan considers the Jesus of history and the Jesus of faith. His intention is «to specify impli-

---

116 «Christology Today», 82.
117 «Christology Today», 92.
118 «Christology Today», 78.
119 «Christology Today», 78.

cations of scholarly history for christological thought»[120]. He examines the meaning of the Council of Chalcedon which declares that «Jesus Christ is similar to us in all things except sin». In the light of this declaration, Lonergan affirms that «if we are to think of Jesus as truly a man, we have to think of him as a historical being, as growing in wisdom, age, and grace in a determinate social and cultural milieu, as developing from below as other human beings and from above on the analogy of religious development»[121].

In this article, Lonergan pursues his reflection on development from below upwards in the context of contemporary christology. He clarifies by contrasting the world of immediacy and the world mediated by meaning. He conceives of development from below upwards as being reali-zed by self-transcendence in the world mediated by meaning.

4.3 Creating and Healing in History

In «Creating and Healing in History»[122] of May 13, 1975, Lonergan speaks of the two complementary vectors of human development: the one, from below upwards, creativity; and the other, from above downwards, healing. He considers the vectors of creativity and healing in relation to history. But, as no particular field of history has been specified, he articulates the theme of creativity and healing in terms of human affairs, considered as the stuff of history. He compares two points of view, that of Bertrand Russell and that of Karl Popper, concerning evil in the world. Bertrand Russell's point of view is that our intellectual development has out-run moral development:

> We have become very clever, according to Russell, indeed too clever. We can make lot of wonderful gadgets, including television, high-speed rockets, and an atom bomb, or a thermonuclear bomb, if you prefer. But we have not been able to achieve that moral and political growth and maturity which alone safely direct and control the uses to which we put our tremendous intellectual powers. This is because we now find ourselves in a mortal danger. Our evil national pride has prevented us from achieving the world-state in time. To put this view in a nutshell: we are clever, perhaps too clever, but we also are wicked, and this mixture of cleverness and wickedness lies at the root of our troubles[123].

---

[120] «Christology Today», 81.
[121] «Christology Today», 82.
[122] Published in *IC*, 100-109.
[123] K. POPPER, *Conjectures and Refutations*, 365.

Karl Popper's points to a misguided moral enthusiasm at the root of the evils in the world.

> The main troubles of our times — and I do not deny that we live in troubled times — are not due to our moral wickedness, but, on the contrary, to our often misguided moral enthusiasm : to our anxiety to better the world we live in. Our wars are fundamentally religious wars; they are wars between competing theories of how to establish a better world. And our moral enthusiasm is often misguided, because we fail to realise that our moral principles, which are sure to be over-simple, are often difficult to apply to the complex human and political situations to which we feel bound to apply them[124].

To stress with B. Russell either this mixture of cleverness and wickedness or with K. Popper our misguided moral enthusiasm gets no further than a simple diagnosis. When one speaks instead of creativity and healing, one refers mainly to remedies, to positive courses of action. Lonergan shows the need of creativity in the midst of the world's economic crisis caused by the multinational corporations which, in the long term, are generating a worldwide disaster, because these multinational corporations aim at maximizing profit on a global scale. Taking into account R. Barnet and R. Muller's affirmation that «the new system needed for our collective survival does not exist»[125], Lo-nergan considers elaborating a new economical system as indispensable for our collective survival. And to elaborate this new system means becoming involved in a creative process. When survival requires a system that does not exist, then the need of creating is manifest.

> The creative task is to find the answers. It is a matter of insight, not of one insight but of many, not of isolated insights but of insights that coalesce, that complement and correct one another, that influence policies and programs, that reveal their shortcomings in their concrete results, that give rise to further correcting insights, corrected policies, corrected programs, that gradually accumulate into the all-round, balanced, smoothly functioning system that from the start was needed but at the start was not yet known[126].

Let us remember that the long road of progress is a creative process and that human development occurs to the extent that, at the heart of historical, political and socially determined contexts, new insights, new policies, new plans of action are established in order to resolve existential problems. Nevertheless, «insights can be implemented only if peo-

---

124 K. POPPER, *Conjectures and Refutations*, 366.
125 R. BARNET – R. MULLER, *Global Reach*, 385.
126 «Creativity and Healing in History», 103.

ple have open minds. Problems can be manifest. Insights that solve them may be available. But the insights will not be grasped and implemented by biased minds»[127].

In fact, four kinds of bias, neurosis, individual bias, group bias and the general bias, prevent the emergence of new insights needed. These new insights correct and influence policies, plans, courses of action, and their concrete results gradually lead to a global and balanced system. This global and balanced system favours the process of progress the we have.

> Growth, progress, is a matter of situations yielding insights, insights yielding policies and projects, policies and projects transforming the initial situation, the initial situation giving rise to further insights that correct and complement the deficiencies of previous insights. So the wheel of progress moves forward through the successive transformations of an initial situation are gathered coherently and cumulatively all the insights that occurred along the way[128].

Toward the end of the article, Lonergan conceives development from below upwards as follows: «There is development from below upwards, from experience to growing understanding, from growing understanding to balanced judgement, from balanced judgement to fruitful courses of action, and from fruitful courses of action to the new situations that call forth further understanding, profounder judgment, richer courses of action. But there also is development from above downwards»[129].

As in «Mission and the Spirit» and «Christology Today: Methodological Reflections», in «Creating and Healing in History», Lonergan considers development from below upwards as a dynamic process that evolves from experience to decision, passing through understanding and judgement. But, in the present article, development from below upwards is specified as a creative process in a context of the contemporary economic crisis.

---

[127] «Creativity and Healing in History», 105. «For there is the *bias of the neurotic* fertile in evasion of the insight his analyst sees he needs. There is the *bias of the individual egoist* whose interest is confined to the insights that would enable him to exploit each new situation to his own personal advantage. There is the *bias of group egoism* blind to the fact that the group no longer fulfils its once useful function and that is merely clinging to power by all the manoeuvres that in one way or another block development and impede progress. There is finally the *bias of all good men of common sense*, cherishing the illusion that their single talent, common sense, is omnicompetent» («Creativity and Healing in History», 105).

[128] «Creating and Healing in History», 105.

[129] «Creating and Healing in History», 106.

4.4 Religious Experience

In «Religious Experience»[130] of March 2, 1976, the question exami-ned by Lonergan is that of knowing «in what manner God's love flooding our hearts is a human experience and just how it fits into hu-man consciousness»[131]. By human experience Lonergan means a series of elements which, when grouped, constitute human consciousness which is composed of an «infrastructure and superstructure»[132]. It is exercised within a social and cultural context in which human beings function as a symbolic and rational animals.

In this context, «we are all conscious of our sensing and our feeling, our inquiring and our understanding, our deliberating and deciding»[133]. The making of decisions is realised through commitment. The commit-ted person faces «the problem of personal existence, that is, when one finds out for oneself that one has to decide for oneself what one is to do with oneself, with one's life, with one's five talents or two or lonely one»[134].

Lonergan considers development from below as a develo-pment of human consciousness that coexists with development from above downwards. He describes development from below in these terms:

It proceeds from data of experience through the unifications and relational networks spun by understanding towards a process of verification that ends with a verdict of acceptance or rejection. Moreover, there is a certain neces-sity to this order of development: without the unifications and relational networks spun by understanding there is nothing of a process of verification to test; and without the data of experience there is nothing for understanding to unify or relate. It remains, however, that these operations occur within a context[135] and that this context is all the more complex and extensive the richer the culture and the more nuanced the social arrangements one has[136].

---

130 «Religious Experience» is one of the three Donald Mathers Memorial lectures, given at Queen's Theological College, Kingston, Ontario, March 2, 1976 The two other lectures are «Religious Knowledge» and «The Ongoing Genesis of Methods», published in *IC*, 115-128.

131 «Religious Experience», 125

132 «Religious Experience», 60.

133 «Religious Experience», 117.

134 «Religious Experience», 123.

135 «Nor is this context just some inert datum that attains influence only in the measure that it is noted, understood, verified, evaluated. Rather it exerts a major influence on the interest that motivates our attention, on the language that selects what we can name and study, on the preunderstanding that underpins our further advance,

This social fabric and inherited culture is what Lonergan calls tradition, because the person engaged in development from below upwards must be faithful to tradition, critique its shortcomings and appropriate its values. Being faithful to the tradition, criticising it and appropriating its values make a person authentic. In this quest for self-development, «what is fundamental is human authenticity»[137], grasped more as a task to be accomplished than as a gift to be received.

And if the person engaged in development from below, does not sufficiently take his tradition into account, he risks foundering in unauthenticity. A tension will then exist between the authenticity to be realized and the unauthenticity to be avoided. «The issue is the struggle of authenticity against unauthenticity, and that struggle is part and parcel of the human condition, of our being animals yet equipped to live not just by instinct but principally by the symbols by which we express our self-understanding and our commitments»[138].

The person will succeed in promoting authenticity and in opposing unauthenticity to the extent that he puts into practice the transcendental precepts by being attentive, intelligent, rational and responsible. In other words, we have «to accept ourselves as we are and by dint of constant and persevering attention, intelligence, reasonableness, responsibility, strive to expand what is true and force out what is mistaken in views that we have inherited or spontaneously developed»[139].

In «Religious Experience», Lonergan envisions development from below upwards in strict relation to human authenticity which requires putting the transcendental precepts into practice.

4.5 The Ongoing Genesis of Methods

In «The Ongoing Genesis of Methods»[140] of March 4, 1976, Lonergan elaborates a dynamic methodological approach to the sciences and examines how they are structured and restructured according to their

---

on the opinions that have to be revised before anything novel or new can be entertained or accepted.» («Religious Experience», 126).

[136] «Religious Experience», 126

[137] «Religious Experience», 120.

[138] «Religious Experience», 122. «Really the problem is not tradition but unauthenticity in the formation and transmission of tradition. The cure is not the undoing of tradition but the undoing of its inauthenticity» (Religious Experience, 121-122).

[139] F.E. CROWE, «An Exploration», 63, fn. 55.

[140] «Ongoing Genesis of Methods», in *IC*, 146-165.

methods and their fields of research[141]. In «Questions with regard to Method», published in 1980, Lonergan specifies that «the ongoing genesis of methods is precisely the matter of the structure of scientific revolutions»[142].

«The Ongoing Genesis of Methods» examines, first of all, the origin of the dynamic approach to methods that appeared with the scientific revolution of the sixteenth and seventeenth centuries; sec-ondly, the relativism and the possible foundations of methods; thirdly, the increasing specialisation and limitation of methods; fourthly, the growing interest within the human sciences in studying concrete human beings; and finally, the consideration of the dialectic as the method for distinguishing authenticity from unauthenticity.

In dealing with the third point, Lonergan argues that the modern sciences are characterised more by their methods than by their fields of research. It is the method that in engendering laws and principles assures the development of sciences. Considered from a dynamic perspective, these methods themselves are in a process of evolution and development. And «the developments of existing methods are just fresh instances of attending to the data, grasping their intelligibility, formulating the content of the new insights, and checking as thoroughly as possible their validity»[143].

Lonergan comes back to the distinction between the world of immediacy and the world mediated by meaning. The world of immediacy is a world that is very much like «Hume's world in which there is discerned neither permanence nor causality nor necessity. The subject correlative to the world of immediacy is the subject locked up in his immediate experience of sense and of the data of consciousness. His knowledge is just infrastructure, and his actions flow directly from ap-

---

[141] «The *Posterior Analytics* conceived philosophy and science as a single, logically interlocking unity, in which philosophy was to provide the sciences with their basic terms and principles. Instead of directing men's minds to practical results, Aristotle held that science was concerned with the necessary truth, that what can be changed is not the necessary but the contingent, and so the fruit of science can be no more than the contemplation of the eternal truths that are brought to light» («The Ongoing Genesis of Methods», 148). In contrast, Lonergan has a dynamic view of the same matter where «sciences are conceived in terms of methods and fields, and method are not fixed once for all but keep developing, differentiating, regrouping as the exigencies of advance may demand» («The Ongoing Genesis of Methods», 146).

[142] «Questions with regard to Method», in *DIC*, 307.

[143] «The Ongoing Genesis of Methods», 150.

petites. His capacity to communicate is uninformed by intelligence, unguided by reason, uncontrolled by responsibility»[144].

Development from below upwards is described in the context of the «empirical generalized method» which, according to a normative pattern, «moves from experience to understanding, and from understanding to factual judgement»[145]. This normative pattern of the generalised empirical method is made more explicit in the following:

> The normative pattern that relates these operations to one another is the conscious dynamism of sensitive spontaneity, of intelligence raising further questions and demanding satisfactory answers, of reasonableness insisting on sufficient evidence before it can assent yet compelled to assent when sufficient evidence is forthcoming, of conscience presiding over all and revealing to the subject his authenticity or his unauthenticity as he observes or violates the immanent norms of his own sensitivity, his own intelligence, his own reasonableness, his own freedom and responsibility[146].

The operations of sensibility, of intelligence, of reasonableness and responsibility are those which, each in his own consciousness, can personally verify and appropriate. The personal verification and appropriation of these operations «take individuals out of the isolation and privacy of the experiential infrastructure»[147] and engage them in a steadfast fidelity to immanent norms of the human spirit. The steadfast fideli-ty becomes really efficacious and integral only if the subject relies upon authenticity:

> On the authenticity with which intelligence takes us beyond the experiential infrastructure to enrich it, extend it, but never to slight it and much less to violate its primordial role; on the authenticity with which rational reflection goes beyond the constructions of intelligence [...] on the authenticity with which moral deliberation takes us beyond cognitional process into the realm of freedom and responsibility, evaluation and decision, not in any way to annul or slight experience or understanding or factual judgement, but to add the further and distinct truth of value judgements and the consequent decisions demanded by a situation in which authenticity·cannot be taken for granted[148].

---

[144] «The Ongoing Genesis of Methods», 150-151.
[145] «The Ongoing Genesis of Methods», 160.
[146] «The Ongoing Genesis of Methods», 150.
[147] «The Ongoing Genesis of Methods», 151.
[148] «The Ongoing Genesis of Methods», 160.

This authenticity is an achievement of development from below upwards to the extent that, as a quest for cognitive and moral self-
transcendence, it invites individuals to question not only the data of
experiential infrastructure and the insights of intelligence, but also and
above all, to question values, while concretely envisaging how to put
them into practice. In putting them into practice, individuals become
authentic persons, contributing to the advent of progress within their
society. Progress is conceived «as a cyclic and cumulative process. A
situation gives rise to an insight. The insight generates policies, pro-
jects, plans, courses of action. The courses of action produce a new and
improved situation. The new and improved situation gives rise to further insights, and so the cycle recommences»[149]. Like progress, decline
can be cyclic or cumulative. If decline becomes cyclic and cumulative,

> the policies, projects, plans, courses of action that come from creative insight
> into the existing situation have the misfortune of running counter not merely
> to vested interests but to any and every form of human unauthenticity.
> Doubts are raised, objections are formulated, suspicions insinuated, com-
> promises imposed. Policies, projects, plans, courses of action are modified to
> make the new situation not a progressive product of human authenticity but a
> mixed product partly of human authenticity and partly of human obtuseness,
> unreasonableness, irresponsibility[150].

This mixture of authenticity and unauthenticity creates a situation of
conflict and tension. How does one face this situation of conflict between progress favoured by authenticity and decline engendered by unauthenticity? To face this conflict, Lonergan has recourse to the dialectic as a «technique for distinguishing between authentic evaluations,
decisions, actions»[151]. Dialectic can be applied to problems of interpretation just as it can be equally applied to questions related to history. In
the domain of interpretation, this dialectic thus consists in a recognition
of the obstacles, an effort to reverse them and to restore the process of
development.

The dialectic has a twofold hermeneutics: «The hermeneutic of suspicion that pierces through mere plausibility to its real ground; the hermeneutic of recovery that discovers what is intelligent, true, and good
in the obstruction and goes on to employ this discovery to qualify,

---

149 «The Ongoing Genesis of Methods», 157.
150 «The Ongoing Genesis of Methods», 157-158.
151 «The Ongoing Genesis of Methods», 159.

complement, correct earlier formulation of the method»[152]. In having recourse to this twofold hermeneutics, the dialectic has as its essential function to promote authenticity and development as opposed to unauthenticity and decline.

In «The Ongoing Genesis of Methods», develo-pment from below upwards within the framework of the generalized empirical method. Human authenticity which, as a quest for cognitive and moral transcendence, promotes the process of individual and social development.

4.6 1976 Lonergan Workshop

During the *docta ignorantia* session at the Lonergan Workshop[153], Lonergan alludes to the two ways of human development. The literary form of this session is an interview. We will examine some questions and answers from this interview which Lonergan sets down within the context of the functional specialities of theology. The first question is:

> *What would the main contributions of the functional specialities of dialectics and foundations in a methodically transformed theology be to our understanding of the relation of theory and praxis?* The first phase is development from below upwards, if I'm permitted a spatial metaphor to denote the fact that the procedure is from data, through understanding and judgement to decision, and that's the first phase. You are learning what the original texts were in textual criticism, you are learning to understand what the meaning of the texts was in exegesis, you are placing the different texts each in its own period and so on and so forth in history and you are clarifying the oppositions that aren't going to be eliminated by any further empirical work in dialectic[154].

For to Lonergan, the functional specialities of theology can be divided into two phases, namely, the mediating phase, in *oratione obliqua* and the mediated phase, *in oratione recta.* And in each phase, it is a question of «experiencing, understanding and judgment and decision»[155]. He emphasises that both phases, in their complementarity, promote human development. However, it is the first mediating phase alone that constitutes development from below upwards.

---

[152] «The Ongoing Genesis of Methods», 164. Lonergan has taken this twofold dialectic from P. RICOEUR, *De l'interprétation*, 36f.

[153] *Lonergan Workshop* held at Boston College, June 14 to 18, 1976 during a session called *docta ignorantia*. Transcribed by N. Graham, File 885, LRI, 1-119.

[154] 1976 LoWo Transcripts, 6; my emphasis.

[155] 1976 LoWo, 99.

This development from below upwards which proceeds from the data of experience to decision by way of understanding and judgment, is illustrated starting from the textual criticism which evolves progressively from research to dialectic, passed through interpretation and history. As the four levels of intentional consciousness moves from one level to another, likewise the first four functional specialities of theology evolve from one function speciality to another.

The second question concerns the understanding of praxis:

Would you please review for us the central elements of your understanding of praxis. How is this understanding of praxis related to other significant uses of the word, e.g., in Aristotle, Marx, and Habermas? There is development from below upwards, ever fuller attention to ever broader experience, ever better understanding and formulation of the understanding, ever fuller verification of these formulations, ever truer authenticity in one's commitment to intelligence, reasonableness, responsibility, love[156].

Before giving the essential elements of his understanding of praxis[157], Lonergan makes explicit development from below in relation to authenticity that is sublated by a commitment at the levels of intelligence, rationality, responsibility and love. Invited to comment on his understanding of authenticity, Lonergan insists on the fact that it is a question of the subject's own authenticity, exercised at each level of human knowing:

I'm referring to you. You're intelligent, you ask questions. And when the answers do not satisfy you it's because of your intelligence, intelligence in you is a norm. And you are authentic on that level in so far as you ask the question and you are not satisfied with unsatisfactory answers. And you are rational. You want to have sufficient evidence for the answers before you affirm them. And you are authentic in so far as you follow that norm, your own rationality. And you are responsible in so far as you deliberate [...] And that is you, your authenticity[158].

---

156 1976 LoWo, 57.
157 As answer to the use of praxis in Aristotle, Marx and Habermas, Lonergan writes: «In Aristotle you distinguish *theoria*, *praxis* and *poesis*. *Theoria* is speculative intellect, contemplation of the necessary, what is necessarily so [...] *Praxis* and *poesis* deal with the contingent. *Praxis* is conduct, it deals with the contingent. *Poesis* is producing and it deals with the contingent (1976 LoWo, 58). For K. Marx, «it is praxis as a theory [...] As Hegel, Marx is dynamic but his dynamic is not of the concept but of the modes and relations of production» (1976 LoWo, 59).
158 1976 LoWo, 44.

As in «Religious Experience», «The Ongoing Genesis of Methods», in the 1976 Lonergan Workshop too, Lonergan conceives of development from below upwards in relation to the subject's own authenticity which sublates intelligence, rationality and responsibility.

4.7 The Human Good

«The Human Good»[159] is the title of the second chapter of *Method in Theology*[160]. In «The Human Good» of September 1976, Lonergan sums up the major themes of his second chapter on the notion of value judgments, self-transcendence, progress and decline. These different themes are placed in a historical process in which human beings are involved: «It is not something of the past, it is something we are part of, it is human history, it is something in which we are involved now and for the rest of our lives»[161]. But what is new, in the present article, in relation to the second chapter of *Method in Theology*, is the explicitation of the two ways of human development.

Lonergan arrives at the explicitation of development from below upwards by distinguishing the world of immediacy and the world mediated by meaning and values. He deems that there is an evolution from the world of immediacy into the world mediated by values: «The infant lives in a world of immediacy. As the child learns to speak, goes to school, goes to work, marries, he moves more and more into a world mediated by meaning and motivated by values and it is an entirely different world, enormously larger, a world not merely of fact but also of fiction, involving truth but also falsehood, and so on»[162].

The transition from the world of immediacy to the world mediated by meaning and values can be compared to the transition from horizontal development to vertical development: «There are stages of the development and deliberate stages in the development. There is horizontal development within the horizon one has attained; vertical development when one has moved beyond one's present horizon — when someone pulls the rug from underneath your world and you have to move into another»[163].

---

[159] «The Human Good» is a lecture delivered at Saint Mary's University, Halifax, Nova Scotia, September 1976, under the theme «Beyond Relativism». Published in *Humanitas* 15 (1979) 113-26.

[160] *MiT*, 27-55.

[161] «The Human Good», 126.

[162] «The Human Good», 115.

[163] «The Human Good», 120.

It is within this world mediated by values and marked by different horizons of the subject that the two ways of human development are unfolded. «Human development is of two types. There is development from below upwards: experience, understanding, judgments of fact, judgements of value. And that is the way we appropriate, make things our own. On the other hand, there is development from above downwards»[164].

Development from below, composed of experience, understanding, judgements of fact and judgements of value, is also the way of self-appropriation which contributes to the constitution of ourselves as persons. «The immanently generated knowledge, in virtue of one's own inner and outer experience, one's own insights, one's own judgments of fact and value, one has made them oneself on the evidence that one knows»[165].

Lonergan insists, in the social sphere, on the primordial role that insights play in the cyclic process of progress: «Situations give rise to insights revealing new possibilities. New possibilities lead to new courses of action, new courses of action produce new situations and new situations give rise to further insights revealing still further possibilities and so on: a cyclic and cumulative process»[166]. If on the level of intelligence insights promote progress, then biases favour decline. It is up to insights to avoid biases and to restore progress. In fact, «insight is revealing the mistakes of the past, bringing them to light, revealing possibilities for correction, and indeed bringing to light new courses of action. Challenge and response is an ongoing process»[167].

In clarifying cognitive operations, namely, experience, insights, judgments of fact and judgements of value, Lonergan affirms that development from below evolves from questions for intelligence. In other words, as normative and recurrent, these three forms of questions exhibit the inquiring and critical spirit of the human mind. «So the wonder of the investigator, the restlessness of the doubter, the disquiet of the uneasy conscience keeps moving us. Wonder, from the level of experience to understanding and formulation, doubt, to the level of truth and knowledge of reality as mediated by meaning, and the uneasy conscience, to making good resolutions»[168].

---

164 «The Human Good», 120.
165 «The Human Good», 121.
166 «The Human Good», 124.
167 «The Human Good», 124
168 «The Human Good», 118.

The notion of objectivity has to do with grounding our knowledge of reality. «And in what does the objectivity consist? It derives its claim from its self-transcendence. The sense in which objectivity is authentic subjectivity; the subjectivity of a person who is attentive, intelligent, reasonable, responsible authentic human subjectivity»[169]. The question of objectivity regards the world mediated by meaning and motivated by values. Without the knowledge of this world mediated by meaning and values, «you get into moral idealism»[170]. A true objectivity is thus the consequence of an authentic subjectivity which responds to the invitation to human beings to be attentive, intelligent, rational and responsible. Without putting these transcendental precepts into practice, the upward movement of development would be impossible.

In «The Human Good», Lonergan affirms that development from below upwards implies an evolution from the world of immediacy to the world mediated by values. The values of the second world form the object of a self-appropriation which helps persons to become authentic.

4.8 Questionnaire on Philosophy

In 1976, Lonergan responded to a questionnaire on philosophy[171] for a philosophy symposium. In the «Questionnaire on Philosophy», questions dealt with the nature, method, objectives and relevance of philosophy, in their interdisciplinary relations to human sciences in general, and to theology in particular.

In answering the questions, Lonergan makes explicit his understanding of the two ways of human development. The first mention of development from below upwards appears in the context of sublation by the cognitive operations. «Sensitivity sublates vegetal living; intelligence sublates animal living; rational judgement concentrates the creativity of intelligence on truth and reality; deliberation, evaluation, decision, praxis integrate knowing and feeling in the pursuit of the good, of the truly worth while»[172].

---

[169] «The Human Good», 119.

[170] «The Human Good», 120.

[171] A questionnaire was distributed to many Jesuit Professors of Philosophy. The responses to the questionnaire were to be handed on before September 30, 1976. Lonergan did not attend the Symposium, held one year later, at Villa Cavaletti near Rome, from September 8 to 18, 1977. Published in *MJLS* 2 (1984) 1-35.

[172] «Questionnaire on Philosophy», *MJLS* 2 (1984) 7.

In the second reference, development from below upwards seems to be indispensable in the philosophical formation of candidates for the ministerial priesthood.

Do you think that philosophical studies for christians and/or especially for candidates for the priesthood should be different from philosophical studies «tout court», and if so, why? The basic principle seems to be that human development occurs in two distinct modes. If I may use a spatial metaphor, it moves (1) from below upwards and (2) from above downwards. It moves from below upwards inasmuch as it begins from one's personal experience, advances through ever fuller understanding and more balanced judgement, and so attains the responsible exercise of personal freedom[173].

Human development, in its two modes, constitutes the fundamental principle for the formation of future priests. Human development from below upwards of the latter begins first with their personal experience, then moves towards a greater understanding and a balanced judgement in order to finally reach a higher sense of responsibility in the exercise of their personal freedom. The interdependence of the two ways of human development is once more affirmed, but Lonergan specifies that it is only through the first way that assimilation and appropriation of the second way become effective and significant.

Moreover, development from below upwards depends primarily on what Lonergan calls «horizon» of the individuals engaged in this development.

By horizon is meant the totality, the «*Umgreifendes*», within which understanding is sought, judgments of facts are made, and evaluations are accepted. Such a totality dominates our knowing and deciding from the very fact that our questions have their origin in the *a priori* desire to understand, to reach the truth, to know the real, to do what is worth while, that this desire of itself is both comprehensive and concrete, but its specification is attained only through specific questions and the accumulation of specific answers[174].

As in the preceding articles, Lonergan speaks of the interdependence and complementarity of the two ways of human development, by emphasizing the structure of knowing and doing. In effect, «the structure of our knowing and doing expresses the conditions of being an authentic person; but this structure is a matter of being attentive, being intelligent, being reasonable, being responsible; accordingly there are four

---

[173] «Questionnaire on Philosophy», 10.
[174] «Questionnaire on Philosophy», 30.

basic precepts independent of cultural differences»[175]. The four transcendental precepts, independent of cultural differences, must continuously be personally appropriation. It is a matter, Lonergan insists, of «personal appropriation of one's intelligent, rational, and responsible being»[176].

The personal appropriation of the transcendental precepts, a process embodied in the dialectic of history[177], is composed of three components, namely, progress, decline and recovery. Progress occurs when attentiveness, intelligence, rationality and responsibility are put into practice. Decline, on the other hand, appears, when inattention, unintelligence, irrationality, and irresponsibility reign. Lonergan explains his understanding of progress and decline in these terms:

> Progress results only if people are attentive to the results of previous action, only if they are intelligent in devising remedies for previous mistakes, only if they are reasonable and responsible in their decisions to act and to cooperate. But such attentiveness, intelligence, reasonableness, and responsibility are distorted or even blocked by the egoism of individuals and groups and by the bias of practical men of common sense who are ever prone to fancy themselves omnicompetent. Now in the measure that men are inattentive, unintelligent, unreasonable, irresponsible, in the same measure their actions and consequent situations will be marked by unintelligibility of their oversights, their mistakes, their irrationality[178].

Against the conflict between the thesis of progress and the antithesis of decline, redemption is presented as the dialectical synthesis, enabling people to live out their authenticity. Thus, «attentiveness, intelligence,

---

[175] «Questionnaire on Philosophy», 27.

[176] «Questionnaire on Philosophy», 10; see also 21. 32.

[177] «Dialectic has to do with the concrete, with action, with contradiction» («Questionnaire on Philosophy», 15). Concerning the dialectic of history, Lonergan points out two shortcomings of Marx's materialist dialectic as correcting Hegel's dialectic. «From Hegelian idealism he moves to the world of historical praxis. This was a real advance, but its benefit was compromised by Marx's arguing against idealism and concluding to materialism [...] Marx was right in feeling that the Hegelian dialectic needed to be adjusted, but he was content to turn it upside down. What was needed, I should say, was for it to be turned inside out» («Questionnaire on Philosophy», 18).

[178] «Questionnaire on Philosophy», 15. «Further, the more that objective situations are distorted by unintelligent and irrational actions, the less are they capable of giving rise to fresh insights, since all that intelligence can discern in the unintelligible is its lack of intelligibility. So with creativity blocked, the body social becomes the victims of warring egoism and blundering short-sightedness» («Questionnaire on Philosophy», 16).

reasonableness, responsibility, are the conditions of possibility of human authenticity. These conditions are excluded by inattention, obtuseness, unreasonableness, irresponsibility, and such exclusion is the root and substance of human inauthenticity, of man's alienation from his true being. Finally, man's salvation even in this life is the otherworldliness of the theological virtues of faith, hope, and charity»[179]. Redemption, in struggling against the alienation of persons, restores them to true authenticity, in their genuine human development.

In «Questionnaire on Philosophy», the development from below upwards concerns human authenticity that sublates the cognitive operations of experience, understanding, judgement and decision. But this human authenticity only occurs through personal appropriation of the transcendental precepts. As in «Creating and Healing in History», in «Questionnaire on Philosophy» puts in relief, the interdependence of the two distinct modes of development.

4.9 Natural Right and Historical Mindedness

In «Natural Right and Historical Mindedness»[180] of April 16, 1977, Lonergan asserts that in the contemporary context, concrete human reality must take of two components into account, namely, human nature and historical mindedness[181]. If one wants to establish the norms of historicity, they will be found neither in cultural achievements nor in the styles of human life but in the «human spirit as raising and answering questions»[182]. It is in the context of human historicity that Lonergan defines development from below upwards:

---

[179] «Questionnaire on Philosophy», 16.

[180] Lecture at the Fifty-first Annual Meeting of the *PACPA*, 1977. Published in *IC*, 169-183.

[181] Lonergan uses Alan Richardson's term, of historical mindedness from his book, *History Sacred and Profane*, London, 1964. According to Richardson, «since the nineteenth century it has been an axiom of Western thinking that men and their institutions cannot be understood apart from their history, or that to know what a thing is, it is necessary to give an account of its past. This is part of, at least, and a very important part, of the meaning of the statement that we nowadays live in an historical-minded age» (A. RICHARDSON, *History Sacred and Profane*, 32). Concomitant with this historical-minded age, in human studies, «man is to be known not only in his nature but in his historicity, not only philosophically but also historically, not only abstractly but also concretely» («Natural Right and Historical Mindedness», 179).

[182] «Natural Right and Historical Mindedness», 172.

Now what was going forward may be either (1) development or (2) the handing on of development and each of these may be (3) complete or (4) incomplete. Development may be described, if a spatial metaphor is permitted, as "from below upwards": it begins from experience, is enriched by full understanding, is accepted by sound judgement, is directed not to satisfactions but to values, and the priority of values is comprehensive[183].

In this citation, development from below upwards corresponds to what Lonergan calls «development» and «the transmission of development» equates with development from above downwards. Lonergan's conception of development from below upwards here basically the same as in the preceding articles. The only difference is that instead of decision and responsibility, it is a matter of values and even a priority in the scale of values.

But human development from below upwards can be complete or incomplete. It can be incomplete in two ways. First, «development is incomplete when it does not go the whole way upwards: it accepts some values but its evaluations are partial; or it is not concerned with values at all but only with satisfactions; or its understanding may be adequate but its factual judgements faulty; or finally its understanding may be more a compromise than a sound contribution»[184].

Secondly, development from below upwards can be incomplete if it is not based on development from above that promotes the values from which development from below upwards takes root. To avoid development from below upwards being incomplete, one must be involved in a process self-transcendence which implies an intellectual, moral and affective conversion.

As intellectual, this conversion draws a sharp distinction between the world of immediacy and the world mediated by meaning, between the criteria appropriate to operations in the former and, on the other hand, the criteria appropriate in the latter. As moral, it acknowledges a distinction between satisfactions and values, and it is committed to values even where they conflict with satisfactions. As affective, it is commitment to love in the home, loyalty in the city, faith in destiny of man[185].

As in «Mission and the Spirit», human development from below upwards is articulated around «questions for intelligence, questions for

---

[183] «Natural Right and Historical Mindedness», 180.
[184] «Natural Right and Historical Mindedness», 180-181.
[185] «Natural Right and Historical Mindedness», 179.

reflection, and questions for deliberation»[186]. These three forms of questions are connected to each other and presuppose the acknowledgement of the world mediated by meaning. But «knowing a world mediated by meaning is only a prelude to man's dealing with nature, to his interpersonal living and working with others, to his existential becoming what he is to make of himself by his own choices and deeds»[187]. According to Lonergan, each person in quest of human development from below asks himself these three forms of question and «can reveal to any other his natural propensity to seek understanding, to judge reasonably, to evaluate fairly, to be open to friendship»[188].

Nevertheless, putting these norms into practice is not taken for granted because «besides intelligence, there is obtuseness; besides truth there is falsity; besides what is worthwhile, there is what is worthless; besides love there is hatred»[189]. Consequently, one can expect to encounter not only development, but also decline, «not only social order but also disorder, not only cultural vitality and achievement but also lassitude and deterioration, not an ongoing and uninterrupted sequence of developments but rather a dialectic of radically opposed tendencies»[190].

In «Natural Right and Historical Mindedness», Lonergan examines the two ways of human development using the spatial metaphor from below upwards and from above downwards. Development from below upwards, incomplete without the transmission of development from above downwards, is articulated around questions for intelligence, for reflection, and for deliberation.

4.10 Theology and Praxis

In «Theology and Praxis»[191] of June 16, 1977, Lonergan deals with the relationship between theology and praxis. He asks precisely how theology can be envisaged as praxis. To ask how theology is a praxis «is not to ask whether the views of Kant or Schopenhauer, Kierkegaard or Newman, Nietzsche or Blondel, Ricoeur or Habermas are to be made normative in theology. On the contrary, it is to ask a general question

---

[186] «Natural Right and Historical Mindedness», 172.
[187] «Natural Right and Historical Mindedness», 173.
[188] «Natural Right and Historical Mindedness», 182.
[189] «Natural Right and Historical Mindedness», 176.
[190] «Natural Right and Historical Mindedness», 176.
[191] A lecture at the Thirty-second Annual Convention of the *PCTSA*, 1977. Published in *IC*, 1985, 184-201.

and a rather technical one. It is to ask whether there are basic theological questions whose solution depends on the personal development of theologians»[192].

In explaining the two ways of development, Lonergan affirms that the structure of development is twofold : the way up and the way down. The two ways are complementary in such a way that if the way down develops, the way up develops as well. «As it proceeds more and more there develops the capacity to raise questions and to be satisfied or dissastisfied with answers. Such is the spontaneous and fundamental process of teaching and learning common to all. It is at once intelligent and reasonable and responsible»[193].

Commenting on Plato's myth of the cave, he asserts that development from below upwards resembles «the ascent from the darkness of the cave to the light of day [which] is a movement from the world of immediacy that is already out there now to a world mediated by the meaningfulness of intelligent, reasonable, responsible answers to questions»[194]. We move from the world of immediacy into the world mediated by meaning, thanks to the inner light of intelligence, reasonableness and deliberation because:

> It is the inner light of intelligence that asks what and why and how and what for and, until insight hits the bull's eye, keeps further questions popping up. It is the inner light of reasonableness that demands sufficient reason before assenting and, until sufficient reason is forthcoming, keeps in your mind the further questions of the doubter. It is the inner light of deliberation that brings you beyond the egoist's question — What's in it for me? — to the moralist's question — Is it really and truly worthwhile? — and if your living does not meet that standard, bathes you in the unrest of an uneasy conscience[195].

It is at the level of values that Lonergan puts the relationship between theology and praxis. In explaining this relationship, he relies

---

[192] «Theology and Praxis», 185. «To use a distinction made by P. Ricoeur, it is to ask whether issues on which theologians are badly divided call for a hermeneutic of suspicion and a hermeneutic of recovery, hermeneutic of suspicion that diagnoses failures in personal development and a hermeneutic of recovery that generously recognises the genuine personal development that did occur» (*Ibid.*)

[193] «Theology and Praxis», 197.

[194] «Theology and Praxis», 193.

[195] «Theology and Praxis», 193.

upon Aristotle's definition of praxis[196] which results from «our own deliberation and choice under the guidance of the practical wisdom that Aristotle named *phronesis* and Aquinas named *prudentia*»[197]. It is up to theologians to transform theology into praxis to the extent that their personal development results from a free appropriation of virtues such as *phronesis* and *prudentia*.

To give importance to the free appropriation of values arising from human behaviour is a reaction to behaviourism and positivism. The philosophic trend to value moral freedom «appears in Kant's first and second critiques, in Schopenhauer's world as will and representation, in Kierkegaard's reliance on faith and Newman's reliance on conscience, in Nietzsche's will to power, in Blondel's philosophy of action, in Ricoeur's philosophy of will, in Habermas's juxtaposition of knowledge and human interests»[198].

Nevertheless, the theologian in his professional activity should not take the views of the aforementioned philosophers as norms for theological questions. The development of theology depends fundamentally on the theologian's personal development and conversion. In effect, «a theological issue of some importance yet can be genuinely solved only inasmuch as individual theologians undergo an intellectual conversion»[199].

In «Theology and Praxis», Lonergan examines the relationship between theology and praxis. Development from below upwards is conceived as a movement that makes one leave the obscure world of immediacy in order to enter into the world mediated by meaning thanks to the inner light of intelligence, reasonableness and deliberation.

---

[196] In ARISTOTLE's *Nicomachean Ethics*, one reads that *praxis* is shared neither by animals (VI, 2, 1139a 19-20) nor by gods (X, 8, 1178b 7-22). It differs from *poesis* and *technè* (VI, 4, 1140a 1-23). As *phronesis* (VI, 7, 1141b 16), it is concerned with particulars (III, 1, 1110b 6-7). Desire and the *logos* of the end are principles of *proairesis* and *proairesis* is the efficient principle of *praxis* (VI, 2, 1139a 31-33). As hypothesis is the principle of mathematics so the end is the principle of *praxis* (VII, 9, 1151a 16-17).

[197] «Theology and Praxis», 184. For *prudentia* in Aquinas, see *ST*, II-III, q. 48-56. I find restrictive Lonergan's view of praxis. I share instead M. Lamb's viewpoint which extends praxis to the social and political spheres of existence. «My only criticism is the complement that I would have liked Lonergan to go on and relate that personal praxis to social and political praxis. Aristotle mentions how practical wisdom (*phronesis*) not only should guide personal conduct (*praxis*), but also communal economy (*oikonomia*) and politics» (M. LAMB, «Theology and Praxis», 26).

[198] «Theology and Praxis», 185.

[199] «Theology and Praxis», 185.

4.11 Questions with Regard to Method

On March 31, 1980, at the Thomas More Institute in Montreal, in an interview entitled «Questions with regard to Method»[200], Lonergan speaks once more of the two ways of human development:

> *Our first question is one we have been deputed to ask you. It relates to Doran's work[201] on dreams and to readings people have been doing in their courses. Do you take it in dreams there are levels which might correspond to the levels of insight, judgment and decision?* Besides the horizontal process — from sensitivity to images, from intelligent questioning to insights and definitions and theories and hypotheses, from questions for reflection through grasping the sufficient evidence to making judgments, and through grasping the evidence to making judgement, and through moral evaluation and making a decision — helping you is an influence coming from below suggesting relevant images, relevant questions, all the way up[202].

Lonergan reaffirms that the way up evolves from questions for intelligence to questions for reflection, and from questions for reflection to questions for deliberation. These questions for intelligence, reflection and deliberation constitute 'the horizontal process' that includes the four levels of consciousness.

Nevertheless, «as distinctions develop between the different levels, they move to a point where they become their own masters, at home with themselves and capable of doing things for themselves, being on their own, self-actuating. That is where the going from below upwards becomes fully significant in the individual»[203]. The way up is only fully and truly significant if individuals appropriate the horizontal process in becoming themselves, in being masters of their destiny.

As in the preceding articles, in «Questions with regard to Method», Lonergan considers the way up via the horizontal process that evolves from questions for intelligence to questions for reflection and deliberation.

5. Conclusion

By way of conclusion we affirm that in the eleven post-*Method* articles published between 1974 and 1980, Lonergan explains the theme of development from below upwards already operative in *Method in Theo-*

---

[200] Published in *DIC*, 286-314.
[201] R. DORAN, *Subject and Psyche*, 1977.
[202] «Questions with Regard to Method», 286-287.
[203] «Questions with Regard to Method», 311.

logy. In *Method in Theology* as well as in the eleven post-*Method* articles, Lonergan conceives of human development from below upwards as a dynamic process which proceeds from an experiential infrastructure to responsible decision by passing through intelligent understanding and rational judgement. Nevertheless, in the eleven post-*Method* articles there are various and complementary connotations which enrich Lonergan's understanding of development from below upwards.

In the article «Mission and the Spirit», 1974, Lonergan looks at development from below in the context of vertical finality, understood as identical with self-transcendence. A year later, in 1975, he published two articles, namely «Christology Today», and «Healing and Creating in History». In the first, he maintains that the way up is articulated in the world mediated by meaning, and this is effected by means of self-transcendence. In the second article, development from below is explained as analogous to the creative process that unfolds in our historical and social context, marked by biases.

In 1976, Lonergan wrote five articles: «Religious Experience» (March 2), «The Ongoing Genesis of Methods» (March 4), The 1976 Lonergan Workshop (June 14-18), «The Human Good» (September), and the «Questionnaire on Philosophy» (September). In all of them but «The Human Good», development from below upwards is closely connected to human authenticity which sublates the cognitive operations of experience, understanding, judgement and decision. This human authenticity promotes both individual and social progress, while unauthenticity, characterised by biases, favours decline. When decline sets in, then dialectic must be called upon in order to deal with unauthenticity and thereby to restore the process of human development.

In «The Human Good», Lonergan's understanding of the development from below upwards is in general similar to that in «Christology Today: Methodological Reflections» to the extent that, in both articles, human development from below upwards emerges and unfolds within the world mediated by meaning and values. More specifically though, «The Human Good» discusses human development in terms of personally appropriating the operations of one's own experience, insights, judgements of fact and of value.

In 1977, Lonergan re-examines the theme of human development in two articles: «Natural Right and Historical Mindedness» and «Theology and Praxis». In the former, he conceives of human development from below upwards in terms of questions for intelligence, reflection and deliberation. This conception is taken up again in «Questions with

Regard to Method» of March 1980. In «Theology and Praxis», the way up is presented as a process which, with the help of intelligence, rationality and deliberation, enables a person to develop and grow within the world mediated by meaning and values.

CHAPTER II

Human Development from Above Downwards

1. Introduction

For Lonergan, the two ways of human development constitute the
two complementary phases of one and the same human development.
«As progress must take its start from tradition, so tradition must submit
to the critique of progress. But, in principle, the development achieved
through personal experience and the development based on accepting
heritage can be conceived as complementary to one another»[1] · We will
now examine, from a synthetic perspective, human development from
above downwards, first in *Method in Theology*, and then in the post-
Method articles published between 1974 and 1980.

2. *Method in Theology*

If «the way up» implies a movement from below upwards that includes the data, the intelligible, the true and the good, the way down
implies a movement from above downwards that proceeds from the
good to the data through the true and the intelligible. As a matter of
fact, Lonergan writes: «as the many elementary objects are constructed
into larger wholes, as the many operations are conjoined in a single
compound knowing, so too the many levels of consciousness are just
successive stages in the unfolding of a single thrust, the eros of the human spirit. To know the good, it must know the real; to know the real, it

---

[1] *OTN*, 24.

must know the true; to know the true, it must know the intelligible, to know the intelligible, it must attend to the data»[2]

In the same way, as in the development from below upwards, we evolve from experience to values through understanding and judgement, so too as regards development from above downwards, «we can verify in our own history the process of shared values to judgements accepted in trust, judgements we struggle to understand in turn affect our experience in many ways»[3]. Thus, values and judgements can be communicated in an atmosphere of confidence and make intelligible the data of our experience.

Generally speaking, human development from above downwards depends on gift, love, affectivity and tradition. More specifically, human development from above downwards revolves round love in its three-fold manifestation, namely, family love, civic love and divine love.

In this first section of the second chapter, we are going to articulate human development from above downwards with special reference to the fourth (religion) and the tenth chapter (dialectic) of *Method in Theology*. The articulation of this section will have two principal points: first, human love and second, God's love, both as gift, as conversion and as dynamic state.

2.1 *Human Love*

In the first chapter on human development from below upwards, we stated that the human being is in quest of intelligibility and transcendence. He is «his true self inasmuch as he is self-transcending»[4]. And he not only transcends himself at the cognitive level, when he asks himself questions for intelligence and questions for reflection, but also at the moral level, when he asks himself questions for deliberation. Questions for intelligence, understanding, reflection and deliberation show the human being's desire and capacity to transcend himself.

However, his desire for self-transcendence achieves its fruition and «his capacity becomes an actuality when one falls in love»[5]. Thus, in addition to the first two forms of self-transcendence, cognitive and moral, there is affective transcendence. The human person is «self-transcendent affectively when he fell in love, when the isolation of the

---

[2] *MIT*, 13.
[3] *OTN*, 24.
[4] *MIT*, 357.
[5] *MIT*, 105.

individual was broken and he spontaneously functioned not just for himself but for others as well»[6]

For Lonergan, self-transcendence finds its achievement and foundation in love which he defines as «the habitual actuation of man's capacity for self-transcendence»[7] He makes a distinction between three kinds of love: «There is the love of intimacy, of husband and wife, of parents and children. There is the love of one's fellow men with its fruit in the achievement of human welfare. There is the love of God with one's whole heart and whole soul, with all one's mind and all one's strength»[8]

Love, in its threefold manifestation, engages necessarily in interpersonal relationships within the family, and in the civil and religious community. This love remains a fruit of self-transcendence, which starts from knowledge, but goes further, since it is true, according to Blaise Pascal, that «the heart has reasons that reason does not know». Here is what Lonergan understands about Blaise Pascal's quotation:

> Here by reason I would understand the compound of the activities on the first three levels of cognitional activity, namely, of experiencing, of understanding, and of judging. By the heart's reasons I would understand feelings[9] that are intentional responses to values[10]; and I would recall the two aspects of such responses, the absolute aspect that is a recognition of value, and the relative aspect that is a preference of one value over another. Finally, by the heart I understand the subject on the fourth, existential level of intentional consciousness and in the dynamic state of being in love[11]

Thus, Pascal's observation would mean that besides the knowledge of facts that one would expect through experience, understanding and judgement, «there is another kind of knowledge reached through the

---

[6] *MIT*, 289.

[7] *MIT*, 283.

[8] *MIT*, 105.

[9] As intentional responses to values, «feelings are related to their subject: they are the mass and the momentum and power of his conscious living, the actuation of his affective capacities, dispositions, habits, the effective orientation of his being» (*MIT*, 65).

[10] «Feelings that are intentional responses regard two main classes of objects: on the one hand, the agreeable or disagreeable, the satisfying or dissatisfying; on the other hand, values, whether the ontic value of persons or the qualitative value of beauty, understanding, truth, virtuous acts, noble deeds. In general, response to value both carries us towards self-transcendence and selects an object for the sake of whom or of which we transcend ourselves» (*MIT*, 31).

[11] *MIT*, 115.

discernment of value and the judgment of value of a person in love»[12] Beyond the knowledge of facts, there is some knowledge born of love.

If there is some knowledge born of love, how should one interpret the Latin aphorism: *Nihil amatum nisi praecognitum*? (Nothing is loved unless known beforehand). «The truth of this tag is the fact that ordinarily operations on the fourth level of intentional consciousness presuppose and complement corresponding operations on the other three»[13] However, there are two exceptions to this aphorism: one minor exception and one major exception. The major exception is God's gift of his love flooding our hearts. But «there is a minor exception to this rule inasmuch as people do fall in love, and that falling in love is something disproportionate to its causes, conditions, occasions, antecedents. For falling in love is a new beginning, an exercise of vertical liberty in which one's world undergoes a new organisation»[14]

The *nihil amatum nisi praecognitum* is thus transformed into *nihil cognitum nisi prius amatum*. Indeed, being in love occurs as a *sui generis* event, without any proportion. It does not depend on any prior knowledge. It is a new beginning that imparts a new configuration to persons in a love relationship. The truth of this assertion finds an illustration in the threefold manifestation of love, but particularly in the second manifestation, that of intimate love between man and woman.

Both man and woman are invited to give themselves up to one another and to surrender themselves. «It is the love that each freely and fully reveals to the other that brings about the radically new situation of being in love and that begins the unfolding of its life-long implications»[15] Considered as gift and self-surrender to the other, love initiates a radically new and unprecedented situation. For the persons in love, it constitutes the source of all their actions. «A man or woman that falls in love is engaged in loving not only when attending to the beloved but at all times. Besides particular acts of loving, there is the prior state of being in love, and that prior state is, as it were, the fount of all one's actions»[16]

This way of loving and giving up oneself to the other must be welcomed and accepted. And it is only when the love for the other is welcomed and accepted that man or woman feels that he/she can respond to

---

[12] *MIT*, 115.
[13] *MIT*, 122.
[14] *MIT*, 122.
[15] *MIT*, 113.
[16] *MIT*, 32-33.

a corresponding love. «The reception of the love of another person for us changes us in such a way as to enable us to perform operations and experience states which previously were not within our capacity [...] The love of another person for us is somehow constitutive of us»[17]. The welcome of the other's love effects in us a transformation, an expression of ourselves that goes beyond what we can think of or imagine. In short, the love received from the other constitutes us as persons. It leads to a new understanding of one's world.

What is true of intimate love between man and woman can also be so about love between parents and children, of love experienced by persons within a civil or religious community. That is to say, a series of love relationships between *I* and *thou* may form a loving *we* within a society or a church. And this *we*, Lonergan insists, the *we* is «vital and functional»[18], since it creates an atmosphere, a framework wherein love relationships become functional.

Moreover, «prior to the *we* that results from the mutual love of an *I* and a *thou*, there is the earlier *we* that precedes the distinction of subjects and survives its oblivion»[19]. Thus, because the *we* made up of mutual love is vital and functional, it plays the role of promoting «the love that makes families, the loyalty that makes states, the faith that makes religions»[20].

We must, however, admit that the vital function that love fulfills within the family, the nation and religion, is not free from different forms of biases. The different forms of biases or deviations[21] show that interpersonal relationships do not always center around love in its threefold manifestation. These relationships «vary from intimacy to ignorance, from love to exploitation, from respect to contempt, from friendliness to enmity. They bind a community together, or divide it into fac-

---

[17] R. DORAN, «Consciousness and Grace», *MJLS* 11 (1993) 75.

[18] *MIT*, 57.

[19] *MIT*, 57.

[20] *MIT*, 79.

[21] «There are the deviations occasioned by neurotic need. There are refusals to keep on taking the plunge from settled routines to an as yet inexperienced but richer mode of living. There are the mistaken endeavours to quieten an uneasy conscience by ignoring, belittling, denying, rejecting higher values. Preference scales of values become distorted. Feelings soured. Bias creeps into one's outlook, rationalisation into one's morals, ideology into one's thought. So one may come to hate the truly good, and to love the really evil. Nor is that calamity limited to individuals. It can happen to groups, to nations, to blocks of nations, to mankind. It can take different, opposed, belligerent forms to divide mankind and to menace civilisation with destruction. Such is the monster that has stood forth in our day» (*MIT*, 39-40).

tions, or tear it apart»[22]. Human love, as a particular relationship and an actualisation of self-transcendence, urges persons to fight against biases.

Intimate love between a man and a woman can be selfish and limited. Love between parents and children can be truly unbalanced. Love of one's country may be excessively nationalistic. Only «being in love with God is being in love without limits or qualifications or conditions or reservations»[23].

2.2 *God's Love*

If to love is considered as the fruit of self-transcendence, to love God constitutes the peak of self-transcendence. For a better understanding of human development from below upwards, based on the love of God, we divide this second point into three sections: first, God's love as a gift; second, God's love as religious conversion; and thirdly, God's love as a dynamic state.

2.2.1 God's Love as a Gift

The fourth chapter in *Method in Theology*, entitled religion, does not at first deal with the question of God in terms of the gift of God's love. It is only later when it deals with the notion of self-transcendence, that we move from the question of God to the gift of God's love. In fact, the question of God is not a matter of image or feeling, of concept or judgement. It is a question that «rises out of our conscious intentionality, out of the *a priori* structured drive that promotes us from experiencing to the effort to understand, from understanding to the effort to judge truly, from judging to the effort to choose rightly. in the measure that we advert to our own questioning and proceed to question it, there arises the question of God»[24].

There is thus within our *a priori* conscious intentionality not only a region for the intelligible, the true and the good, but also « a region for the divine, a shrine for ultimate holiness. It cannot be ignored»[25]. It is from the heart of this region that the gift of God's love springs up. This

---

[22] *MIT*, 51.
[23] *MIT*, 106.
[24] *MIT*, 103.
[25] *MIT*, 103 «The atheist may pronounce it empty. The agnostic may urge that he finds his investigation has been inconclusive. The contemporary humanist will refuse to allow the question to rise. But their negations presuppose the spark in our clod, our native orientation to the divine» (*Ibid.*).

gift of God's love is not a *bonum acquirendum* that one would attain at the end of a process of reasoning or deliberation. It is a *bonum communicandum* that God gives to all (universal love) and to each (personal love: *cor ad cor loquitur*).

This gift of God's love is free, unconditional, transcultural, absolute and mysterious. It is free since the gift of God's love means « something that God freely bestows. It is given in various measures. But it is ever the same love, and so it ever tends in the same direction, to provide a further factor for continuity»[26]. The gift of God's love is unconditional because God imposes no conditions upon us before He offers us the gift of His love. This gift of God's love is free, without any condition. It is conditioned neither by our knowledge of his love, nor by our capacity to welcome this gift and experience its requirements.

The gift of God's love includes a transcultural element inasmuch as, free and unlimited, it constitutes the factor that urges human beings from all cultures to be involved in the quest for God. And «it is not restricted to any stage or section of human culture but rather is the principle that introduces a dimension of other-worldliness into any culture»[27]. The absolute character of this gift resides in the fact that it urges persons to love God wholeheartedly, with all their soul and thought.

Finally, the gift that God makes of his love assumes a mysterious dimension: «It is this gift that leads men to seek knowledge of God. God's gift of his love is God's free and gratuitous gift. It does not suppose that we know God. It does not proceed from our knowledge of God»[28]. Indeed, the gift of God's love is not a reality that depends on our knowledge of God. Inasmuch as it is conscious without being known, the gift of God's love is an «unmediated experience of the mystery of love and awe»[29], an experience of the *mysterium fascinans et tremendum* (R. Otto).

In Christian terms, the gift of God's love means that God first loved us (I Jn 4, 19) and that in the fullness of time he revealed and offered us his love in Christ (Jn 3, 16). According to St Paul, «the love of God has been poured out into our hearts through the Holy Spirit, which was given us» (Rm 5, 5). This scriptural passage reveals that God gives himself to us, that he pours out his love into our hearts and invites us to

---

[26] *MIT*, 352. See also *PGT*, 10.50.55.58.67.
[27] *MIT*, 283.
[28] *PGT*, 50.
[29] *MIT*, 112.

experience what it means to be unconditionally loved by him. However, an exegesis of Rm 5, 5 demonstrates that «the love of God does not mean our love for God, but rather God's love for us»[30].

The context of this passage deals with reconciliation with God. The initiative of this reconciliation resides in God who pours out his love into our hearts; thus, the gift of God's love from above, poured out in our hearts, constitutes the source of our acts of love from below. It makes the dynamism of our love operative by engaging us not only in love of God, but also in love of one's neighbour. «So the gift of God's love occupies the ground and root of the fourth and highest level of man's intentional consciousness. It takes the peak of the soul, the *apex animae*»[31].

The gift of God's love is offered freely and gratuitously. It waits for a response. It can be accepted as well as be rejected. Am I going «to aid others in integrating God's gift with the rest of their living»[32]? «Will I love him in return, or will I refuse? Will I live out the gift of his love, or will I hold back, turn away, withdraw? Such is the basic option of the existential subject once called by God»[33]. If we answer generously to the gift of God's love, then we are religiously converted.

2.2.2 God's Love as Religious Conversion

The experience of being in love with God presents itself as an experience of growth, of full integration, of self-actualisation. It implies a dynamism that involves all the dimensions of the person, a dynamism of love that manifests itself, in a particular way, in religious conversion. It means that the experience of being in love in a dynamic state with God reveals all its depth and all its riches only if the persons go through a religious conversion. But what is a religious conversion?

By conversion, Lonergan means «a new beginning»[34], a transformation of the subject and his world.

> Normally it is a prolonged process though its explicit acknowledgement may be concentrated in a few momentous judgments and decisions. Still it is not just a development or even a series of developments. Rather it is a resultant

---

[30] J. FITZMYER, «Letter on the Romans», 844.

[31] *MIT*, 107. Lonergan speaks of God's gift of his love that is at the fifth level of intentional consciousness. Concerning the fifth level, see Michael's Vertin's article «Lonergan on Consciousness: Is There a Fifth Level?», *MJLS* 1 (1994) 16-32.

[32] *MIT*, 123.

[33] *MIT*, 116.

[34] *MIT*, 238.

change of course and direction. It is as if one's eyes were opened and one's former world faded and fell away. There emerges something new that fructifies in inter-locking, cumulative sequences of developments on all levels and in all departments of human living[35].

Conversion «opens the way to ever further clarifications and developments»[36]. Indeed, on the level of experience, it modifies all the conscious and intentional operations of the subject. It orients his noticing and fills his imagination. It enriches his understanding, guides his judgements and perfects his decisions and actions.

Conversion can be intellectual, moral or religious. «*Intellectual conversion* is a radical clarification and, consequently, the elimination of an exceedingly stubborn and misleading myth concerning reality, objectivity, and human knowledge»[37].

«*Moral conversion* changes the criterion of one's decisions and choices from satisfactions to values [...] It consists in opting for the truly good, even for value against satisfaction when value and satisfaction conflict»[38].

Religious conversion «is being grasped by ultimate concern. It is other-worldly falling in love. It is total and permanent self-surrender without conditions, qualifications, reservations»[39]. «It is a total being-in-love as the efficacious ground of all self-transcendence, whether in

---

35 *MIT*, 130. «Conversion is existential, intensely personal, utterly intimate. But it is not so private as to be solitary. It can happen to many, and they can form a community to sustain one another in their self-transformation and to help one another in working out the implications and fulfilling the promises of their new life» (*Ibid.*).

36 *MIT*, 240.

37 *MIT*, 238. «Knowing, accordingly, is not just seeing; it is experiencing, understanding, judging, and believing. The criteria of objectivity are not just the criteria of ocular vision; they are the compound criteria of experiencing, of understanding, of judging, and of believing. The reality known is not just looked at; it is given in experience, organised and extrapolated by understanding, posited by judgment and belief» (*Ibid.*).

38 *MIT*, 240. «As children or minors we are persuaded, cajoled, ordered, compelled to do what is right. As our knowledge of human reality increases, as our responses to human values are strengthened and refined, our mentors more and more leave us to ourselves so that our freedom may exercise its ever advancing thrust toward authenticity. So we move to the existential moments when we discover for ourselves that our choosing affects ourselves no less than the chosen or rejected objects, and that it is up to each of us to decide for himself what to make of himself» (*Ibid.*).

39 *MIT*, 240.

the pursuit of truth, or in the realisation of the human values, or in the orientation man adopts to the universe, its ground, and its goal»[40].

It brings our human capacity for self-transcendence to its fullness by initiating a new basis to evaluate and engage in good works. As a matter of fact, Lonergan writes:

> That capacity meets fulfilment, that desire turns to joy, when religious conversion transforms the existential subject into a subject in love, a subject held, grasped, possessed, owned through a total and so an other-worldly love. Then there is a new basis for all valuing and all doing good. In no way are the fruits of intellectual or moral conversion negated or diminished. On the contrary, all human pursuit of the true and the good is included within and furthered by a cosmic context and purpose and, as well, there now accrues to man the power of love to enable him to accept the suffering involved in undoing the effects of decline[41].

By furthering a cosmic context and design, religious conversion constitutes a sublation[42] of intellectual and moral conversion since it urges one, on the intellectual level, to a new awareness of the requirements of intelligence and, on the moral level, to a new perception and adhesion to values. It provides a new *Weltanschauung* and «is the habitual actuation of man's capacity for self-transcendence; it is the religious conversion that grounds both moral and intellectual conversion; it provides the real criterion by which all else is to be judged»[43].

It is a «*principium quo creatum*» (Q. Quesnell), «a stream of love and of sense» (O. Rabut), «the discovery of ourselves as worthwhile and significant because we exist in God's love»[44]. It is a creative reality that urges a new religious convert to a new authentic *modus vivendi*, which

---

[40] *MIT*, 240-241. Religious conversion is situated at the fourth level of conscious intentionality. «It is the type of consciousness that deliberates, makes judgements of value, decides, acts responsibly and freely. But it is this consciousness as brought to a fulfilment, as having undergone a conversion, as possessing a basis that may be broadened and deepened and heightened and enriched but not superseded, as ready to deliberate and judge and decide and act with the easy freedom of those that do all good because they are in love» (*MIT*, 107).

[41] *MIT*, 242.

[42] «I would use this notion in Karl Rahner's sense rather than Hegel's to mean that what sublates goes beyond what is sublated, introduces something new and distinct, puts everything on a new basis, yet so far from interfering with the sublated or destroying it, on the contrary needs it, includes it, preserves all its proper features and properties, and carries them forward to a fuller realisation within a richer context» (*MIT*, 241).

[43] *MIT*, 283.

[44] M. RENDE, *Lonergan on Conversion*, 178.

appears more as a task than a *datum*. Indeed, religious conversion is perceived as a slow process of maturation, «the gradual movement towards a full and complete transformation of the whole of one's living and feeling, one's thoughts, words, deeds, and omissions»[45].

However, religious conversion can be authentic or unauthentic. As authentic, religious conversion assures the passage from unauthenticity to authenticity because «it is a total surrender to the demands of the human spirit: be attentive, be intelligent, be reasonable, be responsible, be in love»[46]. By holding fast to transcendental precepts, authentic persons promote human progress and realise that «religious conversion is dialectical»[47].

Dialectical religious conversion means «not a struggle between any opposites whatever but the very precise opposition between authenticity and unauthenticity, between the self as transcending and the self as transcended. It is not just an opposition within the human reality of individuals and of groups. It is not to be defined simply by some *a priori* construction of categories but also to be discovered *a posteriori* by a discerning study of history. It is not confined to the oppositions we have sketched but down the ages it ranges through the endless variety of institutional, cultural, personal, and religious development»[48]. This inner opposition within human reality shows well that the task of repenting and becoming converted is a lifetime work.

But it happens that the absence of any conversion, whether intellectual, moral or religious, engenders dialectically opposed horizons which may lead to all kinds of biases. What should one do to counteract these biases? According to Lonergan, one should recover the pertinence of intellectual, moral and religious conversions in order to fight these biases. One must have attained «intellectual conversion to renounce the myriad of false philosophies, moral conversion to keep themselves free of individual, group, and general bias, and religious conversion so that in fact each loves the Lord his God with his whole heart and his whole soul and all his mind and all his strength»[49].

And since religious conversion sublates and is the basis of intellectual and moral conversions, Lonergan invokes, in the last analysis, re-

---

[45] *MIT*, 241.

[46] *MIT*, 268. «Authenticity consists in being like him, in self-transcending, in being origins of values, in true love» (*MIT*, 117).

[47] *MIT*, 111.

[48] *MIT*, 111-112.

[49] *MIT*, 270.

course to the three theological virtues[50], faith, hope and charity, in order to overcome biases and restart the process of individual and social progress. God's love effects within us a conversion that urges us to a cooperation with God for the advent of a better social order. Religious conversion urges us to live in a dynamic state of love with God.

2.2.3 God's Love as a Dynamic State

The gift of God's love turns into a dynamic state of love, when it is welcome and accepted, when persons respond to and correspond with God's love, when they integrate the gift of God's love into the rest of their lives. But in what is the character of the dynamic state of God's love? «The dynamic state of being in love has the character of a response. It is an answer to a divine initiative. The divine initiative is not just creation. It is not just God's gift of his love»[51].

A positive response to this divine initiative, to the unconditional gift of God's love consists in accepting this love, in agreeing to be filled with divine love, in surrendering oneself to divine love. Lonergan makes it clear that this surrender, properly speaking, is neither an act nor a series of acts, but rather «a dynamic state that is prior to and principle of subsequent acts»[52]. It is from this dynamic state of love with God that a person's acts of love spring forth. «This dynamic state has its antecedents, causes and conditions, but, once it occurs and as long as it lasts, it is a first principle in our living, the origin and source of lovingness that colours our every thought, word, deed, and omission»[53].

---

[50] Lonergan speaks of the three theological virtues, faith, hope and love that may reverse the cycle of decline. «Faith has the power of undoing decline. Decline disrupts a culture with conflicting ideologies. It inflicts on individuals the social, economic, and psychological pressures that for human frailty amount to determinism. It multiplies and heaps up the abuses and absurdities that breed resentment, hatred, anger, violence. It is not propaganda and it is not argument but religious faith that will liberate human reasonableness from ideological prisons. It is not the promises of men but religious hope that can enable men to resist the vast pressures of social decay. If passions are to quiet down, if wrongs are to be not exacerbated, not ignored, not merely palliated, but acknowledged and removed, then human possessiveness and human pride have to be replaced by religious charity, by the charity of the suffering servant, by self-sacrificing love» (MIT, 117).

[51] MIT, 119. This initiative is not restricted to creation or to God's gift of his love because «there is a personal entrance of God himself into history, a communication of God to his people, the advent of God's word into the world of religious expression» (Ibid.).

[52] MIT, 240.

[53] «The Future of Christianity», in 2C, 153. For R. M Doran, it is the experience of being unconditionally loved by God that is the foundation of the dynamic state of

Moreover, this dynamic state of love sublates our attention, our understanding, our judgements and our decisions. It is the principle of our lives, our intentionality and subjectivity. And if objectivity is considered as the fruit of an authentic subjectivity, «to be genuinely in love with God is the very height of authentic subjectivity»[54]. The experience of being in a dynamic state of love with God, is that of being in unrestricted love. In fact, «all love is self-surrender, but being in love with God is being in love without limits or qualifications or conditions or reservations. Just as unrestricted questioning is our capacity for self-transcendence, so being in love in an unrestricted fashion is the proper fulfilment of that capacity»[55].

In other words, «to be in love is to be in love with someone. To be in love without qualifications or conditions or reservations or limits is to be in love with someone transcendent. When someone transcendent is my beloved, he is in my heart, real to me from within me. When that love is the fulfilment of my restricted thrust to self-transcendence through intelligence and truth and responsibility, the one that fulfils that thrust must be supreme in intelligence, truth, goodness»[56].

The dynamic state of love with God thus becomes the «topmost integrator» of the human being's capacity for love and the fundamental fulfilment of being human. Indeed, the fulfilment that God's love represents is not the satisfaction of an appetite or any sort of desire. It is essentially «the fulfilment of self-transcendence, the fulfilment of human authenticity, the fulfilment that overflows into a love of one's neighbour as oneself»[57]. This fulfilment animates, unifies and transforms all the constitutive dimensions of the human being.

However, although it leads the human being's constitutive dimensions to their fullness, this fulfilment is not the fruit of an objective knowledge or of a judicious choice. On the contrary, «it dismantles and

---

being in love with God: «This experience of being loved unconditionally is our share in the inner life of God, and is the conscious basis of (1) our share in the inner life of God, (2) our consequent falling in love with God, (3) the dynamic state of our being in love with God» (R. DORAN, «Consciousness and Grace», *MJLS* 11 (1993) 54.

[54] *PGT*, 51.

[55] *MIT*, 105-106. «When the love of God is not associated with self-transcendence, then easily indeed it is reinforced by the erotic, the sexual, the orgiastic» (*MIT*, 111).

[56] *MIT*, 109.

[57] B. LONERGAN, «Theology and Man's Future», in *2C*, 147.

abolishes the horizon[58] in which our knowing and choosing went on and it sets up a new horizon in which the love of God will transvalue our values and the eyes of that love will transform our knowing. Though not the product of our knowing and choosing, it is a conscious dynamic state of love»[59].

This fulfilment consisting of a dynamic state of love with God has «its antecedents, its causes, its conditions, its occasions. But once it has blossomed forth and as long as it lasts, it takes over. It is the first principle. From it flow one's desires and fears, one's joys and sorrows, one's discernment of values, one's decisions and deeds»[60]. It means that being in a dynamic state of love with God effects a transvaluation of our values, it «reveals to us values we had not appreciated, values of prayer and worship, or repentance and belief»[61]. In the measure that summit is reached, «then the supreme value is God, and other values are God's expression of his love in this world, in its aspirations, and in its goal»[62].

By perceiving God as the supreme value and the other values *sub specie amoris*, we realise with St John that « as for us, we love, because [God] first loved us» (1 Jn 4, 19) and that «ultimately our spirit will not rest until our loving is boundless, unrestricted loving»[63] ». We realise then with St Paul that «neither death nor life, no angel, no prince, nothing that exists, nothing still to come, not any power, or height or depth, nor any created thing, can ever come between us and the love of God made visible in Christ Jesus our Lord» (Rm 8, 38-39). Why? Because the experience of being affectively and effectively in love with God brings about a great joy, a lasting peace and a supernatural beatitude.

More profoundly, being in a dynamic state of love with God occurs at the heart of one's existence as «a vector, an undertow, a fateful call to a dreaded holiness»[64] inasmuch as it urges one to live without reservations or conditions or qualification. «By such love it is oriented posi-

---

58 «Horizons are the sweep of our interests and of our knowledge; they are the fertile source of further knowledge and care; but they also are the boundaries that limit our capacities for assimilating more than we already have attained» (*MIT*, 237).

59 *MIT*, 106.

60 *MIT*, 105.

61 *MIT*, 122.

62 *MIT*, 39.

63 P. BYRNE, «Spirit of Wonder», 9.

64 *MIT*, 113.

tively to what is transcendent in lovableness»[65] . The person in a dynamic state of love with God then realises that integral human development «is not only in skills and virtues but also in holiness. The power of God's love brings forth a new energy and efficacy in all goodness, and the limit of human expectation ceases to be the grave»[66] .

Thus God's love as a dynamic state is both gift and task. Once welcomed, it overruns the heart and sets up existence in a dynamic state of love. This love takes control of a person's existence ceaselessly urges him to an ever-increasing, ever-authentic religious development. However, this religious development must not be taken for granted.

> Religious development is not simply the unfolding in all its consequences of a dynamic state of being in love in an unrestricted manner. For that love is the utmost in self-transcendence, and man's self-transcendence is ever precarious. Of itself, self-transcendence involves a tension between the self as transcending and the self as transcended. So human authenticity is never some pure and serene and secure possession. It is ever a withdrawal from unauthenticity, and every successful withdrawal only brings to light the need for still further withdrawals[67] .

This dynamic state of love with God requires a person to fight against unauthenticity by promoting authenticity. One realises that the data of this dynamic state of love with God implies a process of conversion and development.

To conclude this section, we have articulated development from above by focusing on the human and divine love operative in *Method in Theology*.

First, relative to human love, we first stated that beyond the self-transcendence in the cognitive and moral order, there is a self-transcendence of the affective order which takes place when one is in a love relationship. Then, we pointed out a threefold manifestation of love, namely intimate love, love for one's country and the love of God. And since any love stands for a surrender, an intersubjective, unprecedented and constitutive occurrence, we have briefly illustrated it with the intimate love between man and woman.

Second, we scrutinised love as religious conversion by demonstrating that religious conversion is constitutive of the dynamic state of love with God. As a transformation of the subject and his world, it consists in loving with a supernatural love. It sublates and grounds intellectual

---

[65] *MIT*, 278.
[66] *MIT*, 116.
[67] *MIT*, 110.

and moral conversion. And when biases occur, finally, it is to religious conversion that one must have recourse since it provides an efficient criterion to evaluate everything and constitutes a real source of altruism toward family, country and religious community.

3. Post-*Method* Articles (1974-1980)

In the articles published between 1974 and 1980, Lonergan explicitly deals with two ways of human development, their complementarity, their coexistence and their integration. If human development from below upwards is a process that appeals to experience, understanding, judgement and decision, in the person's quest for authentic self-transcendence, human development from above downwards is dependent upon gift, love, affectivity and tradition. We can rightly affirm with Frederick Crowe that human development from below upwards is «the way of achievement» and the development from above downwards is «the way of heritage, of gift, of tradition»[68].

3.1 The Mission and the Spirit

It is in the context of an analysis of vertical finality that Lonergan, in «The Mission and the Spirit» examines human development from above downwards, considered as « the experience of a transformation one did not bring about, rather underwent»[69]. The latter only is truly effective thanks to the «vertical finality that heads for self-transcendence»[70]. If this experience of transformation is possible for an individual, it can be so for a whole community of subjects that seeks to develop through solidarity and love. In fact, Lonergan writes:

> There is the topmost quasi-operator that by intersubjectivity prepares, by solidarity entices, by falling in love establishes us as members of community. Within each individual vertical finality heads for self-transcendence. In an aggregate of self-transcending individuals there is significant coincidental manifold in which can emerge a new creation. Possibility yields to fact and fact bears witness to its originality and power in the fidelity that makes families, in the loyalty that makes peoples, in the faith that makes religion[71].

---

[68] *OTN*, 13.
[69] «Mission and the Spirit», 33.
[70] «Mission and the Spirit», 30.
[71] «Mission and the Spirit», 30.

Within a community, intersubjectivity, experienced through solidarity and love, promotes fidelity within families, loyalty among people and faith in religion.

In the section on the human subject, Lonergan distinguishes between three kinds of love, namely, family, civic and universal love. «It is natural to man to love with the domestic love that unites parents with each other and with their children, with the civic love that can face death for the sake of one's fellowmen, with the all-embracing love that loves God above all»[72]. Throughout history, universal love[73] has not folded up within itself, but on the contrary, it has sublated itself as constituting a communication of God's love to humankind. This communication of God's love to humankind is promised but not guaranteed for salvation. This love can be freely accepted or refused. If it is refused, then it is sin that dominates, it is the reign of individual, collective and general bias.

Alienated by sin and biases, people need redemption, salvation and deliverance. They needs charity, hope and faith: «the charity that dissolves the hostility and the divisions of past injustice and present hatred; it comes as hope that withstands psychological, economic, political, social, cultural determinisms; it comes with the faith that can liberate reason from the rationalisations that blinded it»[74].

These three theological virtues enable individuals to fight against biases and dispose them to welcome the love that God communicates to them. This communication of God's love reveals itself as «cognitive, constitutive, and redemptive: it is cognitive, for it discloses in whom we are to believe; it is constitutive, for it crystallises the inner gift of the love of God into overt Christian fellowship; it is redemptive, for it liberates human liberty from thraldom to sin, and it guides those it liberates to the kingdom of the Father»[75].

This cognitive, constitutive and redemptive communication of God's love is qualified by Lonergan not as the *fides ex auditu* but as the *fides ex infusione*. The *fides ex auditu* corresponds to human development from below and the *fides ex infusione* corresponds to human development from above for it «descends from the gift of God's love through religious conversion to moral, and through religious and moral to intel-

---

[72] «Mission and he Spirit», 30.

[73] Lonergan refers to Saint Thomas Aquinas who sustains that independently of man's corrupted nature, the human being naturally loves God above all (*ST*, Ia IIae, q. a. 3 c and ad 1 1 m).

[74] «Mission and the Spirit», 31-32.

[75] «Mission and the Spirit», 32.

lectual conversion»[76]. As in *Method in Theology*, Lonergan establishes a correlation between the gift of God's love and religious, moral and intellectual conversions. In «The Mission and the Spirit», human development from above is conceived as a transformation of love that one has not effected, experienced within intersubjective relations as the , basis of fidelity in families and commitment to country and religion.

3.2 Christology Today: Methodological Reflections

In «Christology Today: Methodological Reflections», Lonergan asserts the complementarity between the two processes of human development. He maintains that the process from below upwards constitutes the ordinary way of human development. But it is not unique and exclusive, because another process of development from above downwards revolves round the transformation of love in its three manifestations: intimate love between man and woman, love of one's neighbour and love of God. «Man's insertion in community and history includes an invitation for him to accept the transformation of falling in love: the transformation of domestic love between husband and wife; the transformation of divine love that comes when God's love floods our inmost heart through the Holy Spirit he has given us (Rm 5:5)»[77].

From this quotation, we understand that God's love is not the unique way of human development from above, but one of the three modes. It means that the other modes of human development are not necessarily linked to God's love. However, for Lonergan, the transformation that God's love brings is *sui generis* and more fundamental than the other two, thus making the development from above more fundamental than the development from below.

> Such transforming love has its occasions, its conditions, its causes. But once it comes and as long as it lasts, it takes over. One no longer is one's own. Moreover, in the measure that this transformation is effective, development becomes not merely from below upwards but more fundamentally from above downwards. There has begun a life in which the heart has reasons which reason does not know. There has been opened up a new world in which the old adage, *nihil amatum nisi prius cognitum*, yields to a new truth, *nihil vere cognitum nisi prius amatum*[78].

---

[76] «Mission and the Spirit», 32.
[77] «Christology Today», 77-78.
[78] «Christology Today», 77.

By taking into account the second prolegomenon which is philosophy, Lonergan negatively criticises Piet Schoonenberg's «traffic laws of
one way street»[79] that «runs counter to the structure and procedures of
the world mediated by meaning»[80]. He positively demonstrates that
there can be a double circulation movement, from below upwards and
from above downwards, in both empirical sciences and human sciences
as well as in theology. In empirical sciences, «one proceeds not only
from the data of observation and experiment to the formulation of laws,
but also from the ranges of theoretical possibility explored by mathe-
maticians to physical systems that include empirical laws as particular
cases»[81].

In theology, too, «one proceeds not only from the data of revelation
to more comprehensive statements but also from an imperfect, analogous yet most fruitful understanding of mystery to the syntheses that
complement a *via inventionis* with a *via doctrinae*»[82]. By attaining revealed truths one attains what exists independently from the theologian
who seeks to understand them. His theological research is not the cause,
for instance, of the truth of faith that asserts that Christ is the second
person of the Trinity. This truth of faith is dependent on divine revelation and precedes any theological investigation. It is in this sense that
Lonergan thinks that revealed truths from above are more fundamental
than the analogical understanding from below of the same truths.

In «Christology Today», human development revolves round love in
its threefold manifestation: intimate love, love of neighbour and God's
love. But the love of God is more fundamental since, once established,
it takes control of human existence.

3.3 Healing and Creating in History

In «Creativity, healing and history», of 13 May 1975, Lonergan insists on complementarity between both vectors, from below and from
above, of human development. Development from above is first understood as revolving around love: «there is also development from above
downwards. There is the transformation of falling in love, the domestic
love of the family, the human love of one's tribe, one's city, one's
country, mankind; the divine love that orientates man in his cosmos and

---

[79] «Christology Today», 79. «We can learn about the Trinity from revelation, but
we are not to begin from the Trinity and proceed to think about Christ» (*Ibid.*).
[80] «Christology Today», 79.
[81] «Christology Today», 79.
[82] «Christology Today», 80.

expresses itself in worship»[83]. Human development from above downwards is centered on the transformation of love through its three manifestations.

Then Lonergan considers healing as corresponding to development from above. And healing, as mediator of the conditions of salvation, must fulfill intrinsic as well as extrinsic requirements. For intrinsic requirements, Lonergan maintains that healing must lead to love by avoiding hatred : «healing must not be confused with the dominating and manipulating to which the reforming materialist is confined by his own principles. It has to be kept apart from religious hatred and heretical sects and from philosophic hatred of social classes»[84]. Complementary to healing as the intrinsic requirement «there is the extrinsic requirement of a concomitant creative process. For just as the creative process, when unaccompanied by healing, is distorted and corrupted by bias, so too the healing process, when unaccompanied by creating, is a soul without a body»[85].

This consideration of human development from above as healing is eventually applied to Christianity. Indeed, Christianity stands not only as an historico-social reality, but also as a spiritual strength, a source of healing that requires to be accompanied with creativity. But throughout history, Christianity has not always managed to embody its role as healer, for instance, during the fall of the Roman Empire.

«Christianity developed and spread within the ancient empire of Rome. It possessed the spiritual power to heal what was unsound in that imperial domain. But it was unaccompanied by its natural complement of creating»[86]. If Christianity, as spiritual and from above, is not accompanied by creativity from below, it cannot contribute to «a new style of human developement»[87].

In conclusion, it is advisable to insist on the interdependence and complementarity between both vectors of human development. We assert with Lonergan that «a single development has two vectors, one from below upwards, creating, the other from above downwards, healing»[88].

---

[83] «Creativity, Healing in history», 106.
[84] «Creativity, Healing in History», 107.
[85] «Christology Today», 107.
[86] «Christology Today», 107.
[87] «Creativity, Healing in History», 106.
[88] «Creativity, Healing in History», 107-108.

3.4 Religious Experience

In «Religious Experience», Lonergan deals with human development, from above downwards, by exploring various ways of being in love. These ways of being in love are inscribed at the heart of personal human existence, whereby persons discover and decide what they are going to do with their lives. And in so doing, they develop, they achieve self-transcendence.

«Commonly such a discovery, such a decision, such a program of self-actualisation becomes effective and irrevocable when one falls in love. Then one's being becomes being-in-love. Such being-in-love is not without its antecedents, its causes, its conditions, its occasions. But once it has blossomed forth and as long as it lasts, it takes over. It becomes the immanent and effective first principle. From it flow one's desires and fears, one's joys and sorrows, one's day-to-day decisions and deeds»[89]·

As in «Healing and Creativity in History», Lonergan harks back to the three manifestations of human development from above centered on love. But here he is more explicit about the three forms of love. The first form is that of intimate love between man and woman, expressed by a married life that bears fruit through procreation:

Being-in-love is most conspicuous in the home: in the love of husband and wife, of parents and children. Love gave rise to the marriage. Love gave rise to the offspring. Love keeps the family an ongoing, joyful affair. Nor is love unconnected with authenticity. A love that is not genuine is not the true love that provides the recurrent theme in our older novels and poems and songs»[90]·

The second form of love is civic love that is practised within one's native country. «Besides love in the home there is love of country. Here too our thinking has taken on the complexity of modern life. He is apt to brush aside as jingoism any old-style allegiance to one's country right or wrong. But in the measure that one does so, not only is one questioning the authenticity of once unquestioned loyalties, but also there is commonly to be found not an abolition but only a displacement of loyalty»[91]· As one can notice, in the first two forms of love, Lonergan stresses authenticity. Authenticity should not be taken for granted,

---

[89] «Religious Experience», 123.
[90] «Religious Experience», 123-124.
[91] «Religious Experience», 124.

like a ready-made recipe. On the contrary, authenticity stands as an historical reality enacted in a dynamic process.

But there remains the third form of love: divine love. «Besides the love of home and the love of country there is a third love. To it there testifies a great religious tradition that proclaims: "Hear, O Israel: the Lord our God is the only Lord; love the Lord your God with all your heart, with all your soul, with all your mind, and with all your strength" (Mc 12:29-30). Of such love St. Paul spoke as God's love flooding our inmost heart through the Holy Spirit he has given us (Rm 5:5)»[92].

This third form of love constitutes an answer to Lonergan's main question, regarding «what manner God's love flooding our hearts is a human experience and just how it fits into human consciousness»[93]. He answers as follows: «because man is a symbolic animal, his development is only partly a matter of his genes. All its higher reaches depend upon his historical milieu with its techniques of socialization, acculturation, education»[94].

The trilogy of socialization, acculturation and education deserves to be made explicit. In social psychology, the term *acculturation* signifies a process of learning through which students receive the culture of their milieu to which they belong. According to Tekippe,

> education is an intelligent and intelligible set of schemes of recurrence by which the patrimony of the past, the treasures of skill, knowing, virtue, are passed on as the legacy of the present, and the foundation for future achievements. It includes attitudes imbibed with mother's milk, the manners and values absorbed in the family, the formal and informal learnings imparted by a school system, the dos and don'ts of fashion, entertainment and advertising[95].

This trilogy of socialization, acculturation and education plays a great part in rendering God's love spread in our hearts a human experience. It means that the gift of God's love, when it is experienced, becomes «the first and dominant principle in one's living»[96]. And when God's love becomes the pre-eminent principle of human existence, not only does this love convey a meaning and reason for existence, but it is already a religious experience. In the Judeo-Christian tradition, God's love remains clearly the feature of authentic religious experience.

---

[92] «Religious Experience», 124.
[93] «Religious Experience», 125.
[94] «Religious Experience», 119.
[95] T. TEKIPPE, «The Crisis of the Human Good», in LoWo, VII, 319.
[96] «Religious Experience», 124.

When religious experience is harmoniously integrated into the rest of human life, the individual is in a new process of development. He evolves from the purgative and illuminative ways to unitive way. In the unitive way, «in which potential conflicts were under control, the full significance of religious commitments was understood and accepted»[97].

Engaging in a religious experience leads ideally to being in love with God, which Lonergan calls religious development. However, because of the existence of evil and of the biases, because of infidelity, there is a provision for «rituals of repentance, confessions of sinfulness, prayers for deliverance, that testify to the desire for re-established authenticity»[98] in order to love our neighbours.

Moreover, an authentic love of God leads in principle to the love of neighbour, experienced either within the family or country. In other words, the religious experience that urges us to love God, who is the author of our love, implies a commitment to love our neighbour, who is the sacrament and icon of God's love. But what type of relationship exits between God's love and familial and civic love?

Firstly, God's love plays *the role of foundation* in relation to familial and civic love «for it grounds both domestic and civic devotion by reconciling us, by committing us, to the obscure purposes of our universe, to what Christians name the love of God in Christ»[99].

Secondly, God's love plays *the role of sublation*. Indeed, at the heart of existence, God's love sublates and transcends family and civic love. This love of God conveys a new configuration and strength to «the love of intimacy that animates the family, the love of one's neighbour that animates people, and the love of God which seems to be characteristic of authentic religious conviction»[100]. Because of these roles of foundation and sublation, played by God's love, Lonergan believes that religious experience is to be harmoniously cultivated and integrated within human experience so that a person can achieve authentic human development.

Lonergan ends this article by asserting that «besides development from below upwards there also is development, if not from above downwards, at least from within an encompassing, enveloping worldview or horizon or blik»[101]. As he underlines the coexistence of the two

---

[97] «Religious Experience», 125.
[98] «Religious Experience», 123.
[99] «Religious Experience», 127.
[100] «Religious Experience», 124.
[101] «Religious Experience», 127.

ways of development, Lonergan affirms that development from above downwards does not stem and evolve *ex nihilo*. It is part of a *Weltanschauung*, of a horizon that does not necessarily relate to a religious sphere.

In «Religious Experience», Lonergan makes explicit the three manifestations of love, by closely relating them to authenticity. Religious experience stands here for the most appropriate mode of expressing God's love which, as a higher integration, plays a foundational sublating role in familial and civic love.

3.5 The Ongoing Genesis of Methods

In this article, Lonergan briefly evokes human development from above by emphasising once more the complementarity between the processes of human development. Development from below is based on development from above, through the processes of socialization, cultural adjustment and education. «We are the products of a process that in its several aspects is named socialization, acculturation, education. By that process there is formed our initial mind-set, worldview, blik, horizon. On that basis and within its limitations we slowly begin to become our own masters, think for ourselves, make our own freedom and responsibility»[102].

Thus, human development from above is basically a received heritage. It is essentially by receiving this social, cultural and educational heritage from above that we achieve our human development from below, becoming freely and responsibly masters of our individual and collective destiny.

By examining the issue of praxis[103], Lonergan asserts that «while empirical method moves, so to speak, from below upwards, praxis moves from above downwards»[104]. When conflicts and biases come about, there is the disintegration of civilisation and the reign of decline.

---

[102] «The Ongoing Genesis of Methods», 156.

[103] According to Lonergan, «since the failure of the absolute idealists to encompass human history within the embrace of speculative reason, the issue of praxis has repeatedly come to the fore. Schopenhauer conceived the world in terms of will and representation. Kierkegaard insisted on faith. Newman toasted conscience. Marx was concerned not merely to know but principally to make history. Nietzsche proclaimed the will to power. Blondel strove for a philosophy of action. Paul Ricoeur has not yet completed his many-volumed philosophy of will, and Jürgen Habermas has set forth the involvement of human knowledge in human interests» («The Ongoing Genesis of Methods, 159-160).

[104] «The Ongoing Genesis of Methods», 160.

Can a people, a civilisation overcome decline? Finally, what is going to suppress rationalisations and decline? When rationalisations lead to breakdowns, faith is required. To face social evil, one needs self-love that is capable of sacrifice.

Considering these situations of decline, Lonergan also invokes praxis as a method that «discerns a radically distorted situation, it retreats from spontaneous to critical intelligence; it begins from above on the level of evaluation and decisions; and it moves from concord and cooperation towards the development of mutual understanding and more effective communication»[105]. Proceeding from above, praxis evolves from the level of decision to that of spontaneous intelligence, while passing through understanding and communication.

To conclude, in «The Ongoing Genesis of Methods», Lonergan generally defines human development from above with reference to the process of socialisation, acculturation and education. Specifically, he demonstrates that praxis as method, evolving from above downwards, can contribute to the study and resolution of conflicts.

3.6 1976 Lonergan Workshop

At the 1976 Lonergan Workshop, Lonergan defines human development from above from the perspective of the functional specialities of theology in *Method in Theology*. Lonergan makes development from above explicit by answering the following question:

What would the main contributions of the functional specialities of dialectics and foundations in a methodologically transformed theology be to our understanding of the relation of theory and praxis? The second phase is development from above downwards. From one's basic options, commitments, horizons, that's where foundations come out. Dialectics moves to foundations in so far as you'll appeal to intellectual, moral and religious conversions. And that becomes the starting point.[106]

Dialectics and foundations are placed at the fourth level, that of decision and responsibility, since they concern values and commitments that theologians discover and appropriate themselves. Dialectics deals with conflicts that appear during theological research, whereas foundations allow an elucidation of the conflicts set forth by dialectics which, in turn, thus, in turn, offers a criterion of selection for doctrines, systematics and communications.

---

[105] «The Ongoing Genesis of Methods», 163.
[106] 1976 LoWo Transcript, 6-7.

If the first mediating phase, *in oratione obliqua*, corresponds to development from below, the second mediated phase of theology, *in oratione recta*, corresponds to human development from above. The latter goes from foundations to communication via of doctrines and systematics.

As a constitutive and fundamental functional speciality appealing to intellectual, moral and religious conversions, dialectics constitutes the intersection of both phases inasmuch as the conversions come to light as the summit of theology's mediating phase and e mediated phase from above. However, Lonergan observes, the second phase, development from above downwards, is essentially a matter of options, commitments and horizons. One must «recognise the existence of development from above because that is what the theologian in the second phase is doing. Just as the horizon can block correct interpretation, block historical interpretation, so it can ground a correct development»[107].

Another question that allows Lonergan to make explicit development from above downwards, always in the context of functional specialities of theology, is the following:

Would you, please, review for us the central elements of your understanding of praxis. How is this understanding of praxis related to other significant uses of the word, e.g., in Aristotle, Marx, and Habermas? But there is also development from above downwards. And it starts from commitment. It formulates what the commitment means, it clarifies the formulation and it clarifies the formulation to every audience [...] This second type of development is praxis. It's a different thing, it's a complementary thing»[108].

As in «The Ongoing Genesis of Methods»», praxis belongs to the second phase of human development from above downwards: «developing from above downwards, that is praxis in the strong sense»[109]. Different from and complementary to the first mode of development from below upwards, praxis has its starting point in commitment, thus providing the theologian with a critical horizon and leading him to action.

---

[107] 1976 LoWo, 21.
[108] 1976 LoWo, 57-58.
[109] 1976 LoWo, 10. «You have praxis in the strong sense in Marx in so far as he says that the critique of religion is the basis of the critique of politics and economics» (1976 LoWo, 22).

Another reference to development from above appears when Lonergan relates the fundamental option as one of the principal categories of theology to moral and religious conversion :

A basic category among contemporary catholic theologians is the «fundamental option». Would you please say something about this reality, how this reality is related to moral and/or religious conversion? Religion constitutes a sublation of morality. It introduces a new principle, it goes beyond morality, it directs it to a higher and fuller end, it enriches, strengthens, perfects it. So religion is this apprehension of values and this value results from falling in love[...] Religion is the sublation that is love of God. It is love with a cosmic dimension [...] The love of God is solidary with an appreciation of God's world, of life, of human community and human history, with faith in its meaningfulness, hope in its redemption and salvation.[110] .

From this quotation, we must keep three points in mind. First, the fundamental option at its root, is dependent upon religion which, from above, sublates and perfects morality. Religion thus constitutes an «ultimate foundation» of morality by introducing it into the realm of love. Secondly, religion contributes to the apprehension of values that becomes effective and permanent when a person begins to love. And there are many ways of loving which culminate in divine love. Thirdly, divine love implies a faith and a hope that contemplate the realisation of God incarnated in history.

As in «The Ongoing Genesis of Methods», in the 1976 Lonergan Workshop, Lonergan regards praxis as human development from above downwards. However, in the present article, this praxis is specifically analysed from the perspective of functional specialities of theology. Further, Lonergan insists not only on the complementary character of sciences but also on their interdisciplinary aspect.

What institutional implications regarding the good of order in the Church would you see arising from your chapter on Communication» in Method? The sciences operate from above downwards and from below upwards. From above downwards, theology becomes interdisciplinary, learning from and exerting influence on other human disciplines [...] So that interdisciplinary aspect, from above downwards, from below upwards, innovation at the grass roots, leading to innovations in the higher integrations. In other words, the higher integrations are integrations of what is below and it is below that the big innovations are going on[111] .

---

[110] 1976 LoWo, 26-28.
[111] 1976 LoWo, 77-78.

3.7 The Human Good

In «The Human Good», Lonergan considers knowledge as a common fund, as heritage to receive and appropriate for oneself: «human knowledge is not individual enterprise; it is a common fund on which everyone draws according to his capacity and everyone checks and disputes when he finds it wrong»[112].

Human knowledge, perceived as a common fund, is dependent on development from above and implies a transmission of the common fund through the threefold process of acculturation, socialization and education.

> There is development from above downwards, the benefits of acculturation, socialization, education, the transmission of the tradition. Without that transmission of the tradition there would be no transmitting what anyone did achieve, we would always start at square one. So there is the component of the transmitting of past achievement and that is from above downwards. [...] On the other hand, if there is simply tradition, without that personal appropriation of drawing upon one's own experience, having one's insight validated by one's own experience, and so on, then one is not on one's own[113].

As in «The Ongoing Genesis of Methods» of 4 March 1976, Lonergan harks back to the trilogy of acculturation, socialization and education that allows, in a well determined social context, the transmission of the values of the tradition. Although it is dependent on human development from above, the transmission of the values of tradition by itself does not guarantee true human development. «There is need then to take seriously the double task of the creation and the handling on of values: the attentive, intelligent, reasonable, and responsible production of terminal values, and the love and loyalty to a tradition that receives and guards and hands on the heritage of hard-won-values»[114].

There must be therefore, concomitantly to this transmission, «a personal appropriation of drawing upon one's own experience, having one's insights validated by one's experience»[115]. This transmission of the values of tradition from above must be sustained from below by experience, understanding, judgement and decision. By making this transmission explicit, Lonergan comes to consider belief as part of human development from above. According to Lonergan, belief is a

---

[112] «The Human Good», 122.
[113] «The Human Good», 120.
[114] F.E. CROWE, «An Expansion», 48.
[115] «The Human Good», 120.

judgement whereby one appropriate from other persons their experiences, acts of understanding, judgements of fact and value judgements. This makes possible the progress of personal and collective knowledge, by making available the insights and judgements accumulated throughout centuries.

But belief from above is inseparable from the fabric of our immanently generated knowledge[116] from above. They are interdependent and complementary. This immanently generated knowledge and beliefs are not in two separate compartments. «You can't separate them out; there is a symbiosis. We have no possibility of sorting out how much of each of our judgements rests on what we know and how much is influenced by the context given us by our language, our milieu over the years, what is then accumulated over the centuries, the millennia»[117].

There is therefore an integration, a symbiosis between both forms of knowledge: «belief and immanently generated knowledge». While making a distinction between them, one does not exactly know to what extent, immanently generated knowledge from below depends on belief from above and vice-versa.

In «The Human Good», Lonergan once again examines the ways of human development by insisting on their interdependence. Let us note that it is the first time that Lonergan mentions belief as being dependent upon human development from above. In this article belief consists in a transmission of tradition seen as a cultural heritage. As such, belief does not have, as, an exclusively religious dimension.

3.8 Questionnaire on Philosophy

In «Questionnaire on Philosophy», Lonergan asserts that true human development includes two distinct and complementary modes: one proceeds from below upwards and the other from above downwards.

Do you think that philosophical studies for Christians and/or especially for candidates for the priesthood should be different from philosophical studies «tout court», and if so, why? The basic principle seems to be that human development occurs in two distinct modes. If I may use a spatial metaphor, it moves (1) from below upwards and (2) from above downwards [...] It moves from above downwards inasmuch as one belongs to a hierarchy of groups

---

[116] As a mode of knowledge, belief differs from immanently generated knowledge. Immanently generated knowledge is based on belief. See «The Human Good», 121.
[117] «The Human Good», 121.

and owes allegiance to one's home, to one's country, to one's religion[118].

Development from above downwards appeals to a group's tradition where members are socialised, acculturated and educated. Another point is the interdependence and the coexistence of the two ways of human development. By answering the question about philosophical studies, Lonergan shows that both modes of human development constitute a fundamental and indispensable principle in the training of candidates for ministerial priesthood.

In tackling the question of the nature of philosophy, in its relation to theology, Lonergan deems that ethical existence is not only the level of decision-making, but also that of the threefold manifestation of love.

In the light of what you think to be the nature of philosophy (and of theology) can you state clear reasons why philosophical studies should be a necessary part of preparation for the priesthood and/or the training of a Jesuit[119]? Now such existential ethics undergoes a transformation when God's love floods our hearts through the Holy Spirit he has given us: for such love is unrestricted. It is the love described by St Paul in the thirteen chapter of his first letter to the Corinthians; it is the love to which Ignatius of Loyola directs those that follow his spiritual exercises[120].

From the threefold manifestation of love, familial, civic and divine, Lonergan makes explicit the love of God which, unrestricted and universal, effects a transformation of existential ethics. Moreover, the love of God engages in a process of sublation.

Such Christian praxis is the dynamic of creativity and freedom in which individually men make themselves and collectively they make the world in which they live. In that dynamic must be recognised (1) developing intelligence as the principle of progress, (2) the evils of individual and group egoism and the arrogance of omnicompetent common sense as the principles of alienation and decline and (3) faith, hope, and charity as the principles of recovery from alienation and decline[121].

If, for development from below, Lonergan speaks of the sublation of cognitive operations, for development from above, it is a question of sublation effected by God's love, not only at of the individual level, but also at the level of the christian and human community. This love of

---

[118] «Questionnaire on Philosophy», 10.
[119] «Questionnaire on Philosophy», 3.
[120] «Questionnaire on Philosophy», 7.
[121] «Questionnaire on Philosophy», 19.

God, manifested in the christian and human community, stands in an historical process called christian praxis.

Individually and socially, persons are engaged in a dialectic of progress, decline and redemption. Redemption expresses the love of God, incarnated in Jesus Christ, mediator of salvation. The reception of this love, both sublating and salvific from God leads to religious conversion. «By religious conversion, which is the foundation of the other two, I mean the habitual acceptance of God's gift of his love flooding our hearts through the Holy Spirit he has given us»[122].

The gift of God's love from above allows those who welcome it to be morally and intellectually converted. That is why attentiveness, intelligence, rationality and responsibility constantly remain the conditions of possibility of human authenticity, of full human development. Their exclusion or negation constitute the basis, the root of human unauthenticity. In the last analysis, a person's salvation in this life resides in the appropriation and practice of theological virtues of faith, hope and charity.

In «Questionnaire on Philosophy», Lonergan asserts that the way up is effected, within tradition, through the threefold process of socialization, acculturation and education. This threefold process takes place in an atmosphere of love and Christian praxis.

3.9 Natural Right and Historical Mindedness

In this article, what Lonergan calls development is synonymous with human development from below and the transmission of development corresponds to human development from above that he explains as follows:

> It works from above downwards: it begins in the affectivity of the infant, the child, the son, the pupil, the follower. On affectivity rests the apprehension of values. On the apprehension of values rests belief. On belief follows the growth in understanding of one who has found a genuine teacher and has been initiated into the study of the master of the past. Then to confirm one's growth in understanding comes experience made mature and perceptive by one's developed understanding. With experiential confirmation the inverse process may set in[123].

Indeed, apprehension of value depends on affectivity. Yet this apprehension of value is achieved through feelings as intentional responses

---

[122] «Questionnaire on Philosophy», 11.
[123] «Natural Right and historical Mindedness», 181.

to values. They allow us to welcome «the ontic value of a person or the qualitative value of beauty, of understanding, of truth, of noble deeds, of virtuous acts, of great achievements»[124].

Human development from above therefore begins in the child's affectivity, develops in the apprehension of values and beliefs, to reach a deeper understanding and a confirmation of experience. If development from below upwards proceeds from experience to decision, through understanding and judgement, development from above downwards evolves from affectivity, through belief and understanding to experience. In other words, Frederick Crowe writes, «it may start with a heritage of values and judgements and proceed through to a more mature experience. As values may be created, so also may they be handed on; as judgement may result from weighing the evidence, so also may they be accepted in trust; as understanding may puzzle over what is observed, so it may puzzle over what is believed to be true»[125].

Thus, development from above is prior to development from below. As a matter of fact, the processes of socialization, acculturation and education transmit a set of values and beliefs to the individual even before he is capable of assuring his development from below. Thus, development from above promotes values and beliefs within which development from below can take place.

Fundamentally, human development from above evolves in a context of love and confidence. It is perceived as «heritage, faithfully preserved and responsibly handed on (*traditum*) by parent, teacher, church, society, and received in trust by child or pupil, with acceptance of the role of heir to a community patrimony»[126]. Like development from below upwards, the transmission of development from above downwards can be complete or incomplete.

For the transmission of development to be complete, there must be, on the part of an individual, an appropriation of what has been transmitted to him, an appropriation of the values of the beliefs held by his tradition. Then, he becomes an autonomous person and master of oneself. «One is on his own, one can appropriate all that one has learnt by proceeding as does the original thinker who moved from experience to understanding, to sound judgement, to generous evaluation, to commitment in love, loyalty, faith»[127].

---

[124] *MIT*, 38.
[125] *OTN*, 24.
[126] *OTN*, 63.
[127] «Natural Right and Historical Mindedness», in *IC*, 181.

But it may happen that the process of the transmission of development from above downwards is incomplete. And if the process is incomplete, there is no effective appropriation of tradition. For instance, in the field of education, the lack of development from above in a teacher constitutes a stumbling block in his attempt to understand and impart the riches of tradition to his students[128], from the cradle of development from below.

In order to overcome this stumbling block, through the transmission of the riches of tradition, Lonergan proposes to have recourse to dialectics of history to understand individuals' and peoples' progress and decline. «Its unfolding is the actual course of events, its significance is the radical analysis it provides, its practical utility in the invitation it will present to collective consciousness to understand and repudiate the waywardness of its past and to enlighten its future with the intelligence, the reasonableness, the responsibility, the love demanded by natural right»[129].

Thus, dialectics, through its analysis, helps to discern and repudiate the biases of the past and appropriate the riches of tradition. And among the riches of tradition, Lonergan mentions the fact of being in love that is beyond questions for intelligence, reflection and deliberation. «The point beyond is being-in-love, a dynamic state that sublates all that goes before»[130]. By asking the question about values, Lonergan shows that the eros of the human spirit finds its climax in love. «For self-transcendence reaches its term not in righteousness but in love and, when we fall in love, then life begins anew. A new principle takes over and, as long as it lasts, we are lifted above ourselves and carried along as parts within an ever intimate yet ever more liberating dynamic whole»[131].

As in the previous articles, Lonergan harks back to the three kinds of love. The difference is that in the contemporary context, characterised by historical mindedness, Lonergan insists that beyond self-knowledge based on common sense, science and history, there is «knowledge of af-

---

[128] «The teacher may at least be a believer. He can transmit enthusiasm. He can teach the accepted formulations. He can persuade. But he has never really understood and he is not capable of giving others the understanding that he himself lacks. Then it will be only by accident that his pupils come to appropriate what was sound in their tradition, and it is only by such accidents, or divine graces, that a tradition that has decayed can be renewed » («Natural Right and Historical Mindedness», 181).

[129] «Natural Right and Historical Mindedness», 179.

[130] «Natural Right and Historical Mindedness», 175.

[131] «Natural Right and Historical Mindedness», 175.

fectivity in its threefold manifestation of love in the family, loyalty in the community, and faith in God»[132]. He also demonstrates that human development implies an intellectual, moral, and affective conversion. «As affective, it is commitment to love in the home, loyalty in the community, faith in the destiny of man»[133].

In «Natural Right and Historical Mindedness», human development from below consists in a transmission of development and proceeds from affectivity to experience through values, beliefs, understanding. Being part of human historicity, human development from above implies an appropriation of the riches of tradition, through the processes of socialization, acculturation and education.

3.10 Theology and Praxis

In «Theology and Praxis», Lonergan examines the relationship between theology and praxis, maintaining that there are fundamental theological questions that depend on the theologians' personal development. He considers the two ways of human development as two phases, from below upwards and from above downwards.

> The structure of human development is twofold. The chronological prior phase is from above downwards. Children are born onto a cradling environment of love. By a long and slow process of socialization, acculturation, education they are transferred from their initial world of immediacy into the local variety of the world mediated by meaning and motivated by values. Basically this process rests on trust and belief. But as it proceeds, more and more there develops the capacity to raise questions and to be satisfied or dissatisfied with answers. Such is the spontaneous and fundamental process of teaching and learning common to all. It is at once intelligent and reasonable and responsible[134].

This quotation gathers, in synthetic form, the main features of human development from above downwards, put forth two months earlier in the article «Natural Right and Historical Mindedness». Let us emphasise three points. First, Lonergan asserts that human development from above downwards is chronologically before the second. Thus it constitutes the foundation whereon rest present and future realisations. «And this, of course, takes time; it is a matter of slow growth, of di-

---

[132] «Natural Right and Historical Mindedness», 179.
[133] «Natural Right and Historical Mindedness», 179.
[134] «Theology and Praxis», 197.

rected effort, of persevering application. There seems a need for gift to precede achievement»[135].

Secondly, the first phase from above downwards is effected thanks to the threefold process of socialization, acculturation and education. This threefold process, both in its genesis and term, occurs fundamentally in an environment of love.

> There is a dynamic at work, effecting development from above. Just as the upward development was powered by the capacity and the drive towards intelligibility, truth, and the good, so the downward development is powered by the love and responsibility of the educator for the child, and the corresponding love for, and ensuing trust in, the educator on the part of the child. This form of communication begins and ends, is given and received, in love[136].

Thirdly, the setting up and development of the second phase, which rests on faith and confidence, realise in children a transfer from their world of immediacy to the world mediated by values, thus promoting the development of the first phase, the unfolding of pertinent questions and answers.

In «Theology and Praxis», human development is achieved thanks to the process of socialization, acculturation and education. It springs up and reaches fruition in an environment where love and confidence prevail.

3.11 Questions with Regard to Method

In this article, Lonergan makes explicit his conception of human development from above. We resume, in the form of interview, some questions and answers relative to the way down. *«Since you speak of redemption[137] in the «Healing and Creating» lecture, it seemed that the metaphor for healing, «from above downwards», might be taken to mean God or God's grace.* Certainly»[138].

> *But at other times you talk about a from above downward movement, the origin of which is affectivity?* Well, it is both. What God does is God's operative grace. Operative grace is plucking out the heart of stone (Ezechiel) and putting in a heart of flesh. *So (without denying God) we can understand, in*

---

[135] «Theology and Praxis», 197.
[136] *OTN*, 75.
[137] According to Lonergan's dynamic conception of history: «you have progress and then decline. The third step is redemption and that is what Christianity is about» «Questions with Regard to Method», 306).
[138] «Questions with Regard to Methods», 306.

«from above downwards», that the «above» is responsibility. Above that is being in love. That's a further level; you are out of yourself then[139].

From these questions and answers, we draw three points in relation to human development from above. Firstly, the metaphor from above downwards may have its origin in affectivity[140], and consequently, has no religious connotations. Secondly, the metaphor from above downwards can be used to mean either God or his grace. In this sense, it conveys an essentially religious dimension.

Thirdly, the metaphor from above downwards may at once refer to God's affectivity and grace. It is then, in both cases, a call to be in love. And being in love is a higher level that stands at the fourth level and sublates the other three previous levels.

Lonergan harks back to the fact of being in love, by answering the question about the process of higher integrations in *Insight*. He affirms that the horizontal process from below upwards composed of different levels finds its climax in the vertical process from above, in the fact of being in love.

«All terminates at the *dépassement de soi* which is being in love. And being in love is of different kinds : the domestic love of the family, the urban or national or universal love of mankind, and the love of God, which pulls you out of the finite universe»[141]. Once again, the three kinds of love are mentioned, but, more than the threefold manifestation of love, it is a matter of a threefold way of being in love, «to falling in love with your family, your country, mankind, God»[142].

One last important mention of human development from above downwards appears in the acquisition of new ideas. *The appeal for the scholar to have a new idea is that in the from above downwards? For other people? I suppose so. In other words, what is from below upwards for the person is from above downwards for another?* Yes, that is perfectly true, there are different reference points[143].

How should one understand this apparently contradictory answer, which affirms that «what is from below upwards for the person is from above downwards for another» In the field of education, that can be understood as follows: for an educator, the acquisition of a new idea, of an

---

[139] «Questionnaire on Philosophy», 306.
[140] «Fundamentally it is affectivity: their parents, their brothers and sisters, getting along and being good boy and good girl» («Questions with Regard to Method»., 310).
[141] «Questions with Regard to Method», 310.
[142] «Questions with Regard to Method», 287.
[143] «Questions with Regard to Method», 311.

insight springs up as an answer to the questions one asks oneself. And the acquisition of a new idea by the educator belongs to human development from below upwards. But the students' reception of this new idea imparted by the educator, obviously is dependent upon development from above downwards.

In «Questions with Regard to Method», Lonergan deals mainly with human development from above in the light of God's love. Development from above downwards, the vertical process, is the crowning of human development from below upwards inasmuch as development from above introduces people into the field of human and divine love.

4. Conclusion

As a summary conclusion to the first part, we have asserted that the aim of truly human development does not consist exclusively in a cumulative progress or in an achievement of self-transcendence. It consists neither only in an effective transformation of love in its triple manifestation, nor in the faithful transmission of the values carried out by a tradition. The aim of human development comprises in the complementarity of the two ways of human development, in their integration: «Both ways are normal, one to achievement, the other to reception; and since we are all our lives receiving and achieving, the full normality is the complementarity of the two»[144].

An intrinsic demand connects the two ways and ideally leads them towards full human development: «*ex partita vita in unitam consurgere*». Indeed the way up and the way down of development constitute two processes of one and the same reality called «the truly human development» Furthermore, «the truly human development is of conscious subjects moving cumulatively through their operations to the self-transcendence of truth and love»[145]. In studying human development we have distinguished the two processes but without separating them, and we have done so for the sake of clarity and method. While we have stressed their unity and complementarity from the outset, nevertheless, «as progress must take its start from tradition, so tradition must submit to the critique of progress. But, in principle, the development achieved through personal experience and the development based on accepting heritage can be conceived as complementary to one another»[146]. There-

---

[144] *OTN*, 166.
[145] «Christology Today», 76.
[146] *OTN*, 24.

fore, it seems appropriate to highlight this unity and complementarity as it appears in *Method in Theology* and in post-*Method* articles.

In *Method in Theology*, the unity of both ways is required to achieve authentic human development. In fact, just as «the way up» *rises from* experience to understanding, judgment and decision, similarly the way down» *descends* from decision to judgment, understanding and to experience. «As the many operations are conjoined in a single compound knowing, so too the many levels of consciousness are just successive stages in the unfolding of a single thrust, the eros of the human spirit. To know the good, it must know the real; to know the real, it must know the true; to know the true, it must know the intelligible; to know the intelligible, it must attend to the data»[147].

Chapter One of *Method in Theology*, dealing exclusively with development from below, remains absolutely incomplete without development from above of chapters 4 (religion) and 10 (dialectic) of the same work. Thus, the four transcendental precepts which structure development from below are completed by a the fifth one: «be in love», of development from above.

When Lonergan discusses the two phases of theology, *in oratione obliqua* and *in oratione recta*, he speaks of a reciprocal dependence: «There is, then, reciprocal dependence within each of the two phases, and this was only expected since the four levels of conscious and intentional operations (which determine the four specialities in each phase) are themselves interdependent. There is dependence of the second phase on the first for the second confronts the present and the future in the light of what has been assimilated from the past»[148].

In all eleven post-*Method* articles, Lonergan highlights the complementarity, symbiosis and interdependence of the two ways of human development. The article «Mission and the Spirit» deals with the proximity of the two modes of development: «Besides the *fides ex auditu* there is *fides ex infusione*»[149]. In «Christology Today: Methodological Reflections», «the ordinary process i.e., from below upwards is not the exclusive process»[150], because there also exists development from above downwards.

In «Healing and Creating in History», Lonergan stresses the interdependence of the creative process and the healing process. «Intrinsic to

147 *MIT*, 13.
148 *MIT*, 142-143.
149 «Mission and the Spirit», 32.
150 «Christology Today», 76.

the nature of healing, there is the extrinsic requirement of a concomitant creative process. For just as the creative process, when unaccompanied by healing, is distorted and corrupted by bias, so too the healing process, when unaccompanied by creativity, is a soul without a body»[151]. In «Religious Experience», he insists on the coexistence of the two paths of human development: «Besides development from below upwards there also is development from above downwards»[152].

In «The Ongoing Genesis of Methods», the processes of socialization, acculturation and education from above constitute a solid base for the development from below. «By that process there is formed our initial mind-set, worldview, blik, horizon. On that basis and with its limitation we slowly begin to become our own masters, think for ourselves, make our own decisions, exercise our own freedom and responsibility»[153]. In the 1976 Lonergan Workshop, Lonergan affirms that the higher developments from above sublate the innovations from below. «In other words, the higher integrations are integrations of what is below and it is from below that big innovations are going»[154].

In «The Human Good», «there is a «symbiosis between immanently generated knowledge and belief»[155], an interdependence between «vertical development» or the transmission of tradition and «horizontal development» or personal appropriation. This symbiosis and interdependence between the two ways of development are explained in the «Questionnaire on Philosophy». «The two modes of development are interdependent. But only through the second does the first take one beyond the earliest stages of development. Only through the first is there any real assimilation and appropriation of the second»[156].

In «Natural Right and Historical Mindedness», there exists a strict complementarity between development and the handling on of development. One is incomplete without the other and vice-versa. They call on each other reciprocally. «Development is incomplete when it does not go the whole way upwards [...] The process of handling on can be incomplete»[157], if it is not accompanied by the process of development.

In «Theology and Praxis», Lonergan comes back to the mutual dependence of the two phases of development by affirming that «the

---

[151] «Healing and Creating in History», 107.
[152] «Religious Experience», 126.
[153] «The Ongoing Genesis of Methods», 156.
[154] The LoWo Transcripts, 78.
[155] «The Human Good», 120.
[156] «Questionnaire on Philosophy», 10.
[157] «Natural Right and Historical Mindedness», 180-181.

structure of individual development is twofold»[158]. In the last article, «Questions with Regard to Method», Lonergan states that «besides the horizontal process, there is being in love»[159] i.e., the vertical process. In the light of what has been said, we confirm the thesis according to which the ideal of truly human development consists in the integration and complementarity of the two ways of development.

For the human being develops from below upwards through his creativity and self-transcendence, but he also develops from above downwards by accepting God's love that sublates his desire for creativity and for self-transcendence.

Given this complementarity, one can ask what is the specific relationship between the two ways of human development. The complementarity of the two ways seems to be the chief fruit of Lonergan's thought:

> Of his post-*Method* works most students of Lonergan would probably agree with Frederick E. Crowe, S.J., that the chief fruit is his ever shaper elucidation of the two complementary rhythms of development with the healing vector moving from above downwards (i.e., of being-in-love with God, believing, evaluating, judging, understanding, experiencing), and the creative vector moving from below downwards (i.e., experiencing, understanding, reflecting, believing and loving)[160].

On the basis of this complementarity between the two vectors of human development, we can ask ourselves, in a specific way, what type of relationship exists between these two vectors. In «Christology Today: Methodological Reflections», Lonergan maintains that if the transformation by God's love is real, then «development becomes not merely from below upwards but *more fundamentally* from above downwards»[161]. «Human development more commonly is from below upwards but *more importantly* it is from above downwards»[162]. Indeed, «a life has begun where the heart has its reason which reason ignores. A new world in which the old adage, *nihil nisi amatum prius cognitum*, yields to a new truth, *nihil cognitum nisi prius amatum*»[163].

In the article «The Ongoing Genesis of Methods», «the way down» is the foundation for «the way up». In the 1976 Lonergan Workshop, de-

---

[158] «Theology and Praxis», 196.
[159] «Questions with Regard to Method», 310.
[160] F. LAWRENCE, «Bernard Lonergan», 263.
[161] «Christology Today», 77, my emphasis.
[162] «Christology Today», 79., my emphasis.
[163] «Christology Today», 77.

velopment from above is seen as a higher integration of the innovations produced by development from below. In the «Questionnaire on Philosophy», the relationship between the two processes is discussed in terms of their mutual enrichment because it is only through the second mode of development that one can transcend the initial stages of development, and it is only through the first that the assimilation and appropriation the second become effective.

In «Natural Right and Historical Mindedeness», development from above is given a chronological priority over development from below. Indeed, «on affectivity rests the apprehension of values»[164] within which the process of socialization, acculturation and education from below develops.

In «Theology and Praxis», development from above is once again given chronological priority: «*The chronologically prior phase is from above downwards*»[165]. Why? Because the second phase, which basically rests on love and trust, contributes to the emergence and development of the first phase.

Thus in *Method in Theology* as well as in the eleven post-*Method* articles, there is both complementarity and integration between the «way up» and the «way down,» between tradition and innovation, between the gift of love and its reception, between healing and creativity. Nevertheless, in *Method in Theology* as in these articles, human or divine love from above both grounds and sublates the creative process from below. So, «love, then, as it was the original gift in the way of heritage, is also the crowning element in the way of achievement»[166]. Human or divine love from above integrates and unifies progress from below. Through the various conflicts inherent to existence, love promotes the emergence of a new style of human development.

---

[164] «Natural Right and Historical Mindedness», 181.
[165] «Theology and Praxis», 196, my emphasis.
[166] *OTN*, 96.

SECOND PART

ANTICIPATION OF THE TWO WAYS OF HUMAN DEVELOPMENT IN *INSIGHT*

CHAPTER III

Anticipation of Development from Below in *Insight*

1. Introduction

Among Lonergan's philosophical writings, *Insight* constitutes his masterpiece. According to Frederick Crowe, «*Insight* is an inhumanely rigorous work»[1] and according to Joseph de Finance, «c'est une synthèse constructive et créatrice»[2] *Insight* is an extremely coherent personal and original work with human understanding as its main focus. Lonergan sums up the *telos* of his work in a sentence: «*Thoroughly understand what it is to understand, and not only will you understand the broad lines of all there is to be understood but also you will possess a fixed base, an invariant pattern, opening upon all further developments of understanding*»[3]

It is about a correct, true, and grounded understanding of all that is to be understood: an *épistème*. This *épistème* develops between two mutually complementary sides: on one side, it leads to an exploration of the general procedures of human intelligence and of the essential structures of its object, and on the other side, it invites the subject to become personally conscious of the structure, the working and the implications of his own intellectual activity. Consequently, *Insight* is nothing like a treatise, It neither aim at communicating ready-made results, nor proceeds in a strictly logical manner from first principles or propositions, instead it follows a moving viewpoint.

---

[1] F.E. CROWE, «The Exigent Mind», 20.
[2] J. de FINANCE, «Une étude sur l'intelligence humaine», 136.
[3] *IN*, 22.

As its *telos* is an *épistème*, one understands why *Insight* explores, with originality and coherence, the philosophical areas such as cognitional theory, epistemology, metaphysics, ethics and natural theology. Because of this original and coherent exploration, *Insight* leads one into contemporary philosophical questions about the meaning of human existence and development. It is as a search of human meaning and development that *Insight* interests us because the theme of our dissertation is: Lonergan's two ways of human development, from below upwards and from above downwards.

Lonergan uses the spatial metaphors from below upwards and from above downwards when he speaks of the two heuristic structures of the empirical method: «classical inquiry proceeds from below upwards from measurements through curve-fitting but also from above downwards from differential equations[4] to their solutions»[5]. The differential equations operate from above downwards, the measurements and the empirical correlations work from below upwards. The two structures of the empirical method are complementary.

To explain this double movement and their complementarity, Lonergan also speaks of a scissors-like movement with a lower blade and an upper blade: «the heuristic structure of empirical method operates in a scissors-like fashion. Not only there is a lower blade that arises from data through measurements and curve fitting to formulae, but also there is an upper blade that moves downwards from differential and operator equations»[6]. The lower blade, from below upwards, is constituted of specific determinations such as precise measurements, empirical correlations, and graphics.

One can find, however, in *Insight*, neither the application of the metaphor from below upward and from above downward to the process of the human development as whole, nor the expressions development from below upwards and development from above downwards. Nevertheless, despite the lack of these expressions, we maintain the following thesis: Lonergan's meaning of the two ways of human development, operative in *Method in Theology* and explicit in post *Method* articles, are anticipated in *Insight*.

---

4 «The differential equation is an anticipation of the possible laws relevant to the formulation of a given thing that one is trying to understand. It provides a determination from above downwards on the possible formulae that are to be obtained» (*UB*, 68).

5 *UB*, 87.

6 *IN*, 337.

In this second part, we are going to deal with Lonergan's anticipation of the two ways of human development in *Insight*. This second part has two chapters: a third chapter examines the anticipation of the way up and a fourth chapter considers the anticipation of the way down in *Insight*.

In the introduction of *Insight*, Lonergan reveals his intention: «we are concerned not with the existence of knowledge but with its nature, not with what is known but with the structure of the knowing»[7] So his main interest is not the knowledge but its nature. It is not the known object *(intentio intenta* or *noema)* but the structure and the process by which one comes to know *(intentio intendens* or *noêsis)*. Lonergan's main interest is knowing the cognitional process that proceeds from below upwards. This cognitional process corresponds to the upward movement of human development.

In this third chapter, we will examine the anticipation of the upward development in three main points : first, *Insight* as a moving viewpoint, secondly, the three levels of knowledge, namely, experience, understanding and judgement; thirdly, the fourth level: decision.

2. *Insight*: a Moving Viewpoint

From the introduction, Lonergan qualifies his work as a moving viewpoint: «not only are we writing from a moving viewpoint but also we are writing about a moving viewpoint»[8]. This moving viewpoint is required by the process of development: «As it is clear a book designed to aid development must be written from a moving viewpoint»[9].

This moving viewpoint structures the articulation of the parts and chapters of *Insight*. As a philosophical work, *Insight* is composed of two main parts: insight as activity (chapters 1 to 10) and insight as knowledge (chapters 11 to 20). The two parts are so strictly connected that one can not methodically reach to a personal appropriation of insight as knowledge if one does not first come to a grasp of insight as activity. Insight as activity and insight as knowledge are epistemologically connected.

In the first part, insight is studied as an activity, as an event that occurs within various patterns of other related events. In the second part, insight is

---

7 *IN*, 17.
8 *IN*, 20. That means «earlier statements are to be qualified and interpreted in the light of the later statements» (*IN*, 19).
9 *IN*, 18.

studied as knowledge, as an event that, under determinate conditions, reveals a universe of being. The first part deals with the question, what is happening when we are knowing? The second part moves to the question, What is known when that is happening[10] ?

Lonergan tries in the ten first chapters of *Insight* to help us to answer the question of what is happening when we are knowing. Chapter one clarifies the concept of insight taking examples from mathematics and from natural sciences. These two disciplines are «the fields of intellectual endeavour in which the greatest exactitude is attained»[11] . Chapter two widens the dynamic aspects of the first chapter, dealing with the heuristic structures of the empirical scientific method. Chapter three explains the canons of the empirical method which aim «to reveal the intelligible unity that underlines and accounts for the diverse and apparently disconnected rules of empirical method»[12] .

Chapter 4 examines the complementary of classical and statistical heuristic structures. Chapter 5 analyses the notion of space and time. These chapters «throw considerable light on the precise nature of abstraction, they provide a concrete and familiar context for the foregoing analyses of empirical science, and they form our examination of science to an examination of common sense»[13] .

Common sense in its object (chapter 6) as in its subject (chapter 7) is a specialisation of intelligence in the power of the concrete and of the particular. As a specialisation of intelligence, common sense transcends itself. And «the development of common sense involves a change not only in us, to whom things are related, but also in the things, which are related to us»[14] .

Chapter 8 considers the notion of thing, a «concrete unity-identity-totality», indispensable for the development of scientific thought. «For scientific thought needs, not only explanatory systems, but also description that determines the data which explanation must satisfy»[15] .

---

10 *IN*, 16. In *Insight* (1957), Lonergan speaks of two questions. Ten years later, in 1967, in «Theories of Inquiry», he comes up with three basic questions which he reaffirms in *Method in Theology* (1972). The three basic question are: 1. «What am I doing when I am knowing? 2. Why is doing that knowing? 3. What do I know when I do it? (*MIT*, 25.83.261.297.316). In applying these three basic questions to *Insight*, we affirm that the first eleven chapters deal with the first question. Chapter 12 is an answer to the second question. Chapters 13 to 17, 19, 20 answer the third question.

11 *IN*, 14.
12 *IN*, 94.
13 *IN*, 162.
14 *IN*, 232.
15 *IN*, 273

Nevertheless, the notion of thing does not define the existence of things. It is from the study of the notion of the judgement (chapter 9) and from the reflective understanding (chapter 10) that the affirmation of the experience of things results.

The second part considers insight as knowledge. This second part pivots essentially around chapter 11 which deals with the self-affirmation of the knower. As the self-affirmation of the knower involves the making of correct judgments, Lonergan passes to the structure of the known. Before he explains the notions of being (chapter 12) and of objectivity (chapter 13).

From this epistemological basis, Lonergan derives a metaphysics which, in its method (chapter 14) and in its elements (chapter 15), leads to the study of metaphysics as science (chapter 16) and as dialectic (chapter 17). After the study of metaphysics as dialectic, Lonergan, passing from the order of knowing to that of doing, poses the problem of the possibility of ethics (chapter 18). Ethics, in turn, raises the question of the good as intelligible, as well as the questions of human freedom and moral responsibility.

How, in a moral responsible life, one can give an account of one's existential contingency and the limitation of one's freedom? How can a person find a solution to the problem of evil, in the exercise of his freedom? These questions lead to the problem of general transcendent (chapter 19) and special (chapter 20) knowledge. The solution to the problem of evil of a supernatural order.

The twenty chapters of *Insight* are «written not from above downwards, but from below upwards»[16]. «*Insight* is to aid a process of development»[17] and aims at promoting the subject's development from below upwards of the subject. «Essentially, it is a development of the subject and in, and like all development it can be solid and fruitful only by being painstaking and slow»[18]. This development of the subject and in the subject is not automatic, spontaneous. It is a conquest, a crown-

---

16 *IN*, 17.
17 *IN*, 17.
[18] *IN*, 17. In *Insight*, there are different kinds of development: human development (45.252.412.494.559.567.618.650.652.653.720), intellectual development (198.203-204.302.484.486.596.620.645.745), social development (249.620.745), organic development (484.488), psychic development (493.632.645), historic development (762), scientific development (269), personal development (252.454.650), philosophic development (454.483), development of practical intelligence (233.646.484), material development (239), political development (253), technological development (234-236), mathematical development (18.58.483.484), economic development (234-236.257), sexual development (228.483).

ing of a long, rich and solid enactment that the reader will acquire
through the self-appropriation of his own cognitive operations.

This self-appropriation is the aim proposed by *Insight*: «the aim is
not to set forth the abstract properties but to assist the reader in effecting a personal appropriation of the concrete, dynamic structure immanent and recurrently operative in his own cognitional activities»[19]. Lonergan makes the Socratic imperative of «know-thyself» more precise:
understand what you know, affirm yourself as a knowing subject, reach
up to the self-appropriate the dynamic structures of your experience,
understanding and judging, the three levels of upward human development.

3. **Three Levels of Knowing**

In *Insight*, the ascending human development corresponds to the
cognitional process. To avoid any ambiguity, Lonergan, affirms that his
«primary concern is not the known but the knowing. The known is extensive, but the knowing is a recurrent structure that can be investigated
sufficiently in a series of a strategically chosen instances»[20]. The cognitional process is a dynamic structure that has three levels intrinsically
connected among themselves. Every level includes some distinct but
connected cognitional operations. So there are three levels of the cognitional process: «a level of presentation, a level of intelligence, and a
level of reflection»[21]. In this third chapter, we will first examine these
levels.

3.1 *The Level of Presentation*

The level of presentation of data is the first level of the cognitional
process on which intelligence and reflection are based. Human being
exercises his/her intelligence and his/her reflection upon the data because of «the pure desire». In effect,

> The pure[22] desire is simply the inquiring and critical spirit of man. By mov-
> ing him to seek understanding, it prevents him from being content with mere
> flow of outer and inner experience. By demanding adequate under-standing,
> it involves man in the self-correcting process of learning in which further

---

19 *IN*, 11.
20 *IN*, 12.
21 *IN*, 298.
22 «Because it differs radically from other desire, this desire has been named pure.
It is to be known, not by misleading analogy of other desire, but by giving free rein to

questions yield complementary insights. By moving man to reflect, to seek the unconditioned, to grant unqualified assent only to the unconditioned, it prevents him from being content with hearsay and legend, with unverified hypotheses and untested theories[23].

The pure desire characterised by the human spirit of inquiry, moves us to an adequate understanding of data and to a reflection and a grasp of the virtually unconditioned. This desire is not only pure, but is also a pure desire to know: «the pure desire to know has an objective. It is a desire to know[24]. As mere desire, it is for the satisfaction of acts of knowing, for the satisfaction of understanding, understanding fully, understanding correctly»[25]. This pure desire to know, as an inquiring spirit, is detached and unrestricted. As such, it is at the origin of every question that one asks oneself about the data.

The first level is qualified according to Lonergan as the level of the sensation, «the level of the experiential» and «the level of experience». Let us briefly examine the three aspects of the first level of the presentation of data.

First of all, the first level is the level of the sensation, of the application of the organs of sense to the external data.

Without eyes, there is no seeing; and when I would see with my eyes, I open them, turn my head, approach, focus my gaze. Without ears, there is no hearing; and to escape noise, I must move beyond its range or else build myself soundproof walls. Without a palate, there is no tasting; and when I would taste, there are involved movements of the body and arms, of hands and fin-

---

intelligent and rational consciousness. It is, indeed, impalpable, but also it is powerful. It pulls man out of the solid routine of perception and conation, instinct and habit, doing and enjoying. It holds him with the fascination of problems. It engages him in the quest of solutions. It makes him aloof to what is not established. It compels assent to the unconditioned. It is the cool shrewdness of common sense, the disinterestedness of science, the detachment of philosophy. It is the absorption of investigation, the joy of discovery, the assurance of judgement, the modesty of limited knowledge. It is the relentless serenity, the unhurried determination, the imperturbable drive of question following appositely on question in the genesis of truth» (*IN*, 373).

23 *IN*, 372-373.

24 «By the desire to know is meant the dynamic orientation manifested in questions for intelligence and for reflection. It is not the verbal utterance of questions. It is not the conceptual formulation of questions. It is not any insight or thought. It is not any reflective grasp or judgement. It is the prior and developing drive that carries cognitional process from sense and imagination to understanding, from understanding to judgement, from judgement to the complete context of correct judgements that is named knowledge» (*IN*, 372).

25 *IN*, 373.

gers, of lips and tongue and jaws. Sensation has a bodily basis, and it is linked to bodily movement[26].

The application of the five organs of sense — sight, hearing, touch, taste and smell — to the external data, constitutes «the flow of sensations[27]. As completed by memories and prolonged by imaginative acts of anticipations, becomes the flow of perceptions»[28].

Secondly, the first level is the level of the experiential. «The experiential is the given[29] as given. It is the field of materials about which one inquires, in which one finds the fulfilment of conditions for the unconditioned, to which cognitional process repeatedly returns to generate the series of inquiries and reflections that yield the contextual manifold of judgements»[30]. The given represents the totality of the materials that is examined by the cognitional process.

The knower considers the given as the starting point for inquiry and reflection. It is «the field of fulfilling conditions». «There must be a field of fulfilling conditions. More exactly, since conditions are simultaneous with what they condition, there must be a prior field containing what can become fulfilling conditions. Of themselves, they will be neither conditioning nor conditioned; they will be merely given»[31]. The given as given has nevertheless a twofold characteristic. The first characteristic is that the given is not questionable.

> The given is unquestionable and indubitable. What is constituted by answering questions can be upset by other questions. But the given is constituted apart from questioning; it remains the same no matter what the result of questioning may be; it is unquestionable in the sense that it lies outside the cognitional levels constituted by questioning and answering. In the same fas-

---

26 *IN*, 205.

27 «The choice I cannot make effective is to sense nothing, perceive nothing, imagine nothing. Not only are the contents of these acts imposed upon me, but also consciousness in some degree is inseparable from acts» (*IN*, 354).

28 *IN*, 96. «Perceiving is a function not only of position relative to an object, of the intensity of the light, of the healthiness of eyes, but also of interest, anticipation, and activity» (*IN*, 213).

29 «We are employing the name given in an extremely broad sense. It includes not only the veridical deliverances of outer sense but also images, dreams, illusions, hallucinations, personal equations, subjective bias, and so forth. No doubt, a more restricted use of the term would be desirable if we were speaking for the limited viewpoint of natural science. But we have to acknowledge as given not only the materials into which natural science inquires but also the materials into which the psychologist or methodologist or cultural historian inquires» (*IN*, 406-407).

30 *IN*, 406.

31 *IN*, 361.

hion the given is indubitable. What can be doubted is the answer to a question for reflection; it is a yes or a no. But the given is not the answer to any question; it is prior to questioning and independent of any answers[32].

The given is not questionable because it is situated outside the field of the questioning. It is indubitable in so far as it is not an answer to any question. It is previous to all questioning and independent of any answer. The second characteristic of the given is that it is residual and diffused because it is what is posterior to the exercise of intelligence and reflection upon the data.

The given is residual[33] and, of itself, diffuse. It is possible to select elements in the given and to indicate them clearly and precisely. But the selection and indication are the work of insight and formulation, and the given is the residue that remains when one subtracts from the indicated (1) the instrumental act of meaning by which one indicates, (2) the concepts expressed by the instrumental act, (3) the insights on which the concepts rest Hence, since the given is just the residue, since it can be selected and indicated only through intellectual activities, of itself it is diffuse[34].

Thirdly, the first level is also known as the level of experience for «experience neither defines nor specifies; it only presents»[35]. But, what is presented by experience? Experience « supplies no more than materials for questions; questions are essential to its genesis[36] ». More precisely, «its defining characteristic is the fact that it is presupposed and complemented by the level of intelligence, that it supplies, as it were, the raw materials on which intelligence operates, that, in a word, it is empirical, given indeed but merely given, open to understanding and formulating but by itself not understood and itself ineffable»[37].

The first level is the level of data, of sense or of consciousness up on which the levels of intelligence and of reflection operate. It is the level of the raw materials «for they are what is left over once the fruits of inquiry and reflection are subtracted from cognitional contents»[38]. These

---

32 *IN*, 406.
33 «Empirical residue that 1) consists in positive empirical data, 2) is to be denied any immanent intelligibility of its own, and 3) is connected with some compensating higher intelligibility of notable importance [...] Not only are elements in the empirical residue given positively but also they are pointed out, conceived, named, considered, discussed, and affirmed, or denied» (*IN*, 50).
34 *IN*, 406.
35 *IN*, 457.
36 *IN*, 277.
37 *IN*, 298.
38 *IN*, 407.

raw materials or data are simply given, potentially intelligible, opened to understanding and to reflection. As such, they constitute some materials around which the questions for intelligence and for reflection are formulated.

The data presented are data of sense or of consciousness. «Data of sense include colours, shapes, sounds, odours, tastes, the hard and the soft, rough and smooth, hot and cold, wet and dry, and so forth»[39]. The data of consciousness[40] «consist of acts of seeing, hearing, tasting, smelling, touching, perceiving, imagining, inquiring, understanding, formulating, reflecting, judging, and so forth. As data, such acts are experienced; but, as experienced, they are not described, distinguished, compared, related, defined, for all such activities are the work of inquiry, insight, and formulation»[41].

As acts, the data of consciousness can be experienced, but as experienced, they are neither the fruit of an intelligent understanding nor that of a critical reflection. Confronted with the data of sense or of consciousness, «there is an empirical consciousness characteristic of sensing, perceiving, imagining. As the content of these acts is merely presented or represented, so the awareness immanent in the acts is the mere giveness of acts»[42]. Insight is asked to exercise an attentive experiencing of the data of sense or of consciousness.

This attentive experiencing of data is sustained by a primordial orientation defined by Lonergan as «the pure question». «Though the pure question is prior to insights, concepts, and words, it presupposes experiences and images. Just as insight is into the concretely given or imagined, so the pure question is about the concretely given or imagined»[43]. The pure question corresponds, according to Lonergan, to the wonder that Aristotle considers as the beginning of all sciences and of all philosophy[44].

But, the first level presents the data of sense or of consciousness so that these data may become the object of an intelligent understanding which is the second level, that of intelligence.

---

39 *IN*, 299.
40 In *Insight*, «by consciousness is meant an awareness immanent in cognitional acts» (346). «Consciousness is not some inward look but a quality of cognitional acts, a quality that differs on the different levels of cognitional process [...] Consciousness is given independently of its being formulated or affirmed» (350).
41 *IN*, 359.
42 *IN*, 346.
43 *IN*, 34.
44 ARISTOTLE, *Metaphysics*, I, 1, 980 a 21.

3.2 *The Level of Intelligence*

The level of intelligence is the second level of the cognitional process: «the level of discovery and invention, of catching on and learning, of grasping problems and coming to grasp their solutions, of seeing the point»[45]. According to Lonergan, «intelligence looks for intelligible patterns in presentations and representations»[46]. «It is the source of a sequence of systems that unify and relate otherwise coincidental aggregates of sensible data»[47].This is why «the man or woman of intelligence is marked by the greater readiness in catching on, in getting the point, in seeing the issue, in grasping implications, in acquiring know-how»[48]. As a human faculty, intelligence strives to understand the intelligible relations in the data of sense and of consciousness.

If intelligence is an unrestricted potency, in its actualisation, it is concretely restricted by the data of which it tries to grasp the intelligibility. Thus it is that «the function of human intelligence is not to set up independent norms that make thought irrelevant to fact, but to study the data as they are, to grasp the intelligibility that is immanent in them, to acknowledge as principle or norm only what can be reached by generalisation from the data»[49].

The function of human intelligence does not consist in the foundation of the abstract and independent rules but in the grasp of the imminent intelligibility in the data that one tries to know. On this level cognitional process not merely strives for and reaches the intelligible, but in doing so it exhibits its intelligence; it operates intelligently. «The awareness is present but it is the awareness of intelligence, of what strives to understand, of what is satisfied by understanding, of what formulates the understood»[50].

Intelligence strives for the understanding of data. It is fulfilled by the formulation of this understanding through the questions that it asks. Lonergan distinguishes two kinds of questions: questions for intelligence and questions for reflection. «There are questions for intelligence asking what this is, what that means, why this is so, how frequently it

---

45 *IN*, 334

46 *IN*, 347.

47 *IN*, 292.

48 *IN*, 196.

49 *IN*, 255.

50 *IN*, 346. «On the intellectual level the operator is concretely the detached and disinterested desire to know. It is this desire, not in contemplation of the already known, but headed towards further knowledge, orientated into the known unknown» (*IN*, 555).

occurs or exists. There are also questions for reflection that ask whether answers to the former type of question are correct»[51]. The questions what?, why? how often? are the questions for intelligence.

Thus, the question, Why?[52], leads to a grasp and formulation of a law, a correlation, a system. The question, The question, How often? leads to a grasp and formulation of an ideal frequency from which actual frequencies nonsystematically diverge[53]. The question, What is it? leads to a grasp and formulation of an intelligible unity-identity-whole in data.

The questions for intelligence, namely: What is this?, Why? How often? express the desire to know and they presuppose the data of sense or of consciousness, situated in the first level. And if the first level is a field of fulfilling conditions, the second level is «a level of activity that yields the conditioned as conditioned, the conditioned as linked to its conditions. But this is a level of intelligence, of positing systematic units and systematic relations. Moreover, it will be a freely developing level; without free development questions would not arise»[54].

In establishing the intelligible relations that arise from the data, intelligence aims at defining these data. So, «through questions for intelligence, knowing moves to accumulation of related insights which are expressed or formulated in concepts, suppositions, definitions, postulates, theories»[55]. At the level of the intelligent understanding, we obtain some concepts, some definitions, some hypotheses, some postulates and some theories that present themselves as answers to the questions posed for intelligence. Chapters 1 to 8 of *Insight* deal with questions for intelligence.

According to Lonergan, the knower «is intelligently conscious as one inquires, understands, formulates, and raises further questions for intelligence»[56]. Questions for intelligence strive for understanding through the grasp of insights and their formulation, expressing the intelligibility existing immanent in data of sense and of consciousness. To these

---

51 *IN*, 367-368.

52 «Where does the *why* come from? What does it reveal or represent? Already we have had occasion to speak of the psychological tension that has its release in the joy of discovery. It is that tension, that drive, that desire to understand that constitutes the primordial *why*? Name it what you please — alertness of mind, intellectual curiosity, the spirit of inquiry, active intelligence, the drive to know. Under any name, it remains the same, and is, I trust, very familiar to you» (*IN*, 34).

53 *IN*, 298.

54 *IN*, 361.

55 *IN*, 278.

56 *IN*, 726.

questions for intelligence correspond some objects of thought, or cognitional acts. This is because «the level of intelligence consists in acts of inquiry, understanding, and formulation»[57]. Let us clarify the terms: inquiry, understanding, and formulation and the relations existing among them. According to Lonergan, the human being, especially the scientist, is particularly driven by the desire to inquire, to know, to understand.

> Deep within us, there is a drive to know, to understand, to see why, to discover the reason, to find the cause, to explain. Just what is wanted has many names. In what precisely it consists is a matter of dispute. But the fact of inquiry is beyond all doubt. It can absorb a man. It can keep him for hours, day after day, year after year, in the narrow prison of his study or his laboratory. It can send him on dangerous voyages of exploration. It can withdraw him from other interests, other pursuits, other pleasures, other achievements. It can fill his waking thoughts, hide from him the world of ordinary affairs, invade the very fabric of his dreams. It can demand endless sacrifices that are made without regret though there is only the hope, never a certain promise, of success[58].

The desire to inquire and to know, to understand to know, to explain and to find the cause, cannot be doubted. It characterises what Lonergan calls the orientation of inquiring intelligence.

> The guiding orientation of the scientist is the orientation of inquiring intelligence, the orientation that of its nature is a pure, detached, disinterested desire simply to know. For there is an intellectual desire, an eros of the mind. Without it there would arise no questioning, no inquiry, no wonder [...] Inasmuch as this intellectual drive is dominant, inasmuch as the reinforcing or inhibiting tendencies of other drives are successfully excluded, in that measure the scientific observer becomes an incarnation of inquiring intelligence, and his precepts move into coincidence with what are named data of sense[59].

The orientation of inquiring intelligence is manifested by intellectual curiosity, by the eros of the human spirit that leads individuals to pose some questions, to strive to know, to explain, to understand. This investigation pursued by intelligence presupposes some elements that are the object of investigation. Moreover, intellectual investigation is at the base of the cognitional process. Without it, there would not be knowledge. It must, consequently, be considered as a necessity, a pre-requisite in the cognitional process. «Inquiry is itself a presupposition, for it

---

57 *IN*, 298.
58 *IN*, 28.
59 *IN*, 97.

implies that there is something to be known by understanding the data»[60] .

Inquiry involves the presence of data of sense or of consciousness to be understood. But, before understanding, inquiry proceeds to a selection of pertinent data because «prior to inquiry there can be no intelligent discrimination and no reasonable rejection»[61] . Inquiry is considered as a stage in the cognitional process. So, «coming to know is a process; it advances by stages in which inquiry yields insights only to give rise to further insights that lead to further insights and still further insights. At each stage of the process it is helpful to fix what has been reached and to formulate in some fashion what remains to be sought»[62] .

The second level is also qualified as the level of understanding and of formulation. In his introduction to *Insight*, Lonergan points out that understanding is one of the main concerns of his philosophical work. He indicates that to commit oneself to the process of understanding is to commit oneself to a continuous development. «Thoroughly understand what it is to understand, and not only will you understand the broad lines of all there is to be understood but also you will possess a fixed based, an invariant pattern, opening all further developments of understanding»[63] .

First, let us explain what Lonergan intends by understanding. Understanding is not another kind of sensation, but it works by taking into account the content of sensation, and the data given by the first level. The spirit of inquiry, characteristic of the human intelligence, aims at understanding the data. «Understanding grasps in given or imagined presentations and intelligible form emergent in the presentations. Conception formulates the grasped idea along with what is essential to the idea in the presentations»[64] . Thanks to understanding conception grasps the essential and immanent idea of the data. Without these data, there is neither understanding nor conception and formulation.

But, without understanding there would not be the formulation that expresses what has been conceived and understood. Thus «the formulation of understanding yields concepts, definitions, objects of thought, suppositions, considerations»[65] . The concepts, the definitions, the objects of thought, the suppositions and the considerations are different

---

60 *IN*, 128.
61 *IN*, 407.
62 *IN*, 577.
63 *IN*, 22.
64 *IN.*, 300.
65 *IN*, 298.

ways of expressing understanding. In other words, through formulation, ones expresses what you have conceived, defined, thought, supposed, and considered. Moreover, «formulation expresses not only what is grasped by understanding, but also what is essential to the understanding in the understood»[66]. This means that in the formulation, there are always some elements that are the results of the inquiry and of understanding.

Nevertheless, in the cognitional process, the different ways of formulating the understanding, namely, concepts, definitions, hypotheses, objects of thought, suppositions and considerations do not concern only the particular and the concrete but the universal and the abstract. «For inasmuch as we are understanding, we are abstracting from the empirical residue»[67]. The abstraction is not an impoverishment, not even a negation of data but a grasp of what is essentially significant in the data of sense or of consciousness.

It is only with the grasp of what is essential, significant and pertinent in the data of sense or of consciousness that the subject can go forth into higher stages of knowing. But, «what one does not understand yet, one can learn»[68]. The problem of learning rises on the level of understanding, so that one may learn what one has not understood or what one does do not yet understand.

Understanding is the heart of the cognitional process. And insight appears as an answer to the question for intelligence: What? Why? How often? These questions allow one to know «concrete unities, systematic regularities, or ideal frequencies»[69]. They belong to the insights that are expressed through the hypotheses that, in their turn, will be the object of verification.

Lonergan also considers the second as the level of insight. But what is an insight? Negatively an insight is neither a special kind of sensation or perception, nor any mental activity, neither Descartes' clear and distinct idea, nor Kant's sensible intuition. Positively, an insight is an act of understanding, grasping an idea that unifies and connects the data. By insight Lonergan intends «not any act of attention or advertence or

---

66 *IN*, 298.
67 *IN*, 541. «To abstract is to grasp the essential and to disregard the incidental, to see what is significant and to set aside the irrelevant, to recognise the important as important and the negligible as negligible» (*IN*, 55).
68 *IN*, 646. «Such learning is not without teaching. For teaching is the communication of insights» (*IN*, 197).
69 *IN*, 302.

memory but the supervening act of understanding»[70]. As an act of understanding, insight is a constitutive and fundamental factor in human knowledge.

In fact, the data of sense or of consciousness are to be understood. The objective of inquiry is to understand these data. Insight arises as an answer to this inquiry. «Insights arise in response to an inquiring attitude. There are data to be understood, inquiry seeks understanding; and the insight arises as the relevant understanding»[71].

In so far as the insight is a pertinent understanding of the data, it is at one time both a priori and synthetic. «It is a priori, for it goes beyond what is merely given to sense or to empirical consciousness. It is synthetic, for it adds to the merely given an explanatory unification or organisation»[72]. A priori and synthetic, insight has another characteristic that Lonergan relates to Archimedes' story with his famous *Eureka*. «Insight (1) is a release to the tension of inquiry, (2) comes suddenly and unexpectedly, (3) is a function not of outer circumstances but of inner conditions, (4) pivots between the concrete and the abstract, and (5) passes into the habitual texture of mind»[73].

These characteristics show that insight is the fruit of an intelligent understanding. «Insight results from inquiry and it emerges upon the sensitive flow, in which it grasps some intelligible unity or correlation»[74]. It apprehends an intelligible *eidos* (form) of the concrete data. What insight adds to the data of sense or of consciousness is the unity and the intelligible relations in them.

> By insights one grasps units and correlations; but besides the unity, there are the elements to be unified; and besides the correlation, there are elements to be distinguished and related. Until one gets insight, one has no clue for picking out accurately the elements that are to be unified or related. But once insight is reached, one is able to find in one's own experience just what it is that falls under the insight's grasp and what lies outside it[75].

Insight allows one to grasp some elements of unity and correlations immanent in the data. Moreover, the knower is the one who through his insights, assures the unity and the correlations of the data that present themselves. «Insights yields correlations, definitions, and inferences. It

---

70 *IN*, 3.
71 *IN*, 308.
72 *IN*, 5.
73 *IN*, 28.
74 *IN*, 632.
75 *IN*, 582.

is in terms of such formulations that are framed the further questions that will complement and modify the previous insights by later insights. In like manner the later insights receive their formulation, which is presupposed by the further questions that lead to a still fuller understanding»[76].

If the questions for intelligence favour the emergence of insights, these, in turn, are expressed in definitions, unities and correlations explaining the data. These different formulations of insights, once verified, give place to further questions that require complementary insights and a more adequate understanding. The upward movement from the pertinent questions to the complementary insights, and from the complementary insights to a more adequate understanding is what Lonergan calls the development of intelligence. This development of the intelligence can be verified in the social sphere where insight becomes a source of progress.

> Insight brings to light the cumulative progress. For concrete situations give rise to insights which issue into policies and courses of action. Action transforms the existing situation to give rise to further insights, better policies, more effective courses of action. It follows that if insight occurs, it keeps recurring; and at each recurrence knowledge develops, action increases its scope, and situations improve[77].

But in every human being there are insights that favour the cumulative process of progress. There are also some oversights that produce unintelligent actions contributing to cumulative of decline. «Oversight reveals the cumulative process of decline. For the flight from understanding blocks the insight that concrete situations demand. There follow unintelligent policies and inept courses of action. The situation deteriorates to demand still further insights, and as they are blocked, policies become more unintelligent and action more inept»[78].

Intelligence produces a series of insights that contribute to progress. In contrast, bias produces oversights. Bias leads human subjects to refuse to understand or to ask pertinent questions in concrete situations. Thus it blocks the emergence of new insights and favours decline. Intelligence and bias renders the dialectical subject's development. They are as mutually exclusive as are progress and decline.

---

76 *IN*, 334.
77 *IN*, 8.
78 *IN*, 8.

A source of bias lies, according to Lonergan, in granting the priority not to the pure desire to know but to the desire of sensibility. The dialectic of intelligence and bias originates in the immanent tension in the subject between intellectual desire and sensible desire. Intelligence and sensibility represent two dimensions of the human nature called to work together in the cognitional process. «Intellectual development rests upon the dominance of a detached and disinterested desire to know. It reveals to a man a universe of being in which he is but an item, and a universal order in which his desires and fears, his delight and anguish are but infinitesimal components in the history of mankind»[79]. Ideally intelligence, as higher integration, sublates the lower integration, i.e. sensibility. In case of conflict, the priority must be granted to intelligence so that the human being continues to promote his intellectual development by his insight.

In chapter 7, Lonergan shows that there is a dialectical tension between two opposite principles, namely intelligence and spontaneity:

> For man does not live exclusively on the level of intersubjectivity or on the level of detached intelligence. On the contrary, his living is a dialectical resultant springing from those opposed but linked principles; and in the tension of that union of opposites, the root of egoism is readily to be discerned. For intelligence is a principle of universalization and of ultimate synthesis; it understands similars in the same manner; and it gives rise to further questions on each issue until all relevant data are understood. On the other hand, spontaneity is concerned with the present, the immediate, the palpable[80].

In other words, «besides the detached and disinterested stand of intelligence, there is the more spontaneous viewpoint of the individual subjected to needs and wants, pleasures and pains, labour and leisure, enjoyment and privation[81]». This dialectical tension between intelligence and spontaneity finds its «ground in a duality in man himself»[82]. More precisely,

> Philosophic evidence is within the philosopher himself.[...]It is his own grasp of the dialectical unfolding of his own desire to know in its conflict with other desires that provides the key to his own philosophic development and reveals his potentialities to adopt the stand of any of the traditional or the new philosophic schools. Philosophy is the flowering of the individual's ra-

---

79 *IN*, 498.
80 *IN*, 245.
81 *IN*, 240.
82 *IN*, 240.

tional consciousness in its coming to know and to take possession of itself[83]

We note, finally, that insight moves at the level of thinking. «Inasmuch as we think intelligently, the properties of our thought reflect the properties of our insights»[84]. Insight, as object of thought, is neither true nor false. To decide the truth or falsity of an insight, one must reach the third level, that of reflection.

3.3 *The Level of Reflection*

The second level of intelligence, presupposing and completing the level of experience, is itself assumed and completed by the third level, that of the reflection. So, after attentive experiencing and intelligent understanding, reflection constitutes the third level of the cognitional process. In *Insight*, the level of reflection is mainly studied in chapters 9 (The Notion of Judgement) and 10 (Reflective Understanding).

Just as the acts of understanding are insights, so the act of reflection is also an insight. «As they meet questions for intelligence, it meets questions for reflection. As they lead to definitions and formulations, it leads to judgement. As they grasp unity, or system, or ideal frequency, it grasps the sufficiency of the evidence»[85]. Reflection manifests the critical attitude of the mind in order to understand better and to make judgements.

So, «reflection asks whether understanding and formulation are correct and judgement answers that they are or are not»[86]. Reflection asks if the understanding and its formulation are correct. At the end of reflection, judgement supervenes to affirm if they are correct or to deny if they are not. For Lonergan there are three main determinations concern the notion of judgement.

3.3.1 First Determination

The first determination arises when judgement is expressed in a proposition. According to Lonergan, a proposition is not a sentence, which can be declarative, interrogative, optative or exclamatory. But only a declarative phrase corresponds to a proposition. «A first determination of the notion of judgement is reached by relating it to propositions. A proposition, then, may be an object of thought, the content of

---

83 *IN*, 454.
84 *IN*, 173.
85 *IN*, 304.
86 *IN*, 300.

an act of conceiving, defining, thinking, supposing, considering. But a proposition also may be the content of an act of judging; and then it is the content of an affirming or denying, an agreeing or disagreeing, an assenting or dissenting»[87]. So described, a proposition can express the object of a thought or the content of an act of conceiving. It can also express the content of an affirmation or of a negation.

3.3.2 Second Determination

The second determination relates the notion of judgement to questions[88] for reflection. As questions for intelligence that require an intelligible explanation, the questions for reflection, Is it true? Are you sure? Is it so? have as answers a yes or a no. They are formulated through a judgement. «Our second determination of the notion of judgement is, then, that judging is answering yes or no to a question for reflection»[89].

In a general way, judgment is a mental operation by which one affirms or denies the content of a proposition. In a particular way, judgement is an answer to a question for reflection. As such, the judgement neither defines nor specifies. It affirms or denies what has been defined or specified. «All that judgement adds to the question of reflection is the yes or no, the "is" or the "is not"»[90]. By affirming this *is* or *is not*, judgement posits, *de facto*, a virtually unconditioned[91]: «Every judgement raises a further question; it reveals a conditioned to be a virtually unconditioned, and by that stroke it reveals conditions to happen to be fulfilled; that happening is a matter of fact»[92].

Judgement requires both a conditioned and a fulfilment of conditions. The virtually unconditioned that confirms the realisation of conditions results from the act of reflective understanding. The truth of a judgement depends on the grasp and the affirmation of the virtually

---

87 *IN*, 296-297.

88 «By questions for intelligence and reflection are not meant utterances or even conceptual formulation. By the question is meant the attitude of inquiring mind that effects the transition from the first level to the second, and again the attitude of the critical mind that effect the transition from the second level to the third » (*IN*, 299).

89 *IN*, 297. Chapters 9 et 10 of *Insight* deal with questions for reflection..

90 *IN*, 390. In affirming that this is, judgment makes more than a synthesis: «Judgement is not a synthesis of terms but the unconditioned positing of such a synthesis. Corresponding to judgements there is not a synthesis of forms but the absolute of fact» (*IN*, 390).

91 «The formally unconditioned has no conditions whatever. The virtually unconditioned has conditions but they are fulfilled» (*IN*, 305).

92 *IN*, 676.

unconditioned which has great importance in the philosophy of Lonergan. «The concept of virtually unconditioned is of cardinal importance in Lonergan's philosophy enabling him to avoid Hegel's conclusion that thought ultimately has nothing to think of but itself, without embroiling him with Kantian 'things in themselves such as somehow exist in utter transcendence of our cognitional processes»[93] .

In contrast to Hegel's Absolute Spirit and Kant's noumenon (thing in itself), Lonergan thinks that in a true judgement one effectively grasps a virtually unconditioned that, *de facto*, is. We notice that the questions for intelligence and the questions for reflection are epistemologically complementary and interdependent. They ask and complete themselves. In which sense? According to Frederick Crowe, «Lonergan has taken Aristotle's two basic questions *an sit* and *quid sit*, linked them sharply to the *duae operationes intellectus* of St. Thomas, understanding and reflection, and made them central to his account of the dynamism of cognitional activity» [94] .

In fact, every question for intelligence leads to a question for reflection in the cognitional process. The questions for intelligence (What is it?) lead us to raise questions for reflection (Is it so?).

> Every answer to a question for intelligence raises a further question for reflection. There is an ulterior motive to conceiving and defining, thinking and considering, forming suppositions, hypotheses, theories, systems. That motive appears when such activities are followed by the question, Is it so? We conceive in order to judge. As questions for intelligence, What?, and Why? and How often? stand to insights and formulation, so questions for reflection stand to a further kind of insight and judgement[95] .

If we conceive to judge, the question for reflection: Is it so? does not yet constitute a judgement. The answer: It[96] *is so*, which is a judgement. There is an evolution from What is it? of inquiry to *Is it so?* of reflection, and from the question for reflection (Is it so?) to the judgement (It is so). «There is presupposed a question for reflection, Is it so? There follows a judgement, It is so. Between the two there is the marshalling and weighing of the evidence»[97] .

---

93 H. MEYNELL, *An Introduction*, 49.
94 *ALI*, 16. See also ARISTOTLE *Posterior Analytics*, II, 1, 89 b 22-38.
95 *IN*, 298.
96 «The "it" of the judgement is not a bare "it". On the contrary, it is the conditioned, known as conditioned, that through the fulfilment of its conditions is grasped as virtually unconditioned» (*IN*, 361).
97 *IN*, 304.

According to Lonergan, every judgement requires: «(1) a conditioned, (2) a link between the conditioned and its conditions, and (3) the fulfilment of the conditions»[98]. Before the affirmation of the unconditioned in the judgement, the cognitional process is not complete. When one makes a judgement, the question, It is so? promotes the cognitional process to another level, that of reflection. «Reflection is the complementary process of checking. One understands, and now one wishes to know whether what is understood is correct. One has grasped the point, and one asks whether it is right. One has seen how the successive steps hang together, and one is out to make sure that what hangs together is really cogent[99].

Critical reflection is a process of checking, leading to a judgement based on examining and weighing the sufficiency the evidence, of grasping the fulfilment of conditions that yields a virtually unconditioned to be affirmed in judgement. Hypotheses and insights of the second level must be verified, validated on the third level. They must undergo the process of verification to see whether if they are correct or not, whether they correspond to reality or not. Without the process of verification, you cannot affirm nothing, you can not judge correctly.

> The process of checking reveals in human knowledge, beyond experience and understanding, a third, distinct, constitutive level that is both self-authenticating and decisive. It is self-authenticating: rational reflection demands and reflective understanding grasps a virtually unconditioned; and once that grasp occurred, one cannot be reasonable and yet fail to pass judgement. Again this level alone is decisive: until I judge, I am merely thinking; once I judge, I know[100].

Before the judgement, one experiments, understands, thinks, reflects, checks, and verifies. It is only after verification (checking) that one can make a judgement. But what is the aim of checking? The aim of checking is to grasp the unconditioned, to judge and in judging, to attain the real. So, «the real is the verified, it is what is to be known by knowing, constituted by experience and inquiry, insight and hypothesis, reflection and verification»[101]. Judgement, by which I wait for the real, results from understanding, reflection and checking. «Inevitably, the achievement of understanding, however stupendous, only gives rise to

---

98 *IN*, 305
99 *IN*, 334-335.
100 *IN*, 364.
101 *IN*, 277.

the further question, Is it so? Inevitably, the process of understanding is interrupted by the checking of judgement»[102] .

In the cognitional process, judgement is not exercised *ex nihilo*. It relies on the previous stages of experience, of understanding and of checking. It means that experience, understanding, checking and judgement are intrinsically connected such that without experience, there would be no understanding, without understanding, there would be no checking, and without checking, there would be no judgement. There is more: without judgement, there is no knowledge but only objects of thought, conjecture, hypotheses. «What we know is that to pronounce a judgement without a reflective grasp is merely to guess; again what we know is that, once that grasp has occurred, then to refuse to judge is just silly»[103] . Here, the subject in search of knowledge and development does not accept any assertion or proposition, without asking before about the truth or the value contained in this assertion or proposition.

But what do I know when I make a judgement? According to Lonergan, when I make a judgement, I know what is, I know being. To pose a correct judgement is to affirm that something is actually and really so. To make a judgement is to know something about being. And «being has been conceived as the objective of the detached and disinterested desire to know, and more precisely, as whatever is to be known through intelligent grasp and reasonable affirmation»[104] . Being is not a concept or an idea but an absolute in which objectivity is the fruit of an intelligent grasp and of rational affirmation. The judgement made to know something about being is a judgement of fact. And fact[105] is concrete and intelligible.

---

102 *IN*, 355.

103 *IN*, 304.

104 *IN*, 470. «Though being is known only in judging, the notion of being is prior to judging. For prior to any judgement there is reflection, and reflection is formulated in the question, Is it? That question supposes some notion of being, and strangely enough, it is prior to each instance of our knowing being. Not only, then, does the notion of being extend beyond the known but also it is prior to the final component of knowing when being is actually known» (*IN*, 377).

105 «Fact combines the concreteness of experience, the determinateness of accurate intelligence, and the absoluteness of rational judgement. It is the natural objective of human cognitional process. It is the anticipated unity to which sensation, perception, imagination, inquiry, insight, formulation, reflection, grasp of the unconditioned, and judgement make their several, complementary contributions» (*IN*, 355).

3.3.3 Third Determination

The third determination of the notion of judgement involves a personal and responsible commitment of the one who judges.

> A third determination of the notion of judgement is that it involves a personal commitment. As Rochefoucauld remarked, «Everyone complains of his memory but no one of his judgements»[106] [...] One is ready to confess to a poor memory because one believes that the memory is not within one's power. One is not ready to confess to poor judgement because the question for reflection can be answered not only by yes or no but also by I don't know; it can be answered assertorically or modally, with certitude or only probability [...] A judgement is the responsibility of the one that judges. It is a personal commitment[107].

The one who judges is responsible for his judgement. And the judgement that expresses truth or falsity involves the responsibility of the one who makes a judgement. Judgement involves a personal commitment. «As related to persons, judgement is a personal act, a personal commitment [...] Judgement is something entirely yours; it is an element in personal commitment in an extremely pure state. Because it is so personal, so much an expression of one's own reasonableness apart from any constraint, because all alternatives are provided for, it is entirely one's own responsibility, one does not complain about one's bad judgements; one is responsible for them»[108].

The judgement is a personal act that involves an undeniable responsibility, an inescapable personal commitment. When a person reflects and grasps the sufficiency or the insufficiency of evidence, he is invited to make a judgement, to take a stand about the truth or the falsity of his reflection. «It is on this third level that there emerge the notions of truth and falsity, of certitude and the probability that is not a frequency but a quality of judgement. It is within the third level that there is involved the personal commitment that makes one responsible for one's judgements. It is from this third level that come utterances to express one's affirming or denying, assenting or dissenting, agreeing or disagreeing»[109].

At the level of reflection, we reflect, marshal the evidence, pass the judgement on the truth or falsity of our insights. And in passing some

---

106 Maxim 89, in F. Duc de la ROCHEFOUCAULD, *Reflections, or Sentences*, 265.
107 *IN*, 297.
108 *UB*, 113.
109 *IN*, 298-299.

judgement on the truth or falsity of our insights, we acknowledge our-selves as responsible subjects of our own judgement. Because, it in-volves to responsibility, judgement is described as «a total increment in cognitional process, that brings to a close one whole step in the develo-pment of knowledge»[110]. Nevertheless, even if judgement is a total in-crement in the cognitional process, it remains that it constitutes only an important contribution to the whole process of knowledge. In fact, since the cognitional process is a unified structure, judgement is a further level that takes into account previous levels of understanding and of presentation of data.

Moreover, judgements are not isolated. A new prior judgement, even if it is correct, is exercised within the context of prior judgements. «Hence, when a new judgement is made, there is within us a habitual context of insights and other judgements, and it stands ready to eluci-date the judgement just made, to complement it, to balance it, draw distinctions, to add qualifications, to provide defence, to offer evidence or proof, to attempt persuasion»[111].

A new judgement is dependent on previous judgements that nuance it, qualify it and complete it. And a new judgement may serve as a basis for further judgements. But is not to be taken for granted. A new judgement can be in conflict with the other judgements. «Existing judgements may be found to conflict, and so they release the dialectical process. Again, they do not conflict, they may not be completely inde-pendent of each other, and so they stimulate the logical effort for organ-ised coherence»[112]. The contextual aspect of judgement appears as the fruit of a progressive accumulation of insights and of judgements.

These insights and judgements may become the object of a self-appropriation. For Lonergan, the human being reaches self-appropriation «insofar as I am aware of myself as experiencing, inquir-ing intelligently, and judging rationally»[113]. And it is only through in-telligent inquiry and rational judgement that the human being performs self-appropriation in order to develop his knowledge. Furthermore, one cannot reach self-appropriation if one does not affirm oneself as a knower.

---

110 *IN*, 301.
111 *IN*, 302. «The business of the human mind in this life seems to be, not the contemplation of what we know, but the relentless devotion to the task of adding increments to a merely habitual knowledge» (*IN*, 303).
112 *IN*, 302.
113 *UB*, 131.

But what does Lonergan mean by the self-affirmation of the knower? Chapter 11 of *Insight*, entitled 'the self affirmation of the knower' is a key chapter. It crowns the first part (insight as activity) and inaugurates the second part (insight as knowledge). Insight as activity (chapters 1 to 10) can be considered as phenomenology of knowing[114]. In fact, the later is an objective description of the cognitive operations used in mathematics, in empirical sciences and in common sense. It is only at chapter 11 that the subject is invited to make a decisive and constitutive act of self-affirmation.

Already, in the introduction to *Insight*, Lonergan underlines the capital importance of the knower: «Our concern is the knower that will be the source of further additions and revisions»[115]. At the end of the second chapter, he reveals his ambition: «Our ambition is to reach neither the known nor the knowable but the knower»[116]. To affirm that what is at stake is neither the known nor the knowable implies that without the knower, there is no way of reaching the known and the knowable. The knower is the centre around which gravitate the known and the knowable. The self-affirmation of the knower is required to give an account of human knowledge. But what does Lonergan mean by the self-affirmation of the knower? «By the "self" is meant a concrete and intelligible unity-identity-whole. By "self-affirmation" is meant that the self affirms and is affirmed. By "self-affirmation of the knower" is meant that the self as affirmed is characterised by such occurrences as sensing, perceiving, imagining, inquiring, formulating, reflecting, grasping the unconditioned, and affirming»[117].

«The self» is a concrete and intelligible unity-identity-whole that, in affirming itself, performs the cognitive operations of hearing, perceiving, imagining, searching, understanding, formulating, reflecting, grasping the unconditioned and affirming it. The self-affirmation of the knower shows that the knower is able not only to perform different cognitive operations but is also capable of a cognitive act of self-affirmation when answering the question «Are you a knower»[118]? In

---

114 *TDH*, 20.
115 *IN*, 12.
116 *IN.*, 91.
117 *IN*, 343.
118 «There are several features of the question, Are you a knower? That should be noted. The question is not asking, Are you necessarily a knower? The question is not, Were you always a knower? Or, Will you always be a knower? Rather, the question asks you to make a concrete judgement of fact, here and now» (J. FLANAGAN, *The Quest for Self-Knowledge*, 11).

fact, makes this act of self-affirmation through a judgement of fact. And in affirming this act, we affirm ourselves. Better, we affirm ourselves in affirming.

We have underlined the existing interdependence among the three levels of the cognitional process of experience, understanding, and judgement. But, these three levels stand if there is a subject who experiments, understands, and judges. The knowing subject is, in Kantian terms, transcendental i. e. the condition of possibility of all cognitive operations, the centre of gravity of the process of knowing.

> There must be, then, a concrete unity-identity-whole that experiences the given, that inquires about the given to generate the free development of systematic unities and relations, that reflects upon such developments and demands the virtually unconditioned as its ground for answering yes or no. It is this concrete unity that asks, Is it so? It is this concrete unity that initiates the free development by asking about the given, What is it? Why is it? How often does it exist or happen? It is this concrete unity that grasps and formulates the conditioned as conditioned and that appeals to the given to grasp the virtually unconditioned and to affirm it rationally and absolutely[119].

The knower is transcendental because he is a concrete unity-identity-whole, that experiences, searches, understands, formulates, reflects, grasps the unconditioned and affirms it. The knower is the one who asks questions for intelligence and for reflection and gives answers. The knower is the one who transcends himself and realises himself in a progressive way and appropriates the three dynamically related levels of cognitional process.

We maintain that an upward human development invites the knower to progress in an attentive, intelligent and reasonable way, from the presentation of data to judgement and from understanding to reflection. So «knowing consists in experiencing, understanding and judging»[120]. If, in *Insight*, there are three explicit levels of knowing, what can we discover about the fourth level, that of decision?

---

119 *IN*, 361-362.
120 *IN*, 302. Progress of science follows the same patterns as the one of human knowledge. «The advance of science is a circuit: from data to inquiry, from inquiry to the formulation of premises and the deduction of their implications, from such formulation to material operations which yield fresh data and in the limit generate the new set of insights named a higher viewpoint» (*IN*, 190).

4. The Level of Decision

In *Insight*, Lonergan mentions only three levels of knowing explicitly: can one rightly speak of decision and responsibility in *Insight*? What does Lonergan mean by decision? In chapter 18 of *Insight*, «The Possibility of Ethics», Lonergan gives his understanding of decision in six characteristics. The first characteristic is that decision is an act of willing «Decision itself is an act of willing[121]. It possesses the internal alternatives of either consenting or refusing. It may also possess external alternatives, when different courses of action are considered simultaneously, and then consent to one and refusal of the others constitute a choice»[122].

The second characteristic makes of decision a further stage of reflection. Decision is an actualisation of reflection. «Reflection leads to further insights that reveal the alternative possibilities of the concrete situation [...] Reflection never settles; it can determine that a given course of action is valuable, pleasurable or useful; but only decision makes the course actual; nor does the decision follow because the reflection ends, but the reflection ends because the decision is made»[123].

Reflection examines the reasons for a possible action to be realized and determines if this action is valid, nice or useful. It prepares the event of the decision. But the decision does not happen because the reflection is ended. The latter ends because the decision is made. «What ends reflection is the decision. As long as I am reflecting, I have not decided yet. Until I have decided, the reflection can be prolonged by further questions. But once I have decided and as long as I remain decided, the reflection is over and done with»[124].

The decision is thus perceived as a term, an end to process of reflection. It aims at doing (acting) or not, taking into consideration the reasons made clear by the reflection: «the decision, then, is not a consequent but a new emergence that both realises the course of action or rejects it»[125].

To highlight the four other characteristics, Lonergan makes a comparison between judgement and decision. The third characteristic fo-

---

121 «Will is the bare capacity to make decisions. Willingness is the state in which persuasion is not needed to bring one to a decision. Willing is the act of deciding» (*IN*, 646).
122 *IN*, 636.
123 *IN*, 714-715.
124 *IN*, 635.
125 *IN*, 642.

cuses the nature of decision: «decision, then, resembles judgement inasmuch as both select one member of a pair of contradictories; as judgement either affirms or denies, so decision consents or refuses [...] and both decision and judgement are rational, for both deal with objects apprehended by insight, and both occur because of a reflective grasp of reasons»[126]. As for judgement, one affirms or denies, so too, for decision, one approves or disapproves. Judgement and reflection reach the insights. Like judgement, decision is also a rational act, and one cannot effectively decide before reflecting and grasping the reasons that motivate a decision.

The fourth characteristic of decision supposes practical insights. For the judgement, one has a direct insight[127] and for the decision, one has a practical insight. The two kinds of insight are similar: «as any direct insight, practical insight results from inquiry and it emerges upon the sensitive flow, in which it grasps some intelligible unity and correlation»[128]. But the similarity does not specify the practical insight. «Practical insights are concerned to lead to the making of being. Their objective is not what is but what is to be done. They reveal not the unities and relations of things as they are, but the unities and relations of possible course of action»[129].

As in the empirical sciences, an insight remains a simple hypothesis inasmuch as it is not confirmed by experimentation, so too, practical insight remains a possible action if it is not motivated by reflection and executed by decision: «the possible courses of action grasped by practical insight are merely possible until they are motivated by reflection and executed by decision»[130]. If the direct insight reveals what *is*, the intelligible relations between the data, the practical insight reveals what *must be*, the course of actions of the actions to be realized. It introduces the power of acting, of action. The practical insight bears fruit in practical reflection,

> Practical reflection is concerned with knowing in order to guide doing. It is an activity that involves an enlarging transformation of consciousness. In that enlarged consciousness the term is not judgement but decision. Consequently, practical reflection does not come to an end once the object and the

---

126 *IN*, 636.
127 «Direct insight meets the spontaneous effort of intelligence to understand [...] It grasps the point, or sees the solution, or comes to know the reason» (*IN*, 44).
128 *IN*, 632.
129 *IN*, 633.
130 *IN*, 643.

motives of a proposed action are known; it comes to an end when one decides in favour of the proposal or against it[131].

Practical reflection enlarges the field of our consciousness in so far as it allows a new realisation in the field of doing. It ends when after deliberation and evaluation, the subject decides what he must do.

The fifth characteristic concerns the actualisation of decision. The actuality of judgement occurs in the affirmation of the virtually unconditioned, of what *is*. But the actuality of the decision happens when some actions are chosen and realised. «Both judgement and decision are concerned with actuality; but judgement acknowledges an actuality that already exists; while decision confers actuality upon a course of action that otherwise is merely possible»[132].

Finally, the sixth characteristic of decision reveals rational self-awareness. We are rationally conscious when we ask questions for reflection, grasp the unconditioned and affirm it in a judgement. But we are also rationally self-conscious when we are attentive as an auto-affirmative unity, when we grasp the different courses of action, reflects upon their value and act in a free and responsible way. So, there is a radical difference between the rationality of judgement and the rationality of decision.

> Judgement is an act of rational consciousness, but decision is an act of rational self-consciousness. The rationality of judgement emerges in the unfolding of the detached and disinterested desire to know in the process towards knowledge of the universe of being. But the rationality of decision emerges in the demand of the rationally conscious subject for consistency between his knowing and his doing[133].

If the rationality of judgement is exercised at the level of knowledge, that of decision requires a consistency between the knowing and the doing. In other words, the subject is rationally self-conscious when they translate in his doing what they have decided. In fact, «the subject is effectively rational only if his demand for consistency between knowing and doing is followed by his deciding and doing in a manner consistent with his knowing»[134].

Rational self-consciousness requires a consistency between knowing and doing. Rational consciousness steps in only to examine and to

---

131 *IN*, 637.
132 *IN*, 638.
133 *IN*, 636.
134 *IN*, 636.

know matter of fact. It is an intelligent and critical knowledge of the reason for one's factual situation. Rational self-awareness however introduces knowledge into the realm of doing: «One's own self-rational consciousness is an accomplished fact in the field of knowing, and it demands in the name of its own consistency its extension into the field of doing»[135]. The demand for consistency between knowing and doing must be operative in the concrete life of individuals. It must be appropriate: «the invitation I issue is to an appropriation of one's own rational self-consciousness»[136].

Nevertheless, an intelligent and critical knowledge of an action does not necessarily involve its execution, its actualisation. From our daily personal experience, we know that there can often be no consistency between our knowing and our doing. It is one thing to know what to do and it is quite another thing to do what you know. In fact, we might know what to do but not do it. To know what one must do is not sufficient for effectively doing it. Besides the knowledge of what to do, we need the will and the motivations to really do it in a free and responsible way. «Because man determines himself, he is responsible; because the course of action determined upon and the process of determining are both contingent, man is free»[137].

Freedom goes together with the responsibility of the one who decides and acts. Let us clarify the two terms briefly. Freedom is a certain form of independence for person to determine themselves. According to Lonergan, «freedom is a kind of contingency. It is contingency that arises from empirical residue that grounds materiality and the non-systematic, but in the order of spirit of intelligent grasp, rational reflection, and morally guided will»[138]. The freedom belongs to the order of spirit. It appeals essentially to intelligence, reflection and will. It defines the state of people who, without constraint, determine themselves. It means that they must know what they want, why they want it and to act in conformity with their will.

In the field of moral action, Lonergan distinguishes two kinds of freedom, namely: essential freedom and effective freedom.

The difference between essential freedom and effective freedom is the difference between a dynamic structure and its operational range. Man is free

---

135 *IN*, 625.
136 *IN*, 14.
137 *IN*, 715.
138 *IN*, 642.

essentially inasmuch as possible courses of action are grasped by practical insight, motivated by reflection, and executed by decision. But man is free effectively to a greater or lesser extent inasmuch as this dynamic structure is open to grasping, motivating, and executing a broad or a narrow range of otherwise possible courses of action. Thus, one may be essentially but not effectively free to give up smoking[139].

Even though the two kinds of freedom are exercised at the level of possible course of actions, the essential freedom as a higher integration sublates the three lower levels: «each element in that integration appears, first, as a possible course of action revealed by insight, secondly, as a value[140] to be weighed by reflection, and thirdly, as an activity only if it is chosen»[141]. The essential freedom becomes an effective freedom when a possible action, perceived as value, is actually chosen, concretised, actualised. So effective freedom supposes essential freedom. With effective freedom, human beings actualise their independence for concrete self-determination.

If after deliberation and evaluation, a person, decides to act and effectively acts, he is free and responsible for his actions. Lonergan has underlined the relation between judgement and responsibility. To judge is to make a personal act, to commit oneself, to be responsible. «Judgement is the responsibility of the one that judges. It is a personal commitment»[142]. If judgement involves a responsibility, decision as a higher step, involves a greater responsibility because not only does one judge but one act.

Here the responsibility lies at the moral level, in so far as this means that it commits a conscious person to act. Moral responsibility requires that the one who acts knows the reasons for his acts. He must also consider himself as the subject responsible for his acts, to accept the blame or the praise for his acts. Why? Because the human person is the main reason for his acts, he is the *id quod operatur*.

At the level of responsibility, it is not only a question of the knower, but it is first of all, a question of the doer, of the moral agent. In fact, «man is not only a knower but also a doer; the same intelligent and rational consciousness grounds the doing as well as the knowing; and

---

139 *IN*, 643.
140 «Value emerges at the level of reflection and judgement, of deliberation and choice» (*IN*, 620); it is the good as the possible object of rational choice» (*IN*, 624). «The good that man does intelligently and rationally is a manifold in the field of experience, ordered by intelligence, and rationally chosen» (*IN*, 626).
141 *IN*, 714.
142 *IN*, 297.

from that identity of consciousness there springs inevitably an exigency for self-consistency in knowing and doing»[143]. This exigency of self-consistency between knowing and doing makes a person a morally self-conscious subject. For such a person, «ethics is concerned with the consistency of knowing and doing within the individual's self-consciousness»[144].

The measure of one's upward development depends on one's control over circumstances and one's capacity to decide and to act accordingly. In fact, «the greater man's development, the greater his dominion over circumstances, and so the greater his capacity to realise possible schemes by deciding to realise their conditions»[145]. Greatness, in the ethic field, resides in the consistency between our knowing and our doing, in the coherence between our thought and our life, in our assumption of our responsible freedom.

To the question whether one can rightly speak of the level of decision and responsibility in *Insight*, we have the following affirmative answer: «in *Insight* there is a discussion of the fourth level of consciousness in terms of decision and ethics»[146]. So, also in *Insight*, there is an upward human development which includes not only experience, understanding and judgement, but also decision and responsibility. Why then does Lonergan explicitly affirm three levels in *Insight* and four levels in *Method in Theology*?

The shift from three to four levels of the cognitional process is explained by an evolution in the thought of Lonergan from 1956 to 1972. Lonergan explains this shift in an interview of 1970.

> I was being sent to Rome and having to deal with students from northern Italy and France and Germany and Belgium who were immersed in continental philosophy. I had to talk meaningfully to them (students), and it involved getting hold of the whole movement of the *Geisteswissenschaften*, from Friedlich Wolff on, to be able to communicate with my students. And it's, of course, something that stretches one[147].

Wanting to teach these students in a meaningful and appropriate way, he could not ignore the movement of *Geisteswissenschaften* tin contrast with the sciences of the nature (*Naturwissenschaften*); Lonergan had come to understand the specific methodology and historicity of

---

143 *IN*, 622.
144 *IN*, 688.
145 *IN*, 252.
146 *2C*, VIII.
147 «An Interview with Fr. Bernard Lonergan», in *2C*, 220.

the human sciences. He was interested mainly in the philosophical movements such as existentialism, phenomenology and hermeneutics. The articles published between 1956 and 1972 show Lonergan's effort to examine and to explain the fourth level.

In 1956, in *De constitutione Christi*, Lonergan writes that «man's finality is to ek-sist»[148]. So that he may have a control on the human being conceived in this way, «such control is realised through the exercise of one's reason and one's personal freedom in order to become genuine, personal, and authentic»[149].

In 1957, Lonergan's *Notes on Existentialism* shows his familiarity with Husserl, Heidegger and an appreciation of Karl Jaspers' and Gabriel Marcel's existentialism. In 1964 appeared *Existenz and Aggiornamento* where Lonergan states that «development is a matter of increasing the number of things that one does for oneself, that one decides for oneself, that one finds out for oneself»[150].

The editors of *A Second Collection* who gathered Lonergan's articles published between 1967 and 1974, underline two themes: «the clear emergence of the primacy of the fourth level of human consciousness, the existential, the level of evaluation and love, secondly, the signification of historical consciousness»[151].

The article *The Subject* of 1968 contains the subtitle *Existential Subject*. In this article, Lonergan clearly affirms the existence of «four distinct but related levels of consciousness within the human subject»[152]. One also finds the themes of sublation[153] and of the existential subject:

> the primacy of the existential does not mean the primacy of result, as in pragmatism, or the primacy of will, as a Scotist might urge, or a primacy of practical intellect, or practical reason, as an Aristotelian or Kantian might phrase it. Results proceed from actions, actions from decisions, decisions from evaluations, evaluations from deliberations, and all five from the existe-

---

148 B. LONERGAN, *De Constitutione Christi*, 14. «Finis autem est ut ex-sistat homo».

149 B. LONERGAN, *De Constitutione Christi*, 17. «Quod dominum cum ipse homo per propriam rationem et propriam libertatem efficere debeat ut vere et proprie et authentice et genuine homo».

150 «Existenz and Aggiornmento», in *IC*, 223.

151 *2C*, VII-VIII.

152 B. LONERGAN, «The Subject», in *2C*, 80.

153 «The levels of consciousness are not only distinct but also related, and the relations are best as instances of what Hegel named sublation, of a lower being retained, preserved, yet transcended and completed by a higher» («The Subject», 80).

ntial subject, the subject as deliberating, evaluating, deciding, acting, bringing about results. The subject is not just an intellect or just a will[154].

Decision as a fourth level sublates the inferior levels that are judgement, understanding and experience. In *Faith and Belief* of 1969, the fourth level is the topmost level of consciousness: «on the topmost level of human consciousness the subject deliberates, evaluates, decides, controls, acts. He is at once practical and existential: practical inasmuch as he is concerned with concrete consciousness of action; existential inasmuch as control includes self-control, and the possibility of self-control involves responsibility for what he makes of himself»[155].

All these articles published between 1956 and 1969 find their crown in *Method in Theology* and in post-*Method* articles where the fourth level becomes a clearly distinct level, a higher level that sublates the three other levels. So, people who wants to promote and sustain their upward human development must integrate the fourth level by which they deliberate, choose, decide and act.

But in *Insight*, «man is in process of development. Inasmuch as he is intelligent and reasonable, free and responsible, he has to grasp and affirm, accept and execute his own developing»[156]. Because the human beings are in a process of development, they are to be intelligent, rational, free and responsible, they must understand and assure their own development, and take into consideration the specific laws of human development. In chapter 15 of *Insight*, Lonergan explains three laws of human development, namely : the law of integration, the law of limitation and of transcendence and the law of authenticity.

First, all human development is affected by the *law of integration*. «The law of integration is a declaration of what is meant by human development»[157]. This law requires that the emergence of a higher integration should unify lower integrations. In fact, «the higher the integration, the greater the freedom from material limitation»[158]. Without integration, there would not be development because «development is a flexible, linked sequence of dynamic and increasingly differentiated higher integrations that meet the tension of successively transformed underlying manifolds»[159].

---

154 «The Subject», 84.
155 B. LONERGAN, «Faith and Belief», 6.
156 *IN*, 659.
157 *IN*, 497.
158 *IN*, 492.
159 *IN*, 479.

Nevertheless, Lonergan points out that while the genesis of development is one thing, its complete integration is another. Generally, this genesis «invites complementary adjustments and advances, and unless they are effected, either the initiated development recedes and atrophies in favour of the dynamic unity of the subject, or else that unity is sacrificed and deformed to make man a mere dumping ground for unrelated, unintegrated schemes of recurrence and modes of behaviour»[160].

Secondly, every human development is under the *law of limitation and transcendence*. «It is the law of tension. On the one hand, development is in the subject and of the subject; on the other hand, it is from the subject as he is now and toward the subject as he is to be»[161]. Because the human being in developing, starts from what one actually is towards what one is not yet, there exists an existential tension between limitation and transcendence. «Transcendence, then, means a development in man's knowledge relevant to a development in man's being»[162].

The tension between limitation and transcendence must take into account contingence, the limitation of the human being. The search for human development, must live through the tension between the desires of spontaneity and the norms of intelligence, between the world of satisfactions and that of values. This tension between limitation and transcendence is immanent in human nature. It is intrinsic and ineluctable: «it is this heightened tension that in human development supplies the content of the compound antithetical law of limitation and transcendence»[163]. One can suppress one's spontaneity and vital needs, yet no one can renounce one's intelligence and responsibility. Consequently, «to inquire and to understand, to reflect and to judge, to deliberate and to choose are as much an exigency of human nature as waking and sleeping, eating and drinking, talking and loving»[164].

Thirdly, in relation to the law of tension, there is the *law of genuineness*. It requires simplicity and honesty, perspicacity and sincerity in human life where illusion and waywardness no loner have more a place. «The law of genuineness can be put as follows. Every development involves a starting-point in the subject as he is, a term in the subject as he

---

160 *IN*, 497.
161 *IN*, 497.
162 *IN*, 659. «All development is development inasmuch as it goes beyond the initial subject, but in man this 'going beyond' is anticipated immanently by the detachment and disinterestedness» (*IN*, 499).
163 *IN*, 499.
164 *IN*, 498.

is to be, and a process from the starting-point to the term. However, inasmuch as development is conscious, there is some apprehension of the starting point, the term, and the process»[165].

But the apprehensions of one's starting-point, process and term may be more correct or less. If they are correct, there is harmonious collaboration between the conscious and the unconscious[166] elements. If they are wrong, there is a conflict. «Such a conflict is inimical to the development, and so we have the conditional law of genuineness, namely, that if a development is conscious, then its success demands correct apprehension of its starting point, its process, and its goal»[167]. The conditional law of development requires a correct apprehension of its starting-point, its process and its term. The law of genuineness invites the human being, in the process the development, to confront effectively the conflicts between conscious or unconscious elements. So,

> Genuineness is the necessary condition of the harmonious cooperation of the conscious and unconscious components of development. It does not brush questions aside, smother doubts, push problems down, escape to activity, to chatter, to passive entertainment, to sleep, to narcotics. It confronts issues, inspects them, studies their many aspects, works out their various implications, contemplates their concrete consequences in one's own life and in the lives of others[168].

The law of genuineness requires the admission of the law of tension into consciousness. It is the necessary condition of the harmonious integration between the conscious elements which orient towards transcendence and the unconscious elements which constitute a limitation. As human development is a movement of independence towards autonomy, the law of genuineness must be taken seriously. «To fail in genuineness is not to escape but only to displace the tension between limitation and transcendence»[169]. So, to be genuine is to sustain one's own development by taking on, in an attentive, intelligent, reasonable and responsible way, the existential tension between limitation and transcendence. To be genuine is to cooperate with one's finality defined

---

165 *IN*, 500.
166 «Unconsciously operative is the finality that consists in the upwardly but indeterminately directed dynamism of all proportionate being. Consciously operative is the detached and disinterested desire raising ever further questions» (*IN*, 501).
167 *IN*, 500.
168 *IN*, 502.
169 *IN*, 503.

as «an upwardly but indeterminately directed dynamism towards ever fuller realisation of being»[170].

5. Conclusion

As a philosophical masterpiece, *Insight* evolves essentially as a moving viewpoint from below upwards. This moving viewpoint is explicit in the articulation of the two parts into which the chapters of *Insight* are arranged The upward human development corresponds to the cognitional process with its three levels, namely: the level of the presentation of data, the level of intelligence and the level of reflection. The first level presents the data of sense or of consciousness. It has been qualified as the level of sensation, of the experiential, and of experience.

The data of sense or of consciousness of the first level are not to be contemplated but to be understood by intelligence. The second level of intelligence intervenes to commit one into inquiry, understanding and formulation of what has been understood. By asking questions of intelligence (what is it? why? how often?), the human being seeks to grasp the unities and intelligible relations immanent in the data. Insights are answers to the questions for intelligence. They are acts of understanding resulting from the exercise of intelligence in relation to the data. But as acts of intelligent understanding, insights are neither true nor false. To determine about their truth or their falsity, one needs to appeal to the third level, that of reflection.

Reflection examines and verifies whether the insights and their formulations are true or false. At the end of the process of verification, judgements affirm or deny their truth or falsehood. In asking questions of reflection (Is it? It is so?) and in answering «is» or «is not», judgment posits a virtually unconditioned. And in affirming a virtually unconditioned in a judgement, can also I affirm myself as a self-knower, as an inescapable transcendental source of all my cognitive operations.

In *Insight*, three levels of the cognitional process are explicit: the level of presentation, of intelligence and of reflection. For the individual, the upward human development evolves from the attentive experience of data to the understanding of these data, and from the understanding of these data to their truth or falsity, expressed through a judgement. We have also examined some aspects of the fourth level, that of decision and responsibility. The fourth level is not yet clearly

---

170 *IN*, 477.

distinct in *Insight*. In 1972, with the publication of *Method in Theology*, it will become the object of later writings.

Though the fourth level is implicit in *Insight*, the upward human development includes decision and responsibility. Whereas judgement appeals to a direct insight, decision supposes a practical insight which requires a consistency between our knowing and our acting. It is by facing this requirement, through effective freedom and responsibility, that we assure our upward human development. As the upward human development is a dynamic event, we have to take into account three specific laws of human development, namely: the law of integration, the law of limitation and of transcendence, and the law of genuineness. To be genuine, the upward human development must integrate the tension between limitation and transcendence.

As a philosophical work, *Insight* is «an invitation to know oneself in the tension of the duality of one's own knowing»[171]. Lonergan's main concern is to promote upward human development conceived as a process that the reader will reach through self-appropriation. «More than all else, the aim of the book is to issue a personal, decisive act»[172]. This personal and decisive act is that of a self-appropriation of the dynamic structure of cognitional operations. «We are concerned not with the abstract properties of cognitional process but with a personal appropriation of one's own dynamic and recurrently operative structure of cognitional activities»[173].

Lonergan's main interest is to invite his reader to the self-appropriation of the dynamic structure of his cognitional operations.

> The dynamic structure to be reached is not the transcendental ego of the Fichtean speculation, nor the abstract pattern of relations verifiable in Tom and Dick and Harry, but *the personally appropriated structure of one's own experiencing, one's own intelligent inquiry and insights, one's own critical reflection and judging and deciding*[174].

Self-appropriation deals not with abstract notions but the dynamic structure of our cognitional operations. It means that we need to discover, to identify, to actualise, and to be familiar with his cognitive operations that make us a human beings capable of attentive experiencing, of intelligent understanding, of critical reflection and of responsible decision. So, «our goal is the concrete, individual, existing subject that

---

171 *IN*, 13.
172 *IN*, 13.
173 *IN*, 17.
174 *IN*, 13.

intelligently generates, and critically evaluates»[175] Nevertheless, the appropriation of the cognitional operations is not as easy as one would like it to be. It is a conquest, a long process, a laborious development: «the labour for self appropriation cannot occur at a single leap. Essentially, it is a development of the subject and in the subject, and like all development it can be solid and fruitful only by being painstaking and slow»[176].

In *Insight*, Lonergan's major interest is not knowledge but its nature, not the cognitional operations but their appropriation by the subject. What fundamentally interests him is the subject who personally appropriates his/she own cognitive operations. And by a personal appropriation of one's cognitive operations, he/she promotes and sustains his/her upward human development, developing from below upwards.

---

175 *IN*, 91.
176 *IN*, 17.

CHAPTER IV

Anticipation Development from Above in *Insight*

1. Introduction

The development from above downwards is a matter of gift, of human or divine love, of belief, of tradition. Can one find an anticipation of development from above downward in *Insight*? We answer affirmatively and in the present chapter we will show that, in *Insight*, there exists an anticipation of the development from above downwards. In order to make explicit this anticipation, we will examine the five following points: first, transcendence and the affirmation of God; second, the problem of evil; third, the notion of belief; fourth, God as supernatural solution; finally, God's love. We will mainly explore chapters 19, 20 and the epilogue of *Insight*.

2. Transcendence and the Affirmation of God

Chapter 19 of *Insight* deals with general transcendent knowledge. Knowledge is transcendent insofar as it reaches the domain of the proportionate being. Lonergan defines it as «the knowledge of God that answers the basic questions raised by proportionate being, namely, what being is and whether being is the real»[1] Before examining God's knowledge of God, we first clarify the term «transcendence».

In a general sense, «transcendence means going beyond»[2], as in the fact of going beyond one's self. This conception of transcendence applies

---

[1] *IN*, 709.
[2] *IN*, 605.

to how the book *Insight* has been written[3]. It is also at issue in the moving beyond of common sense, science toward ethics and metaphysics, and beyond ethics and metaphysics, toward the realm of transcendent being.

> One can go beyond both common sense and present science, to grasp the dynamic structure of our rational knowing and doing, and then formulate a metaphysic and an ethics. Finally, one can ask whether human knowledge is confined to the universe of proportionate being or goes beyond it to the realm of transcendent being; and this transcendent realm may be conceived relatively or absolutely, either as beyond man or as the ultimate in the whole process of going beyond[4].

In a restrictive sense, transcendence means a process that underlies all operations of knowledge. So inquiry, insight and its formulation transcend sensitive experience. Reflection and judgment transcend insight and its formulation to enter into the realm of being. In other words, transcendence expresses the movement by which the human being, imbued by the unrestricted desire to know, to think and to judge, is in perpetual development.

> Transcendence, then, means a development in man's knowledge relevant to a development in man's being. For man is a process of development. Inasmuch as he is intelligent and reasonable, free and responsible, he has to grasp and affirm, accept and execute his own developing. But to grasp his developing is for man to understand it, to extrapolate from his past through the present to the alternative ranges of the future. It is to extrapolate not only horizontally but also vertically[5]

Transcendence is therefore defined as development in the order of knowledge, which is linked to a development in the order of being. But, «being is proportionate or transcendent according as it lies within or outside the domain of man's outer and inner experience. The possibility of transcendent knowledge, then, is the possibility of grasping intelligently

---

[3] «The present work has been written from a moving viewpoint. It began from insight as an interesting event in human consciousness. It went on to insight as a central event in the genesis of mathematical knowledge [...] It went beyond the reproducible insights of scientists to the more complex functioning of intelligence in common sense, in its relations to the psychoneural basis, and its historical expansion in the development of technologies, economies, and polities. It went beyond all such direct and indirect insights to the reflective grasp that grounds judgment. It went beyond all insights as activities to its permanent dynamic structure, to construct an explicit metaphysics and add the general form of an ethics» (*IN*, 658-659).

[4] *IN*, 658.

[5] *IN*, 659.

and affirming reasonably a transcendent being. And the proof of the possibility lies in the fact that such intelligent and reasonable grasp occurs»[6].

The intelligent grasp and the reasonable affirmation of a transcendent being present themselves as the crowning achievement of the process of knowledge. If God is transcendent being, he must be known by intelligent grasp and reasonable affirmation. The source of the affirmation of God as transcendent being is not itself transcendent but immanent. Man is an immanent source of transcendence. Furthermore, «the immanent source of transcendence in man is the detached, disinterested, unrestricted desire to know. As it is the origin of the radical further questions that take him beyond the defined limits of particular issues»[7].

The transcendent general knowledge, whose immanent source resides in the inquiring spirit of man, concerns the knowledge of God that, «according to St Thomas Aquinas, consists in knowing that he is but not what he is»[8]. This transcendent knowledge limits itself to the intelligent and reasonable affirmation of God's existence and not to the specification of his attributes.

> We can conceive God as the transcendent idea and affirm him as the transcendent reality of being not only is continuous with all that has gone before but also is its culmination [...] God is the unrestricted act of understanding, the eternal rapture glimpsed in every Archimedean cry of «Eureka». Understanding meets questions for intelligence and questions for reflection. The unrestricted act meets all at once; for it understands understanding and all the intelligibility based on it; and it understands its own understanding as unrestricted, invulnerable, true[9].

Is God as conceived by Lonergan merely the idea of being transcendent, an unlimited act of understanding? Is he a mere object of thought or is he real? Does God exist? Lonergan's answer goes as follows: «For the real is being, and apart from being there is nothing. Being is not know without reasonable affirmation, and the existence is the respect in which being is known precisely inasmuch as it is affirmed reasonably. Hence it is one and the same thing to say God is real, that he is an object of reasonable affirmation, and that he exists»[10].

God is not merely the transcendent idea of being, nor is he only an unlimited act of understanding. God is really a transcendent being that can

---

[6] *IN*, 663.
[7] *IN*, 659.
[8] *IN*, 657.
[9] *IN*, 706.
[10] *IN*, 692.

be the object of a reasonable affirmation. Lonergan's affirmation of God, though different from that of Saint Anselm, Descartes and Kant, is however similar to Saint Thomas Aquinas who affirms God as the *Ipsum Esse Subsistens*.

The affirmation of God as subsistent being *in se et per se* is not only the *telos*, but also the *archè* of the human *eros*, in quest of intelligent understanding and critical reflection. Since God is the *telos* and the *archè* of the human *eros* and of the universe, he must be «the ground of being; identity of knower and known, the act of understanding that grasps everything about everything»[11]. He is «unrestricted understanding's self-knowledge, primary being, self-explanatory, necessary, unconditioned, without any lack or defect»[12].

God is therefore the first being, absolute, necessary and auto-explanatory, the origin of all things and the formally unconditioned. He is perfect, absolute and without lack of or defect. More precisely, «God is without defect, not because the act of understanding is completed by further acts, but by a single act that at once is understanding and intelligible, truth and affirming, goodness and loving, being and omnipotence»[13].

We therefore notice in Lonergan a movement that goes from God's conception as the unlimited act of understanding to the affirmation of God's reality as the *Ipsum Esse Subsistens*, the *telos* and the *archè* of human *eros* and the universe. However, if God is thus affirmed, how can one justify the existence of evil in the world? How can one reconcile God's goodness with the existence of evil? If one does affirm God as perfect goodness, «how can he reconcile that affirmation with the evil that tortures too many human bodies, darkens too many minds, hardens too many human hearts»[14]?

3. **The Problem of Evil**

Human development takes shape within a contingent world, the locus of his insertion and his becoming. And it is within this development that the problem of evil is raised. The specific investigation of God's goodness facing the real problem of evil, constitutes what Lonergan calls special transcendent knowledge. «Since God is the first agent of every event and emergence and development, the question really is what God is or

---

[11] *IN*, 395
[12] *IN*, 706.
[13] *IN*, 707.
[14] *IN*, 23

has been doing about the fact of evil. The answer to that question we shall name special transcendent knowledge»[15].

Evil is a real fact. Lonergan distinguishes three kinds of evil, namely: physical evil, basic sin and moral evil. By physical evil is meant «all the shortcomings of a world order that consists, insofar as we understand it, in a generalised emergent probability»[16]. In such an order of the world, «the unordered manifold is prior to the formal good of higher unities and higher orders; advance is at the price of risk; security is mated with sterility; and the life of man is guided by an intelligence that has to develop and a willingness that has to be acquired»[17].

Basic sin is a failure of will to choose a set of morally good actions or the will's failure to reject a set of bad actions. «Basic sin is the root of the irrational in man's rational self-consciousness. As intelligently and rationally conscious, man grasps and affirms what he ought to do and what he ought not to do; but knowing is one thing and doing is another»[18]. By moral evil, Lonergan means «the consequences of basic sin»[19] that prevent an individual to achieve willingly what he ought to do.

These three kinds of evil create to a serious problem. As a problem for understanding, all that intelligence can understand about fundamental sin is that there is nothing to understand. Because, basic sin is a case of the irrational. «All that intelligence can grasp with respect to basic sin is that there is no intelligibility to be grasped. What is basic sin? It is irrational. Why does it occur? If there were a reason, it would not be sin. There may be excuses; there may be extenuating circumstances; but there cannot be a reason»[20].

Moral evil is a real fact: «it is not an incidental waywardness that provides the exception to prove a rule of goodness. Rather it is a rule. If it is not a necessary but only a statistical rule, it is no less a fact, and indeed it is a worse fact»[21]. Moral evil is contingent but not necessary. If it were necessary, there would be no responsible exercise of liberty.

The existence of the three kinds of evil constitutes a problem, but it indicates, at the same time, that there is an intelligibility to grasp, a pos-

---

[15] *IN*, 709.

[16] *IN*, 689. «Emergent probability does not denote any sort of efficient cause; it refers to the immanent intelligibility of the design or order in which things exists and even occurs» (*IN*, 720).

[17] *IN*, 689.

[18] *IN*, 698.

[19] *IN*, 698.

[20] *IN*, 690.

[21] *IN*, 715-716.

sible solution to be considered. Thus, «evil is, not a mere fact, but a problem, only if one attempts to reconcile it with the goodness of God; and if God is good then there is not only a problem of evil but also a solution»[22].

If God is good, one may find a solution to the problem of evil. The problem of evil and its solution are to be grasped «within the intelligible unity of the actual order of the universe. And this implies the existence of a heuristic structure»[23]. The existence of a heuristic structure implies some aspects of solution to the problem of evil.

And as the problem of evil is human, the solution should be human. But the moral impotence of human being and the limits of effective freedom do not allow man to solve the problem of evil completely. The complete solution to the problem of the evil will not therefore be human but supernatural. This supernatural solution will be a new and higher integration of the human activity. While examining heuristically, the aspects of the supernatural solution, Lonergan sums them up in these terms:

> Any solution would be one; it would be universally accessible and permanent; it would be some harmonious continuation of the actual order of the universe; it would consist in some reversal of the priority of living over the knowledge needed to guide life and over the good will needed to follow knowledge; this reversal would be effected through conjugate forms that in some sense would transcend human nature, that would constitute a new and higher integration of human activity, that would pertain not to static system but to system on the move, that would be realised with man's apprehension and consent and in accord with the probabilities of world order. Finally, it was seen that these conjugate forms would be some type of charity, of hope, and of belief[24]

To effect to the supernatural solution of the problem of evil, the three conjugate forms, namely: charity, hope and belief are both transcendent and operatively present to promote and to secure human development. But before identifying God as supernatural solution to the problem of evil, it seems suitable to us to clarify the notion of belief that belongs to the development from above.

---

22 *IN*, 716.

23 *IN*, 718. «For there is a heuristic structure whenever the object of an inquiry admits antecedent determinations; and the solution that we are seeking admits antecedent determination; and the solution that we are seeking is an object of inquiry that satisfies the intelligible unity of the actual world order and that solves the problem defined above» (*Ibid.*).

24 *IN*, 740.

4. **The Notion of Belief**

Belief generally means an assent that, like an opinion, includes all the degrees of probability. Thus, to believe is to give credit to a witness, to trust one who knows without verification. According to Lonergan, belief is a kind of knowledge by which one appropriates the attentive experience, acts of understanding and judgements of fact and value of other people. This kind of knowledge differs from that to which an individual acquires by himself by immanently generated knowledge. However,

> the general context of belief is the collaboration of mankind in the advancement and the dissemination of truth. For if there is such a collaboration, then men not only contribute to a common fund of knowledge but receive from it. But while they contribute in virtue of their own experience, understanding, and judgment, they receive not an immanently generated but a reliably communicated knowledge. That receipt is belief[25].

The reception from a «common fund» of knowledge is a matter of belief, of development from above. Belief is received and transmitted through a tradition, in the context of a human collaboration for the advancement and the dissemination of truth. It is not the personal acquisition of knowledge, but the assent, based on trust, that someone grants to another's knowledge. Progressively, belief and immanently generated knowledge accumulate and constitute a common fund, a cultural heritage.

To clarify his conception of belief, Lonergan makes a double comparison first between the act of judging and the act of believing, then between knowledge and belief. The first comparison between the act of judging and the act of believing reveals a resemblance and a difference:

The act of believing resembles the act of judgment in object and in mode, but it differs from it in motive and in origin. It resembles the act of judgment in its object, for it affirms or denies a proposition to be true. It resembles judgment in its mode, for it is a rational utterance of a yes or no that may be pronounced with certitude or with probability. But while judgment is motivated by one's own grasp of the unconditioned, the assent or dissent of belief is motivated by a decision in the pursuit of truth. And while judgment results with rational necessity from reflective grasp of the unconditioned, the assent or dissent of belief results with natural necessity from a free and responsible decision to believe[26].

---

25 *IN*, 725.
26 *IN*, 731.

If the act of believing thus looks like the judgment by its object and its mode, it differs in its motive and its origin. The second comparison concerns knowledge and belief. Knowledge is an affirmation of what one understands correctly through personal experience. Belief, on the other hand, it is not an affirmation, but an acceptance of what other people in whom one reasonably trusts say. This is how «knowing is affirming what one correctly understands in one's own experience. Belief is accepting what we are told by others on whom we reasonably rely. Now every conclusion of science is known by several scientists, but the vast and cumulative collaboration of the scientific tradition would be impossible if every conclusion of science had to be known by every scientist. Belief, then, is an essential moment in scientific collaboration»[27].

Belief is effectively an essential moment in the research and progress of sciences. The scientist is called upon to believe what other scientists have established and verified, otherwise he/she would have to spend a lifetime verifying the validity of their laws and their theories. Scientists not only believe in the research and findings of their predecessors and contemporaries, but also, they must rely on the scientific tradition's elements of cumulative proof. It is as believers and heirs of the scientific tradition that they will proceed to new discoveries with success. Indeed, the great discoveries have always been preceded by a long succession of previous contributions. Hence, the individual development of scientists rests largely on their belief in the scientific tradition.

More deeply, there exists a rich and endless symbiosis between personal knowledge and belief.

The development of the human mind is by the self-correcting process of learning[28], and in that process personal knowledge and belief practice an unrelenting symbiosis. The broadening of individual experience includes hearing the opinions and convictions of others. The deepening of individual understanding includes the exploration of many viewpoints. The formation of individual judgment is a process of differentiation, clarification, and revision, in which the shock of contradictory judgment is as relevant as one's own observation and memory, one's own intelligent inquiry and critical reflection[29].

---

[27] *IN*, 452-453.
[28] «The self-correcting process of learning consists in a sequence of questions, insights, further questions, and further insights that move towards a limit in which no further pertinent questions arise. When we are well beyond that limit, judgements are obviously certain» (*IN*, 325).
[29] *IN*, 728.

From this quotation, we would like to underline two points. First, the development of the human mind rests on the self-correcting process of the training that norm exists between teachers and pupils. Teacher who know elaborate a pedagogy in order to provoke or to communicate insights in pupils who do not know. The entire process of teaching consists in the development and the implementation of pedagogies for learning. Indeed,

> Teaching is a vast acceleration of the process of learning. It throws out the clues, the pointed hints, that lead to insights; it cajoles attention to remove distracting images that obstruct them; it puts the further questions that reveal the need of further insights to complement and modify and transform the acquired store; it grasps the seriation of acts of understanding to begin from the simple and work towards the more complex. But what is done explicitly and deliberately by professional teachers also is done implicitly and unconsciously by parents with their children and by equals among themselves[30].

Secondly, the self-correcting process of learning, based on collaboration and communication, is the setting where this mutual enrichment between belief and acquired knowledge is verified: «the self-correcting process of learning goes on in the minds of individuals, but the individuals are in communication. The results reached by one are checked by many, and new results are added to old, to form a common fund from which each draws his variable share measured by his interests and his energy»[31].

The self-correcting process of learning ends up by forming a common fund that is basically possible object of belief. Indeed, persons can effectively appropriate elements of this common fund if they believe, in an attentive, intelligent and reasonable manner, truths that others have grasped. Besides, belief serves as a background, a foundation for the enrichment and the dissemination of immanently generated knowledge personally acquired, by the exercise of attentive experience, intellectual understanding and critical reflection. So, belief plays a basic role in the acquisition of knowledge and the formation of minds. It remains, however, open to the test repeated constantly of new experiences, new questions, new insights and new judgements.

This symbiosis between knowledge and belief arises from the fact, the existential contingency that the human beings are not capable of knowing everything by themselves. Their attentiveness, understanding and critical

---

[30] *IN*, 315.
[31] *IN*, 315.

reflection are marked by contingency and limitation. Each person would have a tiny and insignificant amount of immanently generated knowledge, if each time he were to limit himself exclusively to what he knew by his own experience, his personal insights and grasps of the unconditioned. «If it were necessary to submit our mentalities to a total explicit analysis; it would be also necessary for us to have twofold lives: a life to live, and another, longer life in which to analyse the life we live»[32].

Human progress shows that there exists an interdependence between knowledge and belief, in human collaboration in the research and propagation of knowledge.

There exists a human collaboration in the pursuit and the dissemination of truth. It implies that in the mentality of any individual there exists in principle a distinction between his judgements which rest on immanently generated knowledge, and his other assents, which owe their existence to his participation in the collaboration. Without some immanently generated knowledge, there would be no contribution to the collaboration. Without some belief, there would be no one that profited by the collaboration[33].

Therefore, without immanently generated knowledge, there would not be any contribution to the human collaboration; in the same way, without certain beliefs, no one would benefit from this collaboration. This mutual enrichment between immanently generated knowledge and belief leads to the following conclusion: «no belief is independent of some items of immanently generated knowledge, so there are extraordinarily few elements of immanently generated knowledge that are totally independent of beliefs»[34]. Beliefs are not independent of some items of immanently generated knowledge, and these are not entirely independent of beliefs.

Since judgements are similar to beliefs by their object and their mode, like judgements, beliefs can be true or false; and the reality of evil and the presence of biases may corrupt immanently generated knowledge as well as belief. Indeed, «the life of man on earth lies under the shadow of a

---

[32] *IN*, 738.

[33] *IN*, 736. «On that collaboration there rest the invention and the development of languages, the erection of schools and universities, the use of scientific methods and the publication of scientific journals, our domestic, economic, and political institutions, and the whole network of communications of the civilised world» (*IN*, 729).

[34] *IN*, 728. «The profound transformation of modern living by modern science is a truth that we accept without immanently generated knowledge of the whole of it by our personal experience, personal inquiry, and personal grasp of the unconditioned» (*IN*, 735).

problem of evil; the evil invades his mind; and as it distorts his immanently generated knowledge, so also it distorts his beliefs»[35]

Then what is to be done in order to eliminate false beliefs, inherent in
the human spirit? The elimination of erroneous belief requires us to determine their origins and their consequences, to train ourselves to recognise them as mistakes, to question their motives and their judgements.
These different strategies can help to eliminate erroneous beliefs. But,
they do not reach the root of the problem.

For the basic problem lies not in mistaken beliefs but in the mistaken believer.
Far more than they, he is at fault. Until his fault is corrected, until his bias is
attacked and extirpated, he will have little heart in applying efficacious method,
little zeal in prosecuting the lesser culprits, little rigor in pronouncing sentence
upon them, little patience with the prospect of ferreting out and examining and
condemning still further offenders. A critique of mistaken beliefs is a human
contrivance, and a human contrivance cannot exorcise the problem of human
evil[36]

If it is true that the key to the solution lies not in mistaken beliefs but
in the subject who believes in these beliefs. A critique of mistaken belief is mostly a human contrivance, and a human contrivance will not
completely exorcise the problem of evil. It is necessary, after this consideration of the notion of belief, to pursue our investigation into God
as the absolutely supernatural solution, capable of radically exorcising
the problem of evil.

5. God as Supernatural Solution

In science belief results from human collaboration in the pursuit and
dissemination of knowledge. Facing the problem of evil, human being
is invited to believe that the solution will consist in a new and higher
collaboration «because the solution is a harmonious continuation of the
actual order, it too will be a collaboration that involves belief, truthful-
ness, accuracy, and immanently generated knowledge. Again, because
the solution is a higher integration, it will be a new and higher collaboration»[37]

As a new and higher integration, the collaboration will provide an an-
tidote to mistakes that the human being is inclined to make. Besides, «the
new and higher integration will be, not simply a collaboration of men

---

[35] *IN*, 736.
[36] *IN*, 738-739.
[37] *IN*, 740-741.

with one another, but basically man's cooperation with God in solving man's problem of evil»[38]. If human beings, by themselves, could achieve this collaboration in solving the problem of evil, there would not be any need of supernatural solution. But, *in concreto*, the problem of evil exists, and we affirm the existence of a supernatural solution. Therefore, «the new and higher collaboration is, not the work of man alone, but principally the work of God»[39].

The new and higher collaboration is mainly God's work that invites the human being to participate in this collaboration. So that his involvement can bring about some fruit, he needs belief. And «because it is a belief within a collaboration of man with God as initiator and main agent, the motive of faith will be the omniscience, goodness and omnipotence of God originating and preserving the collaboration»[40]. Belief makes it possible for the human being to participate in this higher collaboration of which God is the initiator and the main agent. «Because God omniscient is, he knows man's plight. Because he is omnipotent, he can remedy it. Because he is good, he wills to do so. The fact of evil is not the whole story. It also is a problem. Because God exists, there is a further intelligibility to be grasped»[41].

If the human being, in his existential contingency, can neither create the supernatural solution nor preserve it, he must still demonstrate intelligence and rationality, in order to recognise it, to accept it, and collaborate in its realisation and transmission. Because of this collaboration and participation in the realisation and the transmission of the supernatural solution, «there will result a heightening of the tension that arises whenever the limitations of lower levels are transcended»[42]. However, the supernatural solution, as a higher integration, does not eliminate the problem of evil, but assumes it and transcends it.

> The solution will be effective in the sense that it meets the problem of evil not by suppressing the consequences of man's waywardness but by introducing new and higher integration that enables him, if he wills, to rise above the consequences, to halt and reverse the sequence of ever less comprehensive syntheses in which theory keeps surrendering to practice, to provide a new and more solid base on which man's intellectual and social development can

---

[38] *IN*, 741.
[39] *IN*, 741.
[40] *IN*, 742.
[41] *IN*, 716.
[42] *IN*, 747.

rise to heights undreamed of, and perpetually to overcome the objective surd of social situations by meeting abundant evil with a more generous good[43].

The supernatural solution allows the human being to lay a new and efficient foundation for his intellectual and social development. It suppresses neither his waywardness nor his limitations. But as a higher integration it sublates and transforms his development from below while opening up new perspectives for him. When this problem of evil is met by has supernatural solution, human perfection itself becomes a limit to be transcended.

«For if the humanist is to stand by the exigencies of his own unrestricted desire, if he is to yield to the demands for openness set by every further question, then he will discover the limitations that imply man's incapacity for sustained development, he will acknowledge and consent to the one solution that exists, and if that solution is supernatural, his very humanism will lead beyond itself[44].

When the human being ratifies the existence of the supernatural solution, his potentialities expand, his humanism evolves toward self-transcendence. More basically, it is God himself who is the supernatural solution: «God, whose wisdom designed the order of the universe and whose goodness brings a solution to man's problem of evil»[45]. But God as supernatural solution «is a new higher integration of human activity that, in any case, involves some transcendence of human ways and, possibly, complicates the dialectic by adding to the inner conflict between attachment and detachment in man the necessity of man's going quite beyond his humanity to save himself from disfiguring and distorting it»[46].

To avoid disfiguration and distortion of self-transcendence, God, as a new and higher integration, is going to assure effectively a foundation for intellectual and social development. It makes human beings discover the truths and values that they would never have discovered and understood by themselves. «For the supernatural solution not only meets a human need but also goes beyond it to transform it into the point of insertion into human life of truths beyond human understanding, of values beyond human estimation, of an alliance and a love that, so to speak, brings God closer to man»[47]. This alliance that God makes with human being, is

---

43 *IN*, 745.
44 *IN*, 749.
45 *IN*, 723.
46 *IN*, 750.
47 *IN*, 747.

achieved by putting into practice the theological virtues which are faith, hope and charity.

Lonergan considers the three theological virtues as component in the absolutely supernatural solution because, negatively, there is no creature that can consider them natural solutions. Positively, they are absolutely supernatural

> because their sole ground and measure is the divine nature itself. Then faith includes objects beyond the natural reach of finite understanding. Then hope is for a vision of God that exhausts the unrestricted desire of intelligence. Then charity is the transport, the ecstasy and unbounded intimacy that result from the communication of the absolute love that God is himself and alone can respond to the vision of God[48] .

Faith, hope and charity form «an absolutely supernatural living that advances towards an absolutely supernatural goal under the action the action of divine grace»[49] . However, the three theological virtues, absolutely supernatural, would suffer from human imperfection if they were not carried away by the divine transcendence. They help human beings to confess that God exists, that he offers them a solution that they can recognise and accept in the universe: «the solution has to be received by man not merely as intelligent and rational, free and responsible, but also as operating within a harmonious continuation of the present order of the universe»[50] .

Not only human beings as intelligent and rational, welcome the supernatural solution, but they are equally also invited to collaborate, in a free and responsible way, in the advent of a harmonious order of the universe. In this context, the lack of collaboration for the supernatural solution becomes a deviation from God. «True knowledge not only is true but also is an apprehension of the divinely ordained order of the universe, and that doing consistent with knowing not merely is consistent with knowing but also man's cooperation with God in the realisation of the order of the universe. Inversely, error becomes a deviation from God, and wrongdoing takes on the character of sin against God»[51] .

Facing the different forms of biases, God alone, whose willing, knowing and doing coincide perfectly, can offer salvation to human beings, incapable of freeing themselves by themselves. Facing sin, God

---

[48] *IN*, 747.
[49] *IN*, 762.
[50] *IN*, 724.
[51] *IN*, 689.

alone, whose love and goodness are immeasurable, can forgive and restore the human beings the hope of a new search for development and
realisation of themselves.

6. God's Love

While trying to determine, in a more precise way, a suitable solution
to the problem of evil, Lonergan speaks about God's love:

> complete understanding is the unrestricted act that is God; and so the good
> that is willed by good will is God. Moreover, to will the good of a person is
> to love the person; but God is a person, for he is intelligent and free; and so
> good will is the love of God. Further, good will matches the detachment and
> disinterestedness of the pure desire to know, and so good will is a love of
> God that is prompted not only by hope of one's own advantage but simply by
> God's goodness[52].

As good will ideally embraces the detachment and the disinterestedness of the desire to know, it constitutes a hope, produced not by personal
development, but by divine goodness. The actual order of the universe
participates in this divine goodness. However, «the order of this universe
is actual, the order of all others universes are possible, because of the
completeness of the intelligibility, the power of the reality, and the perfection of the goodness and the love of God. It follows that, apart from
the surd of sin, the universe is in love with God; and good will is the opposite of the irrationality of sin; accordingly, the man of good will is in
love with God»[53].

Persons imbued by good will are therefore in love with God who wills
the current order of the universe. Willed by God, because of the perfection of his intelligibility, of his goodness and his love, this actual order of
the universe is a good. People in love with God are going to will the good
that is the current order of the universe. «So to will the order of the universe because of one's love of God is to love all persons in the universe
because of one's love of God»[54]. To will the good of the universe because of one's love for God means loving all persons of the universe because of one's love for God. For the persons who love God, the actual order of the universe then becomes God's epiphany: «the whole world of

---

[52] *IN*, 720.
[53] *IN*, 721.
[54] *IN*, 721.

sense is to be, then, a token, a mystery, of God, for the desire of the intelligence is for God, and the goodness of will is the love of God»[55].

The world is the token of God's goodness and the goodness of the human will consists in loving God, in loving him above all and in all, in loving him with a love that embraces the actual order of the universe and that is extended to all human beings. A person is capable of loving God and his neighbour, not only because he is in love with God, but also, because he is carried by the love of his parents.

> For he was born of his parents' love[56]; he grew and developed in the gravitational field of their affection; he asserted his own independence only to fall in love and provide himself with his own hostages to fortune. As the members of the hive or herd belong together and function together, so too men are social animals, and the primordial basis of their community is not the discovery of an idea but a spontaneous intersubjectivity[57].

Love within the family is affirmed by the conception of the human being who is the fruit of his parents' love and who develops in an atmosphere of affection. While benefiting from love and familial affection, the human being, as a social being, realises that intersubjective relations constitute the primordial foundation of community. Sustained by the parents' love, the human being enters into a love relationships with others. His familial love is going to spread to the dimensions of a community, a state and a nation.

> The bond of mother and child, man and wife, father and son, reaches into a past of ancestors to give meaning and cohesion to the clan or tribe or nation. A sense of belonging together provides the dynamic premise for common enterprise, for mutual aid and succour, for the sympathy that augments joys and divides sorrows. Even after civilisation is attained, intersubjective community survives in the family with its circles of relatives and its accretion of friends[58].

---

[55] *IN*, 711. «Ultimately our human spirit leads us to personal commitment, self-donation, self-surrender in love. Our spirit is ever moving us from what we now understand to further understanding, from the limited amount we know for sure to more comprehensive wisdom; and from the limited acts of loving toward the unrestricted loving which is God» P. BYRNE, «The Spirit of Wonder », 9.

[56] «A man or woman knows that he or she is in love by making the discovery that all spontaneous and deliberate tendencies and actions regard the beloved» (*IN*, 720-721).

[57] *IN*, 237.

[58] *IN*, 237.

The love of neighbour, lived out within the family, the community and the nation, is called to grow and develop. But the love of neighbour would be imperfect, if it were not essentially sustained by transcendent love of God. «Imperfect charity lacks the resources needed to combine both true loving and true transformation of loving. It can be absorbed in the union of the family, in the intersubjectivity of comrades in work and in adventure, in the common sense of fellows in nationality and citizenship, in the common aspiration of associates in scientific, cultural, and humanitarian pursuits»[59].

More than parents' love, it is God's love that brings about a real transformation in love, a fruitful commitment in the universal love that overflows the limits of a family, group and nation. To stay within this universal love is a requirement, an ideal that is not always put in practice in daily life. When people do not put into practice this love of God and one's neighbour, they must amend and repent in so far as «self-sacrificing love of God of one's neighbour is repentant»[60]. The repentance requires an amendment of one's past, a recognition of one's biases, of one's lack of love towards God and one's neighbour.

The repentance we deal with here is not equal to a simple feeling of guilt. It implies an intelligent grasp of one's failures and a firm and deliberate will to correspond in our daily life to God's love: the origin of all goodness and all love towards other human beings.

> For as the intellect rises to knowledge of God, the will is called to love God, and then evil is revealed to be not merely a human wrong but also sin, revolt against God, an abuse of his goodness and love, a pragmatic calumny that hides from oneself and from others the absolute goodness and perfect love that through the universe and through men expresses itself to men. So repentance becomes sorrow. A relation between stages in one's living is transformed into a personal relation to the one above all and in all[61].

A personal relationship with God, marked by sanctions, repentance and sorrow, turns into a new relationship with God, recognised as the Being to be loved above all. «For it is the love of God above all and in all, and love is joy. Its repentance and sorrow regard the past. Its present sacrifices look to the future. It is at one with the universe in being in love with God, and it shares its dynamic resilience and expectancy. As emergent probability, it ever rises above past achievement. As genetic process,

---

[59] *IN*, 748.
[60] *IN*, 722.
[61] *IN*, 722.

it develops generic potentiality to its specific perfection. As dialectic, it overcomes evil by meeting it with good and by using it to reinforce the good»[62].

Repentance, as an act of good will, fights against evil by doing good. But there is in chapters 7, 18 and 20 of *Insight*, the problem of the dialectic between good (progress) and evil (decline) that deserves to be clarified.

In chapter 7, Lonergan states that, by their intelligence persons progress and by their biases, they decline. Thus progress and decline form two components of human history: «while there is progress and while its principle is liberty, there also is decline and its principle is bias»[63]. As dialectic deals with a combination of the concrete, the dynamic and the contradictory, defined as «a concrete unfolding of linked but opposed principles of change»[64], there will be a dialectic between the two linked but opposite components that are progress and decline.

The different forms of bias give rise to different kinds of decline. Thus, when «the general bias» is dominant, we have «the longer cycle» of decline while «the group bias» yields to a «shorter cycle» of decline. «The shorter cycle turns upon ideas that are neglected by dominating groups only to be championed later by depressed groups. The longer cycle is characterised by the neglect of ideas to which all groups are rendered indifferent by the general bias of common sense»[65].

Is there, any evidence in the historical process, that decline is going to invite eventually, in a dialectic manner, its counterposition? How are the members of a community going to face the challenges that the longer cycle of decline presents to them perceived as «a succession of lower viewpoints that heads towards an ultimate nihilism»[66]? According to Lonergan, the remedy has to be the attainment of a higher viewpoint: «there is needed a critique of history before there can be any intelligent direction of history. There is needed an exploration of the movements, the changes, the epochs of a civilisation's genesis, development, and vicissitudes. The

---

[62] *IN*, 722.

[63] *IN*, 620.

[64] *IN*, 242. «Dialectic is adjustable to any course of events, from an ideal line of pure progress resulting from the harmonious working of the opposed principles, to any degree of conflict, aberration, breakdown, and disintegration» (*Ibid*). R. DORAN, in *TDH*, speaks of «dialectic of contraries and of contradictories». See specially chapter 3 on the notion of dialectics, 64f.

[65] *IN*, 252.

[66] *IN*, 259.

opinions and attitudes of the present have to be traced to their origins, and the origins have to be criticised in the light of dialectic»[67].

To face and to surmount decline dialectically, one needs what Lonergan calls cosmopolis. «Cosmopolis is concerned with the basic issues of the historical process»[68], «the business of cosmopolis is to make operative ideas that, in the light of general bias of common sense, are inoperative»[69]. Cosmopolis is a synthetic vision, a higher viewpoint, «a dimension of consciousness, a heightened grasp of historical origins, a discovery of historical responsibility [...] It is the higher synthesis»[70].

In chapter 18, there is a moral perspective on dialectics between progress and decline. Lonergan asks the following question: «is there a need for a moral liberation if human development is to escape the cycle of alternating progress and declines»[71]? His answer is affirmative, and he clarifies the question of effective liberty and moral liberation.

Effective liberty, distinct from essential liberty, is radically affected by moral impotence. Because of moral impotence, effective freedom is finite and limited: «to assert moral impotence is to assert that man's effective freedom is restricted [...] in the profound mode that follows from incomplete intellectual and volitional development»[72]. This moral impotence impedes the exercise of effective liberty and the attainment of moral perfection. It is not however a fatality. It invites human beings to become aware of it, for it sharpens the existential tension between limitation and transcendence.

This consciousness of moral impotence not only heightens the tension between limitation and transcendence but also can provide ambivalent materials for reflection; correctly interpreted, it brings home to man the fact that his living is a developing, that he is not to be discouraged by his failures, that rather he is to profit by them as lessons on his personal weaknesses and as a stimulus to greater efforts; but the same data can also be regarded as evidence that there is no use trying, that moral codes ask the impossible, that one has to be content with oneself as one is[73].

This tension between limitation and transcendence, due to moral impotence and lived at the individual level, is amplified in the social sphere.

---

67 *IN*, 265.
68 *IN*, 265.
69 *IN*, 264.
70 *IN*, 266.
71 *IN*, 618.
72 *IN*, 650.
73 *IN*, 650.

Thus, «to the ethics of the individual conscience there is added an ethical transformation of the home, of the technological expansion, of the economy, and of the polity»[74] Because of this tension the progress of human knowledge does not always correspond to moral progress based on virtue and wisdom. «So we are brought to the profound disillusionment of modern man and to the focal point of his horror. He had hope through knowledge to ensure a development that was always progress and never decline»[75].

By his intelligence, the human being hopes to attain progress, but the different forms of bias, along with moral impotence, hinder the advent of progress and produce decline. The more dominant the biases are, the less the imperatives of intelligence are followed and the more the social situation deteriorates. The deterioration of the social situation poses a problem and reinforces a person's inability to promote and to sustain his own development: «essentially the problem lies in the incapacity for sustained development. The tension divides and disorientates cognitional activity by the conflict of positions and counterpositions. This conflict issues in contrary views of the good, which in turn makes good will appear misdirected, and misdirected will appear good»[76].

Because of dialectics, counterpositions can be reversed if one transcends the tension between intelligence and bias. But intelligence and bias «pertain to the very nature of man, and as long as they exist the problem remains in full force»[77]. The tension between intelligence and bias, inherent in sinful human nature and reinforced by moral impotence, does not allow the human being to solve the problem of moral development. And yet, it is necessary, at the very heart of existence, to find a solution to this problem. As in chapter 7, the solution must be a higher viewpoint, a higher integration:

> The solution has to be a still higher integration of human living. For the problem is radical and permanent [...] It is not met by revolutionary change, nor by human discovery, nor by the enforced implementation of history; it is as large as human living and human history. Further, the solution has to take people just as the are [...] It has to acknowledge and respect and work through man's intelligence and reasonableness and freedom. It may eliminate neither development nor tension yet it must be able to replace incapacity by

---

[74] *IN*, 651.
[75] *IN*, 572.
[76] *IN*, 653.
[77] *IN*, 654.

capacity for sustained development. Only a still higher integration can meet such requirements[78].

In chapter 7, cosmopolis was the higher viewpoint. Now, in chapter 20 «besides higher viewpoints in the mind, there are higher integrations in the realm of being»[79]. This higher integration in the realm of being is made explicit in chapter 20 of *Insight*.

We maintain the thesis of the existence of a supernatural solution to the problem of the evil. Facing the problem of evil, God's love is presented as the supernatural solution. And the suitable dialectical attitude is to render back good for evil. «For it is only inasmuch as men are willing to meet evil with good, to love their enemies, to pray for those who persecute them, that the social surd[80] is a potential good. It follows that love of God above all and in all so embraces the order of the universe as to love all men with a self-sacrificing love»[81].

The free love of God and neighbour is, in turn, dialectical, because it opposes to evil by doing good, and while doing good, it triumphs over evil. As in chapters 7 and 18, dialectics is exercised between good (progress) and evil (decline). The particular difference is that, in chapter 20, the solution to the problem of evil is specifically of a theological order:

> There is a theological dimension that must be added to our analysis of the compounding of man's progress with man's decline. Bad will is not merely the inconsistency of rational self-consciousness, it also is sin against God. The hopeless tangle of the social surd, of the impotence of common sense, of the endlessly multiplied philosophies, is not merely a *cul-de-sac* for human progress; it also is a reign of sin, a despotism of darkness; and men are its slaves[82].

Not only this supernatural solution is theological, but also «the systematic treatment of this solution is itself theological»[83]. This supernatural solution, specifically theological in its nature and its investigation, is extrinsic inasmuch as it is neither the product of human and natural sciences, nor the finite product of an ascending human development. It

---

[78] *IN*, 655.

[79] *IN*, 656.

[80] «Inasmuch as the courses of action that men choose reflect either their ignorance or their bad will or their ineffectual self-control, there results the social surd» (*IN*, 711).

[81] *IN*, 721-722.

[82] *IN*, 714.

[83] *IN*, 767.

comes from above: it is a grace that perfects nature (*gratia perficit naturam*).

Grace perfects nature both in the sense that it adds a perfection beyond nature and in the sense that it confers on nature the effective freedom to attain its own perfection. But grace is not a substitute for nature, and theology is not a substitute for empirical human science. It is a fuller viewpoint that both reinforces the scientist's detached, disinterested, unrestricted, desire to know and reveals the concrete possibility of intelligent and reasonable solutions to human problems. Still, this possibility revealed by theology is not intrinsic but extrinsic[84].

Even though it is extrinsic, grace as the supernatural solution perfects human nature, because the solution «from above» is a restoration of humanity «from below». However, for God's grace to perfect nature effectively, for God's grace to operate in human nature[85] the individual is not only invited to welcome it intelligent, reasonably and morally, but also and especially, religiously. Indeed, it is within a «divinely sponsored collaboration» that the individuals are called to active involvement in the redemptive work of God. It is only by accepting God's love that permeates the universe that human beings reach an unselfish love for God and for humankind.

For every individual person who accepts God as the supernatural solution, «there is to be added the consideration of the cumulative historical development, first of the chosen people and then the catholic church, both in themselves and in their role of the unfolding of all human history and in the order of the universe»[86]. Acceptance of this divine love is at once a gift and a task that challenge human beings to a continual conversion.

Conversion challenges persons to discern dialectically a future marked by a greater conformity and a greater collaboration in God's epiphany. The epiphany of God, Jesus Christ, will not radiate all his shining glory «without effecting a transfiguration of human living, and in turn that transfiguration contains the solution not only to man's individual but also to his social problem of evil»[87].

God, as revealed through Jesus Christ, the Light of the world, is the one who assumes and transfigures the human problem at the individual and social level. In «Insight Revisited», it is again Jesus Christ who is the

---

[84] *IN*, 767.

[85] In his doctoral dissertation, Lonergan studied the relationship between grace and nature. See B. LONERGAN, *Gratia operans*, 1940.

[86] *IN*, 763.

[87] *IN*, 764.

sublime coronation of the theological analysis of history according to Lonergan.

> In my rather theological analysis of human history, my first approximation was the assumption that men always do what is intelligent and reasonable, and its implication was an ever increasing progress. The second approximation was the radical inverse insight that men can be biased, and so unintelligent and unreasonable in their choices and decisions. The third approximation was the redemptive process resulting from God's gift of his grace to individuals and from the manifestation of his love in Jesus Christ. The whole idea was presented in chapter twenty of *Insight*[88].

What Lonergan asserts in 1973, he had already anticipated in *Insight* by affirming that «a theory of development that can envisage not only natural and intelligent progress but also sinful decline, and not only progress and decline but also supernatural recovery»[89]. In short, the dialectical triad progress-decline-liberation[90] of chapters 7 and 18 correspond, in theological terms, to the dialectic triad nature-sin-grace of chapter 20: «to consider man in his performance, and that performance is a manifestation not only of human nature but also of human sin, not only of human sin, not only of nature and sin but also of a *de facto* need of divine grace, not only of a need of grace but also of its reception and of its acceptance or rejection»[91].

However, persons can identify God's grace without deciding to welcome it. It is only when God's grace, revealed by Jesus Christ, is accepted and lived out, that persons involved in truly human development are going to produce abundant fruits of their faith, hope and charity. Then, «we can readily see the workings of transcendent love bringing forth value judgements (faith), decisions to act for others (charity), and a transformed, confident desire (hope)»[92]. The reception and the practice of this transcendent love of God shows that the development from above is mainly God's work.

> For the realisation of the solution and its development in each of us is principally the work of God who illuminates our intellects [...] who breaks the bonds of our habitual unwillingness to be utterly genuine in inquiry and criti-

---

[88] *2C*, 272.

[89] *IN*, 764.

[90] This trilogy has been studied by B. Lonergan between 1933 and 1938. See M. SCHUTE's book , *The Origins of Lonergan's Notion of Dialectic*, 1990.

[91] *IN*, 765.

[92] T. DUNNE, «Faith, Charity, Hope», in LoWo, 5, 65.

cal reflection by inspiring the hope that reinforces the detached, disinterested, unrestricted desire to know and by infusing the charity, the love, that bestows on intelligence the fullness of life[93] .

It is God's love that, finally, opposing evil and decline, confers on the intelligence and human will their fullness of life, enabling people to pursue their quest for integral human development. This development, in the Christian perspective, «will consist in a consuming love of God»[94] .

7. Conclusion

We have just shown that there exists an anticipation of development from above in *Insight*. The human beings, endowed by the desire to know and to transcend themselves, are also the ones asking questions about the existence of a transcendent being. At the end of their questioning, intelligently and reasonably conducted, they affirms God as the coronation of the process of knowledge, the transcendent reality of being, the formally unconditioned, the *Ipsum Esse Subsistens*, the *arché* and the *telos* of the human spirit, the supreme wisdom and goodness. If God is supreme wisdom and supreme goodness, how does one explain the problem of evil? We have then considered, in a heuristic way, the solution to the problem of evil and we have identified God as the supernatural solution.

But before specifying that God is the supernatural solution to the problem of evil, we have examined the concept of belief. Belief is a form of knowledge, based on the trust and the credit that one grants to other persons. As such, belief constitutes an inheritance and differs from the knowledge that individuals acquire by themselves. The act of believing resembles judgement in its object and its mode, but it differs from it in its origin and its motive. This resemblance and this difference show that in the domains of knowledge, there exists a mutual enrichment between belief and immanently generated knowledge.

Better still, this mutual enrichment concerns not only the fields of human knowledge, but it even penetrates the sphere of the divine. Indeed, by his/her immanently generated knowledge, human beings finally affirms God as the supernatural solution to the problem of evil. By belief, we welcome, recognise and accept God as the supernatural solution. But God, as supernatural solution, does not eliminate the problem of evil, but assumes and sublates it. The sublation by God of the problem of evil en-

---

[93] *IN*, 751.
[94] *IN*, 714.

gages persons in a continual self-transcendence and assures a foundation for their intellectual and social development.

However, intellectual and social development should not be taken for granted. There are biases, decline, and evil. Then, how can one promote and sustain true human development? How, in the midst of existence, can one make progress and avoid decline on an individual and social level? Dialectics is then invoked to solve the conflict between progress and decline, between good and evil. As a quest of a solution, the cosmopolis of chapter 7 and the moral liberation of chapter 18 lead ultimately to God's love[95] of chapter 20 as the supernatural solution, in terms of the dialectic between good and evil.

Indeed, God's love effects a real transformation of human love, it opens new horizons that overcome the narrow and limited dimension of the affection and love lived within a family, a group and a nation. God's love remains the supernatural solution in the dialectical confrontation between progress and decline, between good and evil. Only God's love, as «the major factor in the integration and development of the person»[96] can basically reconcile us with ourselves, with others and so restore human development from corruption and distortion.

---

[95] *IN*, 711, 714, 720-721, 747-751.
[96] *PGT*, 59.

GENERAL CONCLUSION

While drawing towards a conclusion to this dissertation, I do not claim to close completely this investigation, essentially and potentially a moving viewpoint. In fact, the end of a philosophical investigation does not constitute the exhaustion of a subject, but rather a suspension on the side of its author. My suspension is a retrospective and critical evaluation. Throughout this dissertation, I have supported the thesis that the two ways of the human development, operative in *Method in Theology*, explicit in the eleven post-*Method* articles, find their anticipation in *Insight*, Lonergan's philosophical masterpiece. In fact, in the first part, I have spelled out the Lonerganian understanding of the development from below (chapter 1) and from above (chapter 2) in *Method in Theology* and in the eleven post-*Method* articles. In the second part, I have examined, in *Insight*, the anticipation of the development from below (chapter 3) and from above (chapter 4).

In the first chapter, in *Method in Theology* as well as in post-*Method* articles, Lonergan conceives development from below as a dynamic process which includes four levels of consciousness and intentionality, namely, empirical, intellectual, rational and responsible. However, in the post-*Method* articles, development from below is specifically articulated around finality, self-transcendence, self-appropriation and human authenticity which sublate cognitive operations of experience, understanding, judgement and decision.

In the second chapter, I have considered development from above downwards in *Method in Theology* and in the post-*Method* articles. In *Method in Theology*, development from above gravitates essentially around love and its triple manifestations, i.e., love of intimacy between husband and wife, love for one's country and love of God. We have then considered God's love as gift, as religious conversion and as dynamic state. In fact, God's gift of his love, once received and lived out, religiously converts and establishes one in a dynamic state of love with God.

In the eleven post-*Method* articles published between 1974 and 1980, development from above presents itself, in specific way, as the triple manifestation of love, as praxis, as cultural heritage, as received, transmitted and appropriated tradition, through the processes of socialisation, acculturation and education.

By way of conclusion, we have first emphasised that the two ways of the human development constitute one and the same reality that Lonergan calls «the truly human development». And this «truly human development» consists in a complementarity and integration of the two ways of development. Secondly, I have shown how Lonergan explains the integration of the two ways of the human development in *Method in Theology* and in post-*Method* articles. Thirdly, I have pointed out that as the way down is chronologically first and more fundamental than the way up inasmuch as the former sublates the latter.

The third chapter deals with the anticipation of development from below upwards in *Insight*. Development from below upwards is defined as a formally dynamic process, composed of four cognitional operations, i.e., experience, understanding, judgement, and decision. The three first operations find their principal anticipation in chapters 9 and 10 of *Insight*. The last operation, that of decision, has its anticipation in chapter 18 of *Insight*. As development from below is an ongoing process, individuals must take into account three specific laws of human development: the law of integration, the law of limitation and transcendence, the law of authenticity.

In *Insight* and in *Method in Theology*, dialectic deals with «the concrete, the dynamic and the contradictory»[1]. It represents a critical instance for resolving the conflict between progress and decline, good and evil. But, in *Insight*, cosmopolis as «the higher synthesis», and moral liberation as «the higher integration» lead ultimately to God's love as «absolutely supernatural solution» to the problem of evil.

In *Method in Theology* and in the post-*Method* articles, between the thesis of progress and the antithesis of decline, the redemptive love of Christ is presented as the dialectical synthesis which allows individuals to seek for their personal value and to live in authenticity. This redemptive love of Christ saves individuals from decline and sin, reverses biases and restores their quest for human development. The redemptive

---

[1] *MIT*, 129; see also *IN*, 242f.

love of Christ, in challenging to put into practice the theological virtues of faith, hope and charity, empowers intelligence and will towards the intelligible, the true, the good and the love for God and for one's fellow creatures.

In the light of dialectic, I argue that the two ways of the human development do not constitute two dialectically contradictory processes, mutually exclusive, whereby one must prefer one process to the detriment of the other. On the very contrary, «these two movements are complementary»[2]. And it is in their complementarity that they contribute to the advent of authentic human development. For «if the movement from below upwards, in conscious development, is not met by a movement from above downwards, development will almost inevitably fall victim to some blend or other of the biases»[3].

The movement from below must go together with the movement from above. There exists thus an integration and a complementarity of the two ways of authentic human development. But this integration is not a given but rather a task, a challenge. According to Frederick Crowe,

> The upward way of development enjoys a luxurious growth, like that of vegetation in the rain forests of tropical lands, takes on as many exotic forms. The downward way of development has not had time to adapt to the new situation, or to bring the moderating influence of a valid tradition into union with the critical spirit of times, so that together they might create a new and viable set of values[4].

In today's world, overwhelmed by science and technology, the upward way of development enjoys enormous progress. But, does this upward development move ahead parallel to a downward development, characterised by the promotion of human and religious values? This does not seem to be the case. Indeed, human beings are discovering that our scientific and technological progress is not always proportionate to our moral development. «He has discovered that the advance of human knowledge is ambivalent, that it places in man's hands stupendous power without necessarily adding proportionate wisdom and virtue»[5].

The upward way of development, illustrated by scientific and technological progress, must be completed by the downward way develop-

---

[2] *IN.*, 338.
[3] *TDH*, 195.
[4] *ALI*, 358.
[5] *IN*, 572.

ment, by the creation and the transmission of corresponding values. The two movements of human development must be unfolded in complementarity and interdependence. For it is only through the upward movement that there is an assimilation and an appropriation of downward movement. And it is only through downward movement that there is a valorisation and sublation of upward movement.

In the Epilogue, Lonergan writes that «however indispensable this work (*Insight*), it is vain unless it is complemented by further labour»[6]. As *Insight* is written from a moving viewpoint, not aiming at communicating ready-made results, it conveys an invitation for further developments. During 1974, interview, Lonergan reveals that after *Insight*, the moving viewpoint still continues: «I've learnt a lot since. It's still a moving viewpoint after *Insight*. I kept on moving»[7].

We hope that, after this philosophical investigation of the two ways of human development, we will devote ourselves to the application or expansion of the two ways of human development in the fields of spirituality, education and political science. We are convinced that the particular context of Africa, in the political, economical, social, and cultural domains, constitutes a privileged philosophical field for the application of the two ways of human development.

«Your interest may quite legitimately be to find out what Lonergan thinks and what Lonergan says, but I am not offering you that, or what anyone else thinks or says, as a basis. If a person is to be a philosopher, his thinking as a whole cannot depend upon someone or something else. There has to be a basis within himself; he must have resources of his own to which he can appeal in the last resort»[8].

---

[6] *IN*, 769.
[7] *2C*, 220.
[8] *UB*, 35.

ABBREVIATIONS

1. Books and articles related to Bernard Lonergan

1C	*Collection*, ed. F.E. Crowe – R.M. Doran, Toronto 1985, CWL 4.
2C	*A Second Collection*, ed. F.J. Ryan – J. Tyrell, London 1974.
3C	*A Third Collection*, ed. F.E. Crowe, London 1985.
CWL	Collected Works of Bernard Lonergan.
DIC	*Dialogues in Celebration*, ed. C. Going, Montreal 1980.
IN	*Insight. A Study of Human Understanding*, ed. F. E. Crowe – R. Doran, Toronto 1992, CWL 5.
MIT	*Method in Theology*, Toronto 1972.
PGT	*Philosophy of God, and Theology*, London 1973.
UB	*Understanding and Being. The Halifax Lectures on Insight*, ed. M. Morelli – E. Morelli, Toronto 1990, CWL 3.

2. Other abbreviations

AfChS	*African Christian Studies*
ALI	F.E. CROWE, *Appropriating the Lonergan Idea*, Washington 1989
ArPh	*Archives de Philosophie*
BP	*Blandyke Papers*
CaM	*Canadian Messenger*
CH.	Chapter/Chapters
Cont.	*Continuum*
Conc (GB)	*Councilium*
Cr.	*Cresset*
CrossCur	*Cross Current*
DESJ	*Delta Epsilon Sigma Journal*
ed.	editor/editors
etc.	et cetera
f.	following
fn.	footnote number

Fs.	Festschrift (studies in honour of)
Gr.	*Gregorianum*
Hor.	*Horizons*
Ibid.	*Ibidem*
IPQ	*International Philosophical Quarterly*
ITQ	*International Theological Quarterly*
Jn	Gospel according to John
LSN	*Lonergan Studies Newsletter*
LRI	Lonergan Research Institute, Toronto.
LoWo	Lonergan Workshop
Mc	Gospel according to Marc
MS	*Miltown Studies*
MJLS	*Method. Journal of Lonergan Studies*
n.	number
NEC	*New Catholic Encyclopedia*
NSchol	*New Scholasticism*
OTN	F.E. CROWE, *Old Things and New*, LoWo 5, Atlanta 1985.
p.	page
PACPA	*Proceedings of the American Catholic Philosophical Association*
PCTSA	*Proceedings of the Catholic Theological Society of America*
PhilS	*Philippines Studies*
pp.	pages
PUG	Pontifical Università Gregoriana
RMet	*Review of Metaphysics*
RP	*Review of Politics*
Rom	St Paul's Letter to the Romans
ScC	*Scuola Cattolica*
Scho	*Schoolman*
ScE	*Science et Esprit*
SPSJ	*Studies in the Spirituality of Jesuits*
SR	*Studies in Religion*
ST	*Summa Teologiae*, Saint Thomas AQUINAS, Bologna 1996
TDH	R.M. DORAN, *Theology and Dialectics of History*, Toronto 1990
Thom.	*The Thomist*
trans.	Translator
TS	*Theological Studies*
Vol.	Volume

BIBLIOGRAPHY

The present bibliography is a selective one. A more complete bibliography, in two volumes, is available in Terry J. TEKIPPE, *Primary Bibliography of Lonergan Sources* (Vol. I), New Orleans 1996. For the sake of clarity, I give the list of Lonergan's Sources in chronological order.

1. **Lonergan Sources**

1928 «The Form of Mathematical Inference», *BP* 283 (1928) 126-137.

«The Syllogism», *BP* 285 (1928) 33-64.

1929 «True Judgement and Science», *BP* 291 (1929) 195-216.

1935 *Pantôn Anakephalaiôsis: A Theory of Human Solidarity, A Metaphysic for the Interpretation of St. Paul, a Theology for the Social Order, Catholic Action, and the Kingship of Christ. Incipient Outline.* LRI, File 713, April 28, 1935.

1940 *Gratia operans: A Study of the Speculative Development in the Writings of Saint Thomas of Aquinas,* Rome 1940. Doctoral Dissertation under the direction of C. Boyer.

1942 «St Thomas' Thought on Gratia Operans», *TS* 3 (1942) 69-88; 375-402; 533-578.

1943 «Finality, Love and Marriage», *TS* 4 (1943) 477-510.

«The form of Inference», *Thought* 18 (1943) 277-292.

1945 *Thought and Reality,* series of weekly lectures at the Thomas More Institute, Montreal, from mid-November 1945 to May 1946. Notes taken by J. M. O'Hara, typescript by T. V. Daly. LRI Library, File 31. Unpublished.

1946 «The Concept of *Verbum* in the Writings of St. Thomas Aquinas», *TS* 7 (1946) 349-392.

De Ente Supernaturali: supplementum schematicum. The Early Writings of Bernard J.F. Lonergan, ed. F. E. Crowe, Toronto 1973.

1947   «The Concept of *Verbum* in the Writings of St. Thomas Aquinas», *TS* 8 (1947) 35-79, 404-444.

1949   «The Concept of *Verbum* in the Writings of St. Thomas Aquinas», *TS* 10 (1949) 3-40, 359-393.

«The Natural Desire to see God». Paper at the Convention of the Jesuit Philosophical Association, Boston, April 18, 1949. Unpublished. LRI, File 56.

1950   Book review of E. Gilson, *Being and Some Philosophers*, *TS* 11 (1950) 122-125.

1951   *Intelligence and Reality*, Notes for lectures at the Thomas More Institute, Montreal 1951. Unpublished.

«Le rôle de l'université dans le monde moderne», *Relations* 11 (1951) 263-265.

«Philosophy and Science», lecture to philosophy students at Loyola College, Montreal April 6, 1951. Unpublished. LRI, File 70.

1952   *Analysis Fidei*, Collegium Christi Regi Torontini 1952. Unpublished.

1954   «Theology and Understanding», *Gr.* 35 (1954) 630-648.

1955   Book review of P. Vanier, *Théologie trinitaire chez Saint Thomas d'Aquin*, *Gr.* 36 (1955) 703-705.

1956   *De Constitutione Christi ontologica et psycologica supplementum confecit Bernadus Lonergan*, Rome 1956.

Review of St. Thomas Aquinatis, *In Aristotelis libros peri hermeneias et posteriorum analyticorum expositio*, *Gr.* 37 (1956) 691.

1957   *Insight: A Study of Human Understanding*, London 1957.

Divinarum personarum conceptionem analogicum evolvit Bernadus Lonergan, Romae 1957.

«Existentialism». Notes for Lectures at Boston College. July 15-19, 1957. Reprinted in Montreal by Thomas More Institute, 1-25. LRI, File 113.

«Mathematical Logic». Lectures at Boston College, July 8-12, 1957. Transcript from the tapes made by N. Graham. Unpublished. LRI, File 101-102

1958   «Insight». Lectures, Summer Seminar at the Institute at Saint Mary's University, Halifax, August 4-15, 1958. LRI File 131.

«Philosophical Differences and Personal Development», *NSchol* 32 (1958) 97.

«*Insight*: Preface to a Discussion», *PACPA* 32 (1958) 71-81.

1959   «Christ as Subject: A Reply», *Gr.* 40 (1959) 242-270.

«The Philosophy of Education». Lectures at Xavier University, Cincinnati, August 3-14, 1959.

«Method in Catholic Theology». Lecture to the Society for the Study of Theology, Nottingham, England, April 15, 1945.

De intellectu et metodo. Course offered to doctorate students. Rome 1959. Notes taken by F. Rossi de Gasperis – P. J. Cahill. LRI Archives Batch V.2.a. Unpublished.

Book review of M. Nedoncelle, *Existe-t-il une philosophie chrétienne?*, *Gr.* 40 (1959) 182-183.

«System and History», LRI Archives Batch V.8, 1959. Unpublished.

1960   *De Verbo Incarnato dicta scriptis auxit B. Lonergan,* Rome, 1960.

Book review of W. Martin, *The Order and Integration of Knowledge*, *Gr.* 41 (1960) 171-173.

«Philosophy of History». Notes for the lecture given at the Thomas More Institute, Montreal 1960. LRI Archives Batch IX.7.a. Unpublished.

1961   *De Deo Trino. Pars analytica*, Rome 1961.

«Knowing and Loving». Lecture in the course, Knowing and Loving, Thomas More Institute, Montreal, September 26, 1961 .

1962   *De metodo thelogiae*. Autograph typescript of notes for the course given at the Gregorian University, Spring Semester 1962. LRI Archives Batch V.1.c. Unpublished.

«Time and Meaning». Lecture to the academic community of Regis College, Willowdale (Toronto), September 25, 1962.

1963   «Metaphysics as Horizon», *Gr.* 44 (1963) 307-318.

De Deo Trino I. Pars dogmatica, Rome 1963.

De Deo Trino II. Pars systematica seu divinarum personarum conceptio analogica, Rome 1963. Third revised edition of *Divinarum personarum conceptionem analogicam evolvit Bernadus Lonergan*, October 1963.

1964   *De Verbo Incarnato*, Romae 1964.

«Existenz and Aggiornamento». Lecture at Regis College, Toronto, September 14, 1964 .

1965   «Subject and Soul», *PhilS* 13 (1965) 576-585.

«Dimensions of Meaning». An Address in the distinguished Lecture Series at the Marquette University, May 12, 1965.

1966   *La notion du verbe dans les écrits de Saint Thomas d'Aquin*, Paris 1966.

«The Transition from a Classicist World-view to Historical Minded-ness». Lecture for the opening of the academic year at the Regis College, Toronto, September 10, 1966.

1967   *Collection: Papers by Bernard Lonergan*, ed. F. E. Crowe, London 1967, CWL 4.

Verbum: Word and Idea in Aquinas, ed. B. Burrell, Notre Dame 1967.

Responses to questions raised in a symposium on «Bernard Loner-gan's Theory of Inquiry vis-à-vis American Thought», held at the University of Notre Dame, Indiana, as part of the *PACPA*'s annual convention, March 28-29, 1967.

«Theology in its new Context». Paper at the Congress of the Theo-logy of Renewal of the Church: Centenary of Canada, 1867-1967, Toronto, August 20-25, 1967.

1968   «The Subject». The Aquinas Lecture for 1968, Milwaukee 1968.

«Belief: Today's Issue», *CaM* (1968) 8-12.

«Natural Desire to see God», in *2C*, 117-133.

1969   «Functional Specialities in Theology», *Gr.* 50 (1969) 485-504.

«Theology and man's future», *CrossCur* 19 (1969) 452-461.

«Faith and Belief». Lecture at the meeting of the American Academy of Religion, Baltimore, October 23, 1969. LRI, File 623.

1970   *Insight: A Study of Human Understanding*, New York 1970.

«The Response of the Jesuit, as Priest and Apostle, in the modern world», *SPSJ* 2 (1970) 89-110.

1971   *Grace and Freedom: Operative Grace in the Thought of Saint Tho-mas Aquinas*, ed. P. Burns, London 1971.

Doctrinal Pluralism, Milwaukee 1971.

1972   *Method in Theology*, London 1972.

1973   *Philosophy of God, and Theology*, London 1973.

1974   *A Second Collection*, ed. J. Ryan – J. Tyrell, London 1974.

«Mission and the Spirit». Paper prepared for *Councilium* and ready before November 1974. (It appears in translation in the Spanish is-sue of *Conc. (GB)* (1974) 203-215.

1975   *3 Lectures*: «The Redemption,» «Time and Being,», «Healing and Creating», Thomas More Institute Papers, Montreal 1975.

1976   The Way to Nicea: The Dialectical Development of Trinitarian Theology, trans. C. O'Donovan, London 1976.

«Mission and the Spirit», in *Experience of the Spirit: To Edward Schillebeeckx on his Sixtieth Birthday*, ed. P. Huizing – W. Bassett, *Conc (GB)* 9 (1976) 67-78.

«The Ongoing Genesis of method», *SR* 6 (1976) 341-355.

«Religious Studies and Theology». The Donald Mathers Memorial Lectures, given at Queen's University, Kingston, Ontario. First Lecture: «Religious Experience», March 2. Second Lecture: «Religious Knowledge», March 3. Third Lecture: «The Ongoing Genesis of Methods», March 4.

«Religious Experience», in *3C*, 113-128.

«Religious Knowledge», in *3C*, 129-145.

«The Ongoing Genesis of Methods», in *3C*, 146-165.

1976 LoWo held at Boston College June 12-18 (1976) 1-119. Docta ignorantia session. LRI, File 885.

1977   «Natural Right and Historical Mindedness». A lecture at the Fifth-first Annual Meeting of the *PACPA*, Detroit, April 16, II (1977) 132-143.

«Theology and Praxis», *PCTSA*, XXXII, 1-16. With Responses by K. Braxton – M. L. Lamb.

«Lonergan's Own Account of Insight», *LSN* 12 (1977) 22-24.

1978   *Insight: A Study of Human Understanding*, San Francisco 1978.

«Religious Experience», in *Trinification of the World*, Fs. F.E. Crowe, Toronto 1978, 71-83.

Pour une méthode en théologie, traduit de l'anglais sous la direction de L. Roy., Montréal 1978.

1979   «The Human Good», *Humanitas* 15 (1979) 113-126.

1980   *Understanding and Being: An Introduction and Companion to Insight*, ed. M. Morelli – E. Morelli, New York 1980.

«Questions with Regard to Method: History and Economics». An Interview with Bernard Lonergan, in *DIC*, Montreal 1980, 286-314.

1982   *Caring about Meaning: Patterns in the Life of Bernard Lonergan*, ed. L. Pierrot – C. Tansey – C. Going, Montreal 1982.

Les voies d'une théologie méthodique. Ecrits philosophiques choisis, traduit sous la direction de P. Lambert – L. Roy, Montréal 1982.

1984   «Questionnaire on Philosophy». Symposium held at Villa Cavaletti in September 1976, *MJLS* 2 (1984) 1-35.

«The Mediation of Christ in Prayer», *MJLS* 2 (1984) 1-20.

L'Insight. Etude de la compréhension humaine, trans. P. Lambert, Montréal 1984.

1985   *Collection*, ed. F. E. Crowe – R. M. Doran, Toronto 1985.

«Love, Finality and marriage», in *1C*, 16-53.

A Third Collection (3C), ed. F. E. Crowe, London 1985.

«Mission and the Spirit», in *3C*, 23-34.

« Christology Today: Theological Reflections», *3C*, 74-99.

«Healing and Creating in History», in *3C*, 100-109.

«Religious Experience», in *3C*, 115-128.

«The Ongoing Genesis of Methods», in *3C*, 146-165.

«Natural Right and Historical Mindedness», in *3C*, 169-183.

«Theology and Praxis», in *3C*, 184-201.

«The Original Preface of Insight», *MJLS* 1 (1985) 3-7.

1990   *Understanding and Being. The Halifax Lectures on Insight*, ed. M. Morelli – E. Morelli, Toronto 1990, CWL 3.

1991   «Lonergan's Own Account of *Insight*», *LSN* 12 (1991) 22-24.

Methode in der Theologie, übersetzt und herausgegeben von J. Bernard, Leipzig 1991.

Pour une méthodologie philosophique. Essais philosophiques choisis, Québec 1991.

1992   *Insight. A Study of Human Understanding*, ed. F. E. Crowe – R. M. Doran, Toronto 1992, CWL 3.

1993   *Topics in Education: The Cincinnati Lectures of 1959 on the Philosophy of Education*, ed. R. M. Doran – F. E. Crowe, Toronto 1993.

«Analytic Concept of History», *MJLS* 11 (1993) 5-35.

Comprendere ed Essere. Le lezioni di Halifax su Insight, ed. N. Spaccapelo – S. Muratore, Roma 1993.

1994   «Philosophy and the Religious Phenomenon», *MJLS* 12 (1994) 121-146.

1995   *Die Einsicht: Eine Untersuchung über den menschlichen Verstand*, I-II, übersetzt und herausgegeben von P. H. Fluri – G. B. Sala, Dartford 1995.

1996   *Philosophical and Theological Papers 1958-1964*, ed. R. C. Croken – F. E. Crowe – R. M. Doran, Toronto 1996.

1997   *The Lonergan Reader*, ed. M. Morelli – E. Morelli, Toronto 1997.

2000   *L'insight: Etude de la compréhension humaine*, trans. P. Lambert, Montréal 2000.

Philosophie de l'éducation, traduit par J. Beauchesne – P. Lambert, Montréal 2000.

Macroeconomics Dynamics: An Essay in Circulation Analysis, Toronto 2000.

2. Secondary Sources

AQUINAS, T., *Summa Teologia*, Bologna 1996.

——, *De Veritate*, Pamplona 1998.

ARISTOTLE, *Nichomachean Ethics*, Indianapolis 1962.

——, *De Anima*, Oxon. 1989.

——, *Metaphysics*, London 1968.

——, *Prior and Posterior Analytics*, Oxford 1957.

BARLET, J., *Familiar Quotations*, Boston 1955.

BARNET R. – MULLER R., *Global Reach: The Power of the Multinational Corporations*, New York 1974.

BAUR, M., «A Contribution to the Gadamer-Lonergan Discussion», *MJLS* 8 (1990) 14-32.

BIOLO, S., «A Lonergan Approach to St. Augustine's Interpretation of Consciousness», *ScE* 31 (1979) 323-341.

BOLY, C., *The Road to Lonergan's Method in Theology: The Ordering of Theological Ideas*, Landham 1991.

BRACKEN, J. A., «Authentic Subjectivity and Genuine Objectivity», *Hor.* 11 (1984) 61-85.

BRAIO, F.P., *Lonergan's Retrieval of the Notion of Human Being. Clarifications of and Reflections on the Arguments of Insight, chapters I-XVIII*, Landham 1988.

BURRELL, D.R., «Lonergan and Philosophy of Religion», *MJLS* 4 (1986) 1-5.

BYRNE, P.H., «The Fabric of Lonergan's Thought», in F. LAWRENCE, ed., LoWo 6, 1-84.

——, «The Spirit of Wonder, Spirit of Love. Reflections on the Work of Bernard Lonergan», *Cr.* 8 (1994) 5-12.

——, «Consciousness: Levels, Sublations, and the Subject as Subject», *MJLS* 2 (1995) 464-484.

COELHO, I.N., *The Development of the Notion of the «Universal Viewpoint in Bernard Lonergan. From Insight to Method in Theology*, Roma 1994.

CONN, W.E., *Conscience: Development and Self-Transcendence*, Birmingham 1981.

CORETH, E., «Immediacy and the Mediation of Being: An Attempt to Answer Bernard Lonergan», in P. MCSHANE, ed., *Language, Truth and Meaning*, South Bend 1972, 4-32.

CRONIN, B., «Religious and Christian Conversion in an African Context», *AfChS* 3 (1987) 19-35.

CROWE, F.E., «On the Method of Theology», *TS* 23 (1962) 637-742.

———, ed., *Spirit as Inquiry*, Fs. B. Lonergan, Minnestova 1964.

———, «The exigent Mind: Bernard Lonergan's Intellectualism», in *Spirit as Inquiry*, Fs. B. Lonergan, Minnestova 1964, 16-33.

———, «Understanding (*Intellectus*)», *NCE*, XIV, 389- 391.

———, *The Lonergan Enterprise*, Cambridge 1980.

———, *Old Things and New. A Strategy for Education*, Atlanta 1985.

———, «The Origin and Scope of B. Lonergan's Insight», in *ALI*, 13-30.

———, «An Exploration of Lonergan's New Notion of Value», in *ALI*, 51-70.

———, «An Expansion of Lonergan's Notion of Value», in *ALI*, 344-359.

———, «Insight: Genesis and Ongoing Context», in F. LAWRENCE, ed., LoWo, 8, 61-83.

———, *Lonergan*, Collegeville 1992.

CRYSDALE, C S., «Development, Conversion, and Religious Education», *Hor.* 17 (1990) 30-46.

DELANEY, H., «The Self-correcting Process in Bernard Lonergan's Heritage», *MS* 24 (1989) 50-54.

DIPIETRO, P.J., *The Supernatural Solution to the Problem of Evil: Bernard Lonergan's Understanding of Grace in Insight and Later Writings*, Boston 1994.

DORAN, R.M., *Subject and Psyche: Ricoeur, Jung and the Search for Foundations*, Washington 1977.

———, *Psychic Conversion and Theological Foundations: Toward a Reorientation of the Human Sciences*, Chico 1981.

———, *Theology and Dialectics of History*, Toronto 1990.

———, «Grace and Consciousness», *MJLS* 11 (1993) 51-75.

———, *Theology and Culture*, Milwaukee 1995.

———, «For a Phenomenology of Rational Consciousness», *MJLS* 18 (2000) 67-90.

DUNNE, T.A. – LAPORTE J-M., ed., *Trinification of the World*, Fs. B. Lonergan, Toronto 1978.

DUNNE, T.A., «Being in Love», *MJLS* 13 (1995) 161-175.

de FINANCE, J., «Une étude sur l'intelligence humaine», *Gr.* 49 (1958) 130-136.

———, *Essai sur l'agir humain*, Rome 1962.

FINAMORE, R., *B. Lonergan e l'educazione. L'alveo in cui il fiume scorre*, Roma 1997.

FITZMYER, J.A., «Commentary on Romans», in *New Jerome Biblical Commentary*, New Jersey 1990, 882-898.

FLANAGAN, J., «Lonergan's Epistemology», *Thom.* 36 (1972) 75-97.

———, «The Self-Causing Subject: Intrinsic and extrinsic Knowing», in F. LAWRENCE, ed., LoWo, 2, II, 33-51.

———, «*Insight*: chapter 1-5», in F. LAWRENCE, ed., LoWo, 8, 85-105.

———, *The Quest for Knowledge*, Boston 1994.

GIDDY, P., «The African University and the Social Sciences: The Contribution of Lonergan's Epistemological Theory», *MJLS* 14 (1996) 133-153.

GOING, M.C., ed., *Dialogues in Celebration*, Montreal 1980.

HEFLING, C., «Redemption and Intellectual Conversion: Notes on Lonergan's Christology Today», in F. LAWRENCE ed., LoWo, 5, 219-261.

HUGHES, G., «A Critique of Lonergan's Notion of Dialectic by Ron McKinney», *MJLS* 1 (1990) 60-73.

KIDDER, P., «Lonergan's Negative Dialectic», *IPQ* 30 (1990) 299-309.

LAMB, M.L., «Theology and Praxis. A Response to Bernard Lonergan», *PCTSA*, XXXII, 17-21.

———, «The dialectics of Theory and Praxis within a paradigm Analysis», in F. LAWRENCE, ed., LoWo, 5, 71-114.

———, *History, Method and Theology. A Dialectical Comparison of Wilhelm Dilthey's Critique of Historical Reason and Bernard Lonergan's Meta-Metaphilosophy*, Missoula, 1978.

LAWRENCE, F., «Political Theology and the Longer Cycle of Decline», in F. LAWRENCE, ed., LoWo , 1, 223-255.

———, «The Human Good and Christian Conversion», in P. MCSHANE, ed., *Searching for Cultural Foundations*, Washington 1985, 86-112.

———, «On the Relationship between Transcendental an Hermeneutical Approaches to Theology», *Hor.* 16 (1989) 342-345.

———, «Bernard Lonergan», *NCE*, XVIII, 262-264.

LIDDY, R.M., *Transforming Light. Intellectual Conversion in the Early Lonergan*, Collegeville 1993.

McCARTHY, M., «Liberty, History, and the Common Good: An Exercise in Critical Retrieval», in F. LAWRENCE, ed., LoWo, 12, 111-145.

McKINNEY, R.H., *The Role of the Dialectic in the Thought of Bernard Lonergan*, New York 1980.

———, «The Hermeneutical Theory of Bernard Lonergan», *IPQ* 23 (1983) 277-290.

MacKINNON, E.M., «Cognitional Analysis and the Philosophy of Science», *Cont.* 2 (1964) 343-368.

McSHANE, P., *Language, Truth and Meaning*, South Bend 1972.

———, *Searching for Cultural Foundations*, Landham 1984.

MARSH, J.L., «Lonergan's Mediation of Subjectivity and Objectivity», *Scho* 52 (1974-1975) 249-261.

MATHEWS, W., «Lonergan's Economics», *MJLS.* 3 (1985) 9-30.

McKINNEY, R., «Lonergan's Notion of Dialectic», *Thom.* 46 (1982) 221-241.

MELCHIN, K.R., «Ethics in *Insight*», in F. LAWRENCE, ed., LoWo, 8, 135-163.

MEYNELL, H., «From Epistemology to Metaphysics», *Thom.* 51 (1987) 205-221.

———, «From Crisis to Insight», *MJLS* 6 (1988) 93-106.

———, *An Introduction to the Philosophy of Bernard Lonergan*, Toronto 1991.

MILLER, J., «All Love is self-Surrender», *MJLS* 13 (1995) 105-119.

MOORE, S., «Philosophical Insight», *Month* 22 (1969) 102-107.

MORELLI, E.., «The Appropriation of Existential Consciousness», *MJLS* 6 (1988) 50-62.

MORELLI, E. – MORELLI, M., ed., *The Lonergan Reader*, Toronto 1997.

MORELLI, M., «The Usefulness of Philosophy», *MJLS* 1 (1983) 82-87.

———, *Philosophy's Place in Culture*, New York 1984.

———, «Lonergan and Existentialism», *MJLS* 6 (1988) 1-17.

———, «The Polymorphism of Human Consciousness and the Prospects for a Lonerganian History of Philosophy», *IPQ* 35 (1995) 379-402

MUHIGIRWA, R., Recension du livre d'*Insight. Etude de la compréhension humaine*, ArPh 61 (1998) 549-550.

NACKAMAPARAMBIL T., *Through Self-Discovery to Self-Transcendence. A Study of Cognitional Self-Appropriation in B. Lonergan*, Roma 1997.

NATALINO, S. – FRANCO, F., *Bernard Lonergan*, Milano 1984.

NEWMAN, J., *An Essay in aid of Grammar of Assent*, London 1947.

NILSON, J. M., *Hegel's Phenomenology and Lonergan's Insight: A Comparison of the Ways of Christianity*, Notre Dame 1975.

————, «Transcendent Knowledge in *Insight*: A Closer Look», *Thom.* 37 (1973) 366-377.

NORDQUEST, D.A., «Lonergan's Cognitional Theory: Toward a Critical Human Science», *RP* 26 (1994) 71-99.

NOVAK, M., «Lonergan's Starting Place: Performance of Asking Questions», *Cont.* 2 (1964) 389-401.

PANNEMBERG, W., «History and meaning in Lonergan's Approach to Theological Method», *ITQ* 40 (1973) 103-114.

PELZEL M., W., *A Genetic Study of the Metaphor of Development «From Below» and «From above» in the Writings of Bernard Lonergan*, Washington, 1994.

POPPER K.R., *Conjectures and Refutations. The Growth of Scientific Growth*, London 1963.

QUESNEL, Q., «Beliefs and Authenticity», in M. LAMB, ed., *Creativity and Method*, Fs. B. Lonergan, Milwaukee 1981, 55-81.

RABUT, O., *L'expérience religieuse fondamentale*, Tournai 1969.

RECK, A.J., «Insight and the Eros of the Mind», *RMet* 12 (1958-1959) 97-107.

RENDE, M.L., *Lonergan on Conversion*, New York 1984.

RICHARDSON, A., *History Sacred and Profane*, London 1964.

RICOEUR, P., *De l'interprétation. Essai sur Freud*, Paris 1965.

duc de la ROCHEFOUCAULD F., *Reflections, or Sentences and Moral Maxims* as given by J. Barlett, *Familiar Quotations*, Boston 1955.

ROY, L., *La foi en quête de cohérence*, Montréal 1988.

————, «Moral Development and Faith: A few Suggestions from Bernard Lonergan», *DESJ* 40 (1995) 44-47.

RYAN, W.F., «Intentionality in Edmund Husserl and Bernard Lonergan», *IPQ* 13 (1973) 173-190.

SALA, G.B., «L'analisi della conoscenza umana in B. Lonergan», *ScC* 94 (1966) 187-213.

————, «La métaphysique comme structure heuristique selon Bernard Lonergan», *ArPh* 33 (1970) 45-71; 35 (1972) 443-467; 555-570; 36 (1973) 43-68; 36 (1973) 625-642.

————, «The *A priori* in Human Knowledge: Kant's *Critique of Pure Reason* and Lonergan's *Insight*», *Thom.* 40 (1976) 179-221.

SALA, G.B., *Lonergan and Kant: Five Essays on Human Knowledge*, ed., R. DORAN, ed., trans. J. Spoerl, Toronto 1994.

SCHEPERS, M., «Human Development: From Below Upward and from Above Downward», *MJLS* 2 (1989) 141-144.

SCHOONENBERG, P., *Il est le Dieu des hommes*, Paris 1973.

SHUTE, M.R., *The Origins of Lonergan's Notion of the Dialectic of History: A Study of Lonergan's Early Writings on History*, Landham 1993.

STEBBINS, M.J, *The Divine Initiative: Grace, World-Order, and Human Freedom in the Early Writings of Bernard Lonergan*, Toronto 1995.

STOLLENWERK, D., *Creating and Healing in the Thought of Bernard Lonergan*, Salamanca 1995.

STREETER, C.M., *Religious Love in Bernard Lonergan as Hermeneutical and Transcultural*, Toronto 1986.

SZASKEIWICZ, J., «Soluzione del Problema Critico nel Pensiero di B. Lonergan», *Aquinas* 27 (1984) 205-214.

TEKIPPE, T.J., *The Universal Viewpoint and the Relationship of Philosophy and Theology in the Works of Bernard Lonergan*, New York 1972.

———, ed., *Primary Bibliography of Lonergan Sources*, New Orleans 1996.

———, ed., *Secondary Bibliography of Lonergan Sources*, New Orleans 1996.

———, «The Crisis of the Human Good», in F. LAWRENCE, ed., LoWo, Atlanta 1988, VII, 313-329.

———, *What Is Lonergan Up to in Insight? A Primer*, Collegeville 1996.

TRACY, D.W., *The Achievement of Bernard Lonergan*, New York 1970.

———, «Theological Models: An Exercise in Dialectics», in F. LAWRENCE, ed., LoWo, Atlanta, 1981, II, 83-108.

VERTIN, M., «Dialectically-Opposed Phenomenologies of Knowing: A Pedagogical Elaboration of Basic Ideal-Types», in F. LAWRENCE, ed., LoWo, Atlanta, 1983, IV, 1-26.

———, «Lonergan's Three Basic Questions and a Philosophy of Philosophies», in F. LAWRENCE, ed., LoWo, Atlanta, 1990, VIII, 213-247.

———, «Knowing, Objectivity, and Reality: *Insight* and Beyond», in F. LAWRENCE, ed., LoWo, Atlanta, 1990, VIII, 249-263.

———, «Lonergan on Consciousness: Is There a Fifth Level?», *MJLS* 12 (1994) 1-36.

YSAAC, W. L. ed., *The Third World and Bernard Lonergan. A Tribute to a Concerned Thinker*, Manila, 1986.

INDEX OF AUTHORS

TABLE OF CONTENTS

TESI GREGORIANA

Since 1995, the series «Tesi Gregoriana» has made available to the general public some of the best doctoral theses done at the Pontifical Gregorian University. The typesetting is done by the authors themselves following norms established and controlled by the University.

Published Volumes [Series: Philosophy]

1. HERRERÍAS GUERRA, Lucía, *Espero estar en la verdad. La búsqueda ontológica de Paul Ricoeur*, 1996, pp. 288.

2. CLANCY, Donal, *Valor y Razón. La constitución de la moralidad en Joseph de Finance y Giusppe Abbà*, 1996, pp. 276.

3. SALATIELLO, Giorgia, *L'autocoscienza come riflessione originaria del soggetto su di sé in San Tommaso d'Aquino*, 1996, pp. 152.

4. CASTILLO, Martín Julio, *Realidad y transcendentalidad en el planteamiento del ploblema del mal según Xavier Zubiri*, 1997, pp. 348.

5. NAICKAMPARAMBIL, Thomas, *Through Self-Discovery to Self-Transcendence. A Study of Cognitional Self-Appropriation in B. Lonergan*, 1997, pp. 296.

6. FINAMORE, Rosanna, *B. Lonergan e L'Education: «l'alveo in cui il fiume scorre»*, 1998, pp. 344.

7. ŚLIWIŃSKI, Piotr, *Il ragionamento per analogia nella filosofia analitica polacca*, 1998, pp. 192.

8. KOBYLIŃSKI, Andrzej, *Modernità e postmodernità. L'interpretazione cristiana dell'esistenza al tramonto dei tempi moderni nel pensiero di Romano Guardini*, 1998, pp. 560.

9. MÁRCIO, Antônio de Paiva, *A liberdade como horizonte da verdade segundo M. Heidegger*, 1998, pp. 216.

10. DA SILVA, Márcio Bolda, *A filosofia da litertação a partir do contexto histórico-social da América Latina*, 1998, pp. 336.

11. PARK, Byoung-Jun Luis, *Anthropologie und Ontologie. Ontologische Grundlegung der transzendetal-anthropologischen Philosophie bei Emerich Coreth*, 1999, pp. 292.

12. LUCHI, José Pedro, *A superação da filosofia da consciência em J. Habermas. A questão do sujeito na formação da teoria comunicativa da sociedade*, 1999, pp. 538.

13. BIDERI, Diogène, *Lecture blondélienne de Kant dans les principaux écrits de 1893 à 1930: Vers un dépassement de l'idéalisme transcendantal dans le réalisme intégral*, 1999, pp. 236.

14. TOTI, Daniela, *Franz Rosenzweig. Possibilità di una fondazione della nuova filosofia nella storia*, 2000, pp. 284.

15. DI NAPOLI, Roselena, *Il problema del male nella filosofia di Luigi Pareyson*, 2000, pp. 332.

16. NDAYE MUFIKE, Jérôme, *De la conscience à l'amour. La philosophie de Gabriel Madinier*, 2001, pp. 368.

17. MUHIGIRWA RUSEMBUKA, Ferdinand, *The Two Ways of Human Development According to B. Lonergan. Anticipation in* Insight, 2001, pp. 200.

TOTI DANIELA

FRANZ ROSENZWEIG

**POSSIBILITA' DI UNA FONDAZIONE
DELLA NUOVA FILOSOFIA NELLA STORIA**

pp. 284   Lit. 28.000 - € 14,46

TESI GREGORIANA SERIE FILOSOFIA 14

DI NAPOLI ROSELENA

IL PROBLEMA DEL MALE
NELLA FILOSOFIA DI LUIGI PAREYSON

pp. 332   Lit. 32.000 - € 16,52

TESI GREGORIANA SERIE FILOSOFIA 15

NDAYE MUFIKE JEROME

DE LA CONSCIENCE A L'AMOUR
LA PHILOSOPHIE DE GABRIEL MADINIER

pp. 368   Lit. 35.000 - € 18,07

TESI GREGORIANA SERIE FILOSOFIA 16

Finito di stampare
nel mese di luglio 2001
dalla
Scuola Tipografica S. Pio X
Via degli Etruschi, 7
00185 Roma